Mozart on the Stage

Mozart on the Stage

János Liebner

PRAEGER PUBLISHERS
New York · Washington

BOOKS THAT MATTER

Published in the United States of America in 1972
by Praeger Publishers, Inc., 111 Fourth Avenue,
New York, N.Y. 10003

Library of Congress Catalog Card Number: 70-190594

Printed in Great Britain

CONTENTS

It is not a mean ambition to wish to touch the hem of Mozart's garment.

Stephen Potter: *Sense of Humour*

He turns a new face to every decade.

Peter Hall on *Hamlet*

Through Mozart one becomes a better man.

Ferenc Fricsay

The Free Artist

AT THE age of six Mozart, like some vaudeville infant prodigy, conquered the courts of Europe. It is said that on one occasion he suddenly turned to an Austrian princess who had been praising his performance. 'Madam, do you love me?' he asked her. 'Do you really love me?' And when the taunting reply came, 'No, I don't love you,' the child burst into tears. Tearful smiles and resigned happiness, innocently tender love, sad beauty and lonely grief — these are all in the perfect forms of Mozart's music. So, too, is all the richness of life with its thousand and one faces, its overwhelming joy and dark, tragic depths.

He composed quickly and easily; the stubborn forms obeyed his creative fingers like pieces of soft wax. He never knew the torments of inspiration, the pains of creation, the terrible suffering Beethoven underwent when handling his resisting material. For Mozart, creation was nothing but joy, a natural and necessary function of life or, indeed, life itself. 'I am content because I can compose — this is my only joy and passion,' he wrote to his father. It would seem as though this harmonious and uncomplicated soul had never been torn by cruel, blind passions; that his emotional life was rich but well-balanced, without excesses and extremes, for he was uncommunicative, shy and self-controlled.

The smooth surface, however, hid tragedy in his soul. 'In all my life I have never known happiness, but neither have I known unhappiness; and for this I am thankful to God.' His was not a brooding nature; instead of analysing life, he accepted it the way it was, with all its contradictions. He acknowledged the ways of the world. Within the framework of music he used the accepted forms with the utmost artistic freedom in order to give expression to his own view of life itself, full and complete.

Nil humani a me alienum puto[1] – this could have been Mozart's motto. Joy and sorrow, good and evil, tragedy and comedy – he saw life as an intermingling of all these; there is no shadow without light, and light is brighter when there is shadow behind it. 'Dramma giocoso'[2] he wrote on the front page of *Don Giovanni,* and expressed with what must then have been a revolutionary term that a work of art should portray life itself. Yet at the same time this definition shows the composer's objective view of his artistic creation. He looks upon his work from the outside, and rises above his subject, above life itself. With forgiving love, wise humour and a great deal of benevolent irony he absorbed the world like a child with eyes wide open, without being shocked at anything. 'I saw four fellows hanged at the dome square. They hang people here just as they do at Lyon,' the fifteen-year-old boy told his mother.

Complete acceptance of the infinite richness of the world, sincere interest in the events of everyday life, the ability to see and recognise aspects of lasting value in the momentary and the insignificant – no really great dramatist could lack these qualities. For Mozart every experience and every subject provided raw material; for him everything was part of life, and the subject of his music was life itself. He did not identify himself with any one of his heroes, because each one of them was himself. Nor did he condemn any of them. He only said to the audience: look, this is what Don Giovanni was like and this is what became of him; this is how he lived and this is how he died. He passed no judgement on his heroes, for they, too, were only a part of the completeness of life; and he did not criticise life, he only described it.

Once, however, he rebelled against life – against the life he was leading. He was twenty-five then, with more than forty symphonies, nearly twenty masses, dozens of operas and numerous vocal and instrumental compositions behind him. His name was known and respected all over Europe and his works were played from London to St Petersburg and from Stockholm to Rome in thousands of theatres, salons and concert halls.

But he himself was a lackey, a servant of the archbishop of Salzburg; eating his meals at the servants' table, preceding the cooks and bakers in the domestic hierarchy, but following the butlers and stewards. And when once his master angrily told him that he was a stupid scamp and a scoundrel, Mozart retorted, 'I'm not going to take that! From now on I will have nothing to do with you!'

A count's pointed patent shoe kicked Mozart down the stairs and out of the archbishop's palace. The heavy gate of the Deutsches Haus was shut behind him, and he found himself in the sunlit Singerstrasse – expelled, ashamed, unemployed, but free and independent. Fortunately he could not yet know that this independence would be the independence of misery, this freedom the freedom to starve. He could not see the end of this road: an unmarked grave in a Viennese cemetery many years later, on a stormy December night with cold rain sweeping empty streets, and no one there, no wife, no friend.

But even had he foreseen all this, would he, or could he have acted differently? 'My honour is more important to me than anything else.' A new spirit was in the European air; the fire of revolution was glowing in the world.

The year was 1781. The North American colonies fought for their independence (with a slogan about the equality of men, and the right of everybody to freedom and happiness), and accepted the first constitution of the new republic. In Paris – from where Mozart had just returned, inspired by the friendship of Rousseau and his circle – revolution was slowly but inevitably ripening. And in the colourful, bustling town of Mannheim – where Mozart had experienced his first, sad love affair – the core of a new national conscience was crystallising. Here the first drama by the twenty-two-year-old Schiller had been performed hardly a month before Mozart's personal rebellion (and in less than a year and a half this military doctor from Stuttgart would also turn his back on a tyrannical and stupid master, the prince of Würtemberg). The

9

play, entitled *Die Räuber* (The Robbers), scourged the existing social order and despotism with flaming pathos, and its motto was a two thousand-year-old maxim of Hypocrates: 'Those who cannot be cured by medicine are cured by iron; and those who cannot be cured by iron are cured by fire.' On the front page were two words with the effect of a trumpet call: *In Tyrannos!*[3]

Mozart was the first composer to shake off the chains of feudal dependence, the unbearable burden of doing creative, artistic work to order; he chose the uncertain career of the 'free' artist (in the bourgeois sense) instead of the safe life of a servant. His was the very first decisive step in breaking with the traditional position of 'servant-musician', obliged to fulfil commissions for music and exposed to a great many influences and criticisms quite irrelevant to art. Haydn was still suffering this humiliating situation in the hands of his princely masters. Mozart not only broke with the tradition, but he also made a decisive step towards the type of outlook Beethoven would have. Beethoven proudly compared himself with sovereigns and had the conscience of a free and independent human being. Mozart's body is resting in a mass grave, but the oeuvre he created is eternal.

Notes
(1) Trans: Nothing that is human is alien from me.
(2) Comic opera, possibly with tragic episodes.
(3) Trans: Against the tyrants.

MOZART was entirely and exclusively a musician. Even in his works written for the stage, emotions, situations, ideas, characters and states of mind – all these owe their expression to the music. Some of his libretti were hardly acceptable as literature, yet they were transformed into drama and poetry by his music. Sándor Hevesi was right when he wrote in one of his essays:* 'A libretto is good if it offers every opportunity for the music to unfold its own dramatic possibilities . . . . A good drama . . . can never be a good libretto for the simple reason that a good drama does not require anything but a good performance, while a good libretto requires first of all good music, and a good performance only in the second place . . . . Without Mozart, the character of Osmin could only have been compared with a Kotzebue hero . . . . Beaumarchais's chambermaid, Susanna, is a quick-speaking, shrewd and crafty person who is first and foremost a very prosaic character. In the last act of the opera Mozart gives her an aria by which this character is elevated into a sphere Beaumarchais could never reach.'

Mozart's dramaturgy, his understanding of dramatic composition, was instinctive: he laid down no definite principles (only a few brief remarks appear here and there in his letters) and no clearly formulated aesthetics. Life was perceived and transformed into music directly, and verbal explanation was unnecessary. In fact, he could only express his feelings through the medium of sound. 'I cannot write poetically: I am no poet. I cannot manipulate the grammar so artistically as to create an effect of light and shade: I am no painter.[1] I cannot express my feelings and ideas through signs

* 'The Paradox of the Opera', Budapest, 1913.

and gestures: I am no dancer. But I can express them with sounds: I am a musician.'*

Mozart has left us no guide to the 'understanding' of his works. Without his explaining their transition in words, his aesthetics and dramaturgy changed greatly during his endless stream of musical compositions. His wonderful flexibility of composition always adapted to the changing requirements of dramatic expression. And so it is left to us to define his aesthetics and dramaturgy on the basis of his works and — attempting the impossible — to express in words what can only be truly expressed through the rich language of music.

In fact, one should only talk about music in the language of music, as Beethoven, for example, spoke about Mozart in his two Magic Flute Variations, or Brahms in his first symphony spoke about Beethoven's ninth. Words are an awkward medium of expression which can only roughly approach the colours and moods of nature and the complex phenomena of the world. The rays of music illuminate the dark corners of human relationships and the secret places of the heart, the ultimate truths of life and death.

Combarieu defined music as 'the art of thinking in sounds'. Mendelssohn wrote: 'If I were unable to express the unspeakable in music, I would stop composing'; and on another occasion: 'Music is too precise for words.' The same thought was put into words by the Russian film director, Pudovkin, who said, 'Only music can reach the deepest layers of the subconscious.'

We will never be led by words to the understanding of the true message of a musical work of art — listening is the only means. The work speaks; the rest is silence.

Although we have no explanatory prefaces or essays by Mozart, we do have a number of excerpts from his letters which enable us to define in the most authentic way — with Mozart's own words — the invariably permanent within the permanently changing: the eternal laws of Mozartian aesthetics and dramaturgy. We get most help from two of

* Letter dated 8 November 1777.

Mozart's letters about *The Abduction* where he points out two basic principles, not only related generally to his aesthetics, but also providing a key to his opera dramaturgy. One of them is *the prevalence of beauty in all circumstances.* The other is *the superiority of music over words.*

Since the language of music is at least as exact but much more expressive than that of poetry, Mozart says, 'it is essential that in an opera poetry should be the obedient daughter of the music', while the libretto should only provide 'a well-constructed plot, and the words should be written with the purpose of serving the music'.* 'For the passions, whether violent or not, must never be expressed in such a way as to cause distaste, and music should never, even in the most terrible situations, hurt the human ear; even then, it should give delight — in other words, it should always remain *music.*'†[2] In his letter he also gave a detailed explanation of how he wanted to express limitless anger in Osmin's first aria — of course employing the purest musical means, that is, with simple changes in tempo and key.[3]

One has first of all to examine the development of dramatic expression in musical language when studying Mozart's dramaturgy. In this process there are a number of cul-de-sacs, and some red herrings. During the past two hundred years people have tried to find *themselves* (or the antithesis of themselves), or something that they lacked yet longed to have with some kind of hopeless nostalgia, in the mirror of the Mozartian oeuvre. From letters, diaries and biographies of two centuries we have accumulated some knowledge of the different, and sometimes even diametrically opposed, theories about Mozart's music.

Beethoven thought that the libretti of *The Marriage of Figaro* and *Don Giovanni* were immoral and distasteful, while their setting to music he regarded as a 'desecration of the sacred art'. On the other hand, Wagner gave Mozart's operas top-rating although he felt that in his symphonic music he missed the dramatic core that fills the perfect forms with life.

* Letter dated 13 October 1781.
† Letter dated 26 September 1781.

13

Then Schumann had a different conception again of Mozart, who in his eyes was like Athene springing full-armed from Zeus's head. For many decades this last conception was prevalent, until recently a total switch occurred. Instead of the former image of the 'uniform and harmonious miracle' torn out of his historical context, he began in the new light to be regarded as an example of 'everyman', helplessly tossed in the turbulent oceans of his age, exposed to dizzy storms of impressions, and affected by various external influences.

From the conglomeration of contradictory opinions and half-truths a new idea of Mozart has gradually emerged, according to which the artist is not separated from the human being, or the creative soul from his age. This conception examines the development of artistic creation. It does not forget the determining roles of past and present. Nor does it ignore the many facets which contribute to the inner harmony of the artist: the succession of rejections and fresh starts, the effect of traditions and environment, the balance of creative forces in continuous battle within the soul. This 'inner harmony' cannot be satisfactorily expressed in words but for lack of a better term is usually called *genius.* This path is the one we will follow, for only this will lead us along the gentle slopes of the early operatic experiments, up the steeper hill-sides, until beyond the clouds we reach the huge peaks that are the last great musical dramas. Following this path, we might even — as the late Hungarian conductor, Ferenc Fricsay, said — 'become better through Mozart'.

Notes

(1) Allusion to the baroque technique of chiaroscuro that used to be a guiding principle not only in painting, but also in other fields of art — including music and stage-craft.
(2) Here are some additional relevant quotations from Mozart's letters. 'In my opera there is music for all kinds of people, except those with long ears.' (6 December 1780)

'. . . at the end of an act: the greatest possible noise for the shortest possible time, so that the audience have no time to cool down before they applaud.' (26 September 1781) '. . . pleasing to the ear. . . some parts can only be appreciated by the connoisseur, but at the same time [this music is] written in such a way that even the less educated should enjoy it without knowing exactly why.' (28 December 1782). (3) Cf. Shakespeare: '. . . for in the very torrent, tempest, and, as I may say, the whirlwind of passion, you must acquire and beget a temperance that may give it smoothness.' (*Hamlet,* act III, scene 2) Mozart knew *Hamlet* well (see his letter of 29 November 1789). It is probable that in 1775 the nineteen-year-old musician, so receptive towards every new and progressive influence, saw the performances of *Hamlet, Romeo and Juliet* and *Richard III* by a visiting company at Salzburg. There is also evidence that in 1784, when Schikaneder's company visited Salzburg to give guest performances of *Hamlet, King Lear, Othello, Macbeth* and *Richard III* (most of the title roles being played by the director himself), Mozart had already been, for five years at least, in close professional contact and on friendly terms with the famous actor, theatre director and impresario. In 1779 for instance, at the time of Schikaneder's earlier guest performance at Salzburg, the idea of a joint opera was even raised (*King Thamos*).

Die Schuldigkeit des ersten Gebotes, III
Apollo et Hyacinthus, La Finta
Semplice, Bastien und Bastienne

THE ROOTS go down deep and far. There is a vast range of great forebears: the two types of Italian opera at that period, seria with its enchanting, bewildering magic of bel canto, and buffa with its healthy, earthbound realism; there is the spectacular French grand opera with its rich orchestral effects, excellent stage technique, and elaborate, precise and often dry declamations; the intimate German Singspiel with its naïve sentimentality and the simplicity of folklore; the reforms of Gluck which shook the very foundations of the old genre; German and Italian instrumental music with its cheerful folk-dances, monumental form constructions, and the strict beauty of polyphony. And first and foremost Shakespeare, who taught Mozart that contrasts are inextricable; that the majestic and the trivial are inseparable, as are the dignified and the funny; that the tragic and the comic are but two sides of the same thing; that the subject of any good drama is life in its entirety.

Mozart's twenty-five works for the stage grew and blossomed from this soil.

Mozart did not accept the authority of the nobility. 'Although I am not a count, there is perhaps more honesty in my heart than there is in the hearts of some counts,' he wrote about Count Arco* who had deeply humiliated him; and his quick answer to Emperor Joseph II, who had objected that there are 'far too many notes' in The Abduction, was: 'There are no less and no more notes in it, Your Majesty, than required.'

* Letter dated 20 June 1781.

And though he would not accept any kind of authority in everyday life, he objected to it even more strongly when it concerned his art. He was fourteen when he attended a performance of *Armida,* a new opera by the great Italian composer of the time, Jomelli, at the San Carlo in Naples. He expressed his opinion in a respectful but unambiguous way: 'It is really beautiful, but from a theatrical point of view too over-refined and old-fashioned.' Even Shakespeare, his greatest example, did not go uncriticised: 'If the ghost's part in *Hamlet* wasn't as long as it is, it would be far more effective.'*

It is only natural that this free and critical spirit could not absorb influence without criticism, and no sacred tradition was regarded by him as unquestionable: 'If we composers followed the old rules – which might have been quite good in their own time when there were no better ones – if we followed them as faithfully as they [i.e. the librettists] do, then the music written by us would be just as unacceptable as their libretti are.'† He had an infallible instinct for picking out the essentials from a vast amount of material, and by first filling the old forms with new contents, and then gradually finding new forms suitable for his own subject matter, he created and recreated opera not only musically but dramaturgically as well.

The first experiment in drama was also a strict examination. The archbishop of Salzburg listened to the stories about the infant prodigy with professional scepticism. Miracles were the exclusive monopoly of the Church and he knew his profession too well to believe in such earthly miracles. He sent an order to the ten-year-old composer to come to his palace and display his talent. Mozart was confined there for a week, to work. The examination piece, an oratorio, entitled *Die Schuldigkeit des ersten Gebotes* (The Obligation of the First Commandment), dispersed any uneasiness the archbishop may have felt, and was exactly what he had expected. It was

* Letter dated 29 November 1780.
† Letter dated 13 October 1781.

17

typically baroque music with rich moods and sentiments which — despite its apparent aspiration to achieve dramatic expression — did not deviate from existing — and therefore compulsory — traditions.

The libretto for Mozart's second work in this genre, a comedy in Latin entitled *Apollo et Hyacinthus,* gave him no more opportunity for dramatic characterisation than the first. This was due to the fact that baroque dramas usually portray a static state of mind and give no room for psychological development. So without a coherent dramatic plot the series of arias and duets is but a loose string of cultured pearls: individually each piece is nice, well-shaped and glittering, but the pearls are not genuine yet.

Mozart was twelve when he wrote his first opera, *La Finta Semplice.* Based on Goldoni's work, the libretto was written by Marco Coltellini, the Italian-born *enfant terrible* of the time who later, following Metastasio, became the *poeta cesareo* of Vienna. It was a great honour for the young Mozart to be able to work with the noted librettist of Traetta and Gluck. (Coltellini, by the way, partly due to his daring ideas for theatrical reform, but mainly because of some sharp satires against the Empress Maria Theresia, soon fell out of official favour and 'emigrated' to St Petersburg. However, the two careers converged once more: in 1775 he adapted for Mozart Calzabigi's *La Finta Giardiniera*). Goldoni's libretto for *La Finta Semplice* was the usual gay opera text, with the stock comic opera characters, scuffles, drunkenness and farcical situations. As for the music, it was the traditional Austro-Italian opera buffa music with skilful character-drawing and charming little melodies. There were, however, hints of greater things to come, among them the three finales. This was the first time when, to close an act, Mozart used the ensemble — this special trouvaille of music with enormous dramatic possibilities quite unimaginable in straight theatre. These finales were of course still miles away from the high-tensioned, carefully-constructed ensembles which carry forward both action and character-development in his later operas. Mozart did not yet feel the hidden dramatic possibilities (he was, after all, only twelve!), but rather imitated the highly refined finale technique of the Viennese Gassman, who had himself learnt his technique from the Italians. But in this early experiment Mozart had taken the first step towards the ensemble-technique that comprises and concludes various scene-units, and in a simultaneous, parallel way describes the different characters, their emotions, and their psychological and physical reactions. It was the first step towards the great dramatic finales of his later operas.

Further features of *La Finta Semplice* look forward to Mozart's later operatic development. There is a certain merging of opera seria and opera buffa elements (some arias of particularly sentimental intonation, as well as an aria seria from *Schuldigkeit,* blend smoothly without any breach in style into the buffo form); the characters of the chamber-maid and the servant are more convincing than the rest of the two-dimensional, shadowy commedia dell'arte figures and are in fact forerunners of the great future buffo characters; and it must be borne in mind that the music was composed to suit the abilities of the available singers — a disadvantage in that it could be restricting, but an advantage when it could enrich the characterisation.

La Finta Semplice was not performed in Vienna, and did not appear in Salzburg until a year later, the reasons being professional jealousy and business interests which proved to be stronger than an emperor's word. But the same year Mozart's first German language Singspiel, what we would call today an operetta, *Bastien und Bastienne* was composed. The origin of the libretto was the one-act comic opera by Jean-Jacques Rousseau, *Le Devin du Village* (The Village Diviner), first performed at Fontainebleu in 1752, and the following year in Paris. The same year the Paris Comédie Italienne performed a witty parody on Rousseau's intermezzo, entitled *Les Amours de Bastien et Bastienne.* The parody was written by Madame Favart, the famous actress, who turned Rousseau's stylised and unreal farmers into lively, flesh-and-blood French peasants. This libretto, then — Madame Favart's parody translated by Friedrich

Wilhelm Weiskern, a Viennese actor, and adapted by a trumpeter at the court at Salzburg, Johann Andreas Schachtner — was given to Mozart, who was still only twelve.

Among its musical forerunners the distant ancestor of *Bastien* is the French opéra comique, while its nearer relations include the Stegreifposse, the improvised farce of the small Viennese theatres, and the German Lied which finds its way now into Mozart's operas for the first time. The innocent, charming pastorale had very little indeed in common with the wigged and richly-perfumed rococo idylls of the French royal courts. The heroes of *Bastien* are real villagers of the Salzburg region, peasant boys and girls. The language of the opera is in fact the one used by ordinary people. And the music of the people is also there: bagpipes playing their characteristic augmented fourths, and from the overture, through the solos, to the ensembles everything breathes the intimate, cosy, warm mood of the Lied. The melodies are simple, beautiful, succinct and clear; the characterisation is sometimes surprisingly witty, the instrumentation transparent and fine, and the whole piece strikingly mature and uniform. Thus one could say that *Bastien* was Mozart's first stage work with a completely individual touch.

Dramaturgically there are two other significant factors regarding *Bastien*. One of them is that this was the first time Mozart had a say in the libretto. He re-wrote Bastienne's aria as well as Colas' magic words, exchanging in the former the flat-sounding *'ist kein Spass im grünen Grass'* for the more expressive *'bringt dem Herz nur Qual und Schmerz'*, while we find Colas using the rhymed, rhythmic nonsense words we know so well from Mozart's own letters. From this time on he regularly made changes in his libretti, and instead of accepting whatever was offered he now had definite ideas and demands.

Another important point came to light in *Bastien*: Mozart finally became convinced that German lyrics and the Italian secco style are incompatible. One requirement of a Salzburg performance of *Bastien* was that all the prose parts be rewritten as rhymed recitatives. He actually set to work, but he felt a breach in style and soon gave up. He never again tried to mix Italian secco with German Singspiel.[1]

Note

(1) *Bastien* was first performed at the garden theatre of Dr Mesmer, the famous or rather infamous Viennese 'magnetiser'. Later Mesmer was comically referred to in the libretto of *Così fan tutte*.

Mitridate, Ascanio in Alba, Lucio Silla, La Betulia Liberata

AFTER THE Italian opera buffa and the German Singspiel, a new form, the first opera seria, appears in Mozart's oeuvre. The libretto of *Mitridate, Rè di Ponto,* based on Racine's tragedy, is a skilful work with a grandiose historical background, a great deal of heroism, depraved wickedness and intrigue-stricken love; all the dramatic contrasts of the baroque chiaroscuro. Absolute good is contrasted here with absolute evil and the dramatic conflict is solved by a classical example of *deus ex machina.* Emotionally the fourteen-year-old Mozart was left unmoved by the complicated and superficial plot, but his unrestrained musical imagination was able to bring to life all these remote – and to him almost entirely unknown – ages, characters and personal relationships.

But his dependence upon the singers was quite perceptible: among all the twenty-two numbers between the overture and the closing chorus there is not one ensemble, and only one duet, while the rest – although essential to the action and growing naturally from the given situation – is a lengthy series of arias, with an enormous number of virtuoso coloratura passages. In this respect (and also in Mozart's handling of the orchestra) *Mitridate* remained below the standard of the average Naples School compositions.

However, it did surpass them in the role given to the recitative, its dramaturgical significance and musical elaboration. During the one-hundred-odd years that had passed since Monteverdi's revolutionary innovation, the Italian secco had degenerated into a crippled, empty tradition which had lost its original dramatic function. The bel canto and the aria had used up all the creative energy and nothing was left for the secco. By then not even the Italians themselves cared for the secco: they regarded it purely as a necessary evil. Necessary because it provided a link between the arioso numbers and so created the illusion of a plot; evil because it interrupted the most important and essential process: the endless flow of melodies, the bel canto. Mozart, however, recognised the enormous dramatic potential hidden in the almost free melodic line of the recitative, and primarily in its unlimited scope for harmony and modulation. With *Mitridate* Mozart takes a great step forward and restores the despised secco to its proper dramatic role representing movement and development.

The only element that one need mention regarding *Ascanio in Alba,* a serenata written shortly after *Mitridate,* is the surprisingly mature musical solution of a complex psychological situation: the recitativo accompagnato in which Sylvia renounces Ascanio, without knowing that he was the husband chosen for her and in spite of her great love for him. This is the first appearance of a complicated conflict, so characteristic of the later Mozart.

There was at this time an extremely significant influence which helped Mozart to cross the wide and deep Rubicon between the static baroque dramaturgy based on chiaroscuro, and operatic realism describing colourful, lively people. Conducted by the young composer, the twenty performances of *Mitridate* at La Scala, Milan, were a series of successes and Mozart was commissioned to write another opera. This kept him in Italy for some time, and there he became acquainted with Jean Georges Noverre, ballet master to the court of Milan, who was at that time giving ballet performances at La Scala.

Noverre introduced two new formal elements into ballet: the *tragic subject* as the material of drama, and *pantomime* as a form of dramatic expression. These necessarily resulted in a breaking down of the stiff baroque contrasts of 'ritornello' and 'position', causing the distance between the two to decrease with the replacement of sudden changes by gradual and more carefully prepared transitions; and in the establishment of logical connections between various characters and various scenes. In fact, it brought about the first breach in the strong wall of chiaroscuro. Noverre's revolutionary principles shook the very foundations of conventional ballet dramaturgy and therefore of conventional operatic dramaturgy as well. One has only to replace 'ritornello' and 'position' by 'recitative' and 'aria', and the principle applies to opera too.

After the success of *Mitridate* Mozart went back to Salzburg and set about composing the recitatives of *Lucio Silla,* the new opera commissioned in Milan. (The terms of the contract stated that the arias had to be composed later with the singers' wishes taken into consideration.) Mozart returned to Milan with the seccos finished. There, however, he faced disappointment: the semi-dilettante poet, Giovanni da Gamerra, the opera's librettist, had already presented the libretto to Metastasio, one of the greatest librettists and admired poets of the age, who had suggested considerable alterations.

Metastasio's suggestions were to be regarded as orders. This was not only because he held great authority (that in itself would never have been accepted by Mozart), but primarily because he had a thorough knowledge of his profession and an exceptional talent for blending words and music into a perfect dramatic unity.[1] His practice was to send to the composer engaged to set his work to music, the melodies which would accompany his rhymed lines; and the grateful composer would actually use these melodies without the slightest scruple, knowing that words and music should ideally originate from one source. At that time a work of art was still public property; the concept of copyright was as yet unknown.

So da Gamerra revised the libretto and Mozart was compelled to recompose the seccos. But no measures, however drastic, could rescue the poor plot of *Lucio Silla.* With the exception of a single lively character and one or two dramatic situations of really tragic depth — even these brought to life primarily by the music — it was an average baroque libretto. And this was at a time when Mozart was maturing into manhood, and could no longer put up with the traditional, stiff compromises of Italian opera seria.

Musically *Lucio Silla* dug deeper and said more in terms of passion, tragedy and the expression of demoniacal darkness than its naïve text; especially in the ensembles where Mozart's hands were not tied to such an extent by conceited and spoilt 'star' castrato singers. For instance, the final trio of the second act – when compared with the traditional opera dramaturgy of the age – provided an almost revolutionary way of expressing simultaneously the contradictory sentiments of the various characters. Unfortunately, although the individual and unusually new *Lucio Silla* had no smaller success among Italian theatre audiences than *Mitridate* had enjoyed, it did not bring Mozart any new commissions from Italy. The 'rules of the game' could not be violated without punishment!

Mozart, sixteen by that time, handled with a conscious dramatic sense the various transitional phases between prose and verse: secco, recitativo accompagnato, and stromentato which is only one step removed from the arioso from which the character aria develops (this latter, however, does not appear before *The Marriage of Figaro*). At moments of high dramatic tension the orchestra is already able to talk, confirming, supplementing, or perhaps substituting for the human voice, sometimes even contradicting the spoken words – and all in order to produce a more accurate psychology, not to be found in the text.[2] *Lucio Silla* was the first dramma per musica in the series of Mozart's operas, and this three-act battle-ground – where a struggle began between the obsolete expressionless opera seria form and the more human romantic subject matter requiring new means of expression – provides evidence that the seed sown by Noverre had fallen onto fertile soil and taken root there.

Although it is not a stage work, the oratorio *La Betulia Liberata*, composed earlier than *Lucio Silla* but not performed until fifteen years later, represented a dramaturgically significant step. Considering the difference in form and

25

content between the azione sacra³ and the closely related opera seria (less action, no love interest), Metastasio's text provided an excellent opportunity for the composer to give a profound portrayal of complex emotional conflicts. The elaborate seccos, constructed with care, reveal various musical phrases behind which 'even the movements [of the actors] became apparent'.* Metastasio assigned a particularly important role to the choir, representing the people; all three choruses were essential parts of the action – indeed they promoted the action – and in addition they represented the three peaks of the oratorio: the hopeless misery of the oppressed people (number 4), turned into new hope and confidence by Giudetta's (Judith's) heroic deed (number 8), crowned by the happy thanksgiving hymn upon liberation (number 15). Musically and dramaturgically alike, these three choral parts were extremely important. The closing chorus of the oratorio is the most important of all, showing that even in this inflexible genre Mozart could unerringly find an adequate form in which to express the dramatic subject matter: the endless melody sung by Giudetta, a heroic woman fighting for her people, illustrating her feelings flying with the freedom of a bird above the gregorian melody of the chorus.

* Abert, *W.A. Mozart,* Leipzig, 1924.

Notes

(1) 'Metastasio very deeply and thoroughly knows, understands and feels rhythm in music. His superb verses have an unequalled sound-effect, and his language is enchantingly sweet,' a textbook of his time wrote about him, while a contemporary of his made the following characterisation of the *poeta cesareo*: 'Elegance, kindness, loftiness, accuracy, purity, easiness and harmony: all these can be found in him:

Corneille's heroic eagle-flight and Racine's tame tenderness.'
(2) Rousseau wrote: 'The excited actor is carried away by passion to such an extent that he is almost unable to speak; he stutters, stopping here and there, gasping for breath, while the orchestra "talks" for him. Pauses filled in this way affect the audience much more than if the actor himself explained all the things that are explained by the orchestra.' Remember, too, Gluck's profound saying: 'The violas never lie.'
(3) Sacred musical drama.

König Thamos, La Finta Giardiniera, V
Il Rè Pastore

HAVING returned from Italy Mozart spent the summer of the year 1773 in Vienna. There he made the acquaintance of Freiherr von Gabler, former intendant of the Vienna Opera, who offered his five-act 'heroic dramatic tragedy' for Mozart to set to music. Mozart composed four intermezzos and choral pieces for this work, entitled *Thamos, König in Aegypten* (King of Egypt): a mixture of old Egyptian religious mysticism and modern freemasonic symbolism. Six years later, for Schikaneder's touring company, he partly rewrote it and also added more choral pieces, intermezzos and a melodrama.[1]

The *Thamos* music has double significance. It was the forerunner of the much more important allegory — embracing the whole of life — of *The Magic Flute,* both in the words and also occasionally in its almost demoniacal music. The Hymn to the Sun in *Thamos* reminds us of the closing chorus in *The Magic Flute,* and the string syncopation during the sun-rise recalls the first appearance of the Queen of the Night.

Also of dramaturgical significance is the fact that *Thamos* was the first of Mozart's stage-works where he was not hide-bound by very definite wishes of particular singers at a particular theatre, or by the already-planned dramaturgy of a more or less completed libretto. Nothing now came between Mozart and the realisation of his musical ideas.

The next opera buffa, *La Finta Giardiniera* was the most successful of Mozart's early operas. At the same time it had the worst libretto: a second-rate commedia dell'arte with dull stock characters and disguises, and farcical situations. But the

28

music – as was the case earlier and will be later too – achieved much greater depth. Charm and elegance are its characteristics, and exquisite melancholy and tenderness. Moments of pathos in this work seem more appropriate to opera seria.

This double character of *La Finta Giardiniera* foreshadows later developments, principally *The Marriage of Figaro*. The well-constructed finales producing dramatic characterisation also remind one of this later opera; after all, every aspect of opera buffa has its roots in commedia dell'arte. For a few breath-taking moments the stiff marionette-like figures come to life; heated passions and dark emotions whirl across the stage, and the music, which a moment ago was so smooth and charming, now reveals tragic depths. In one scene Mozart managed to reach a height from which he could look down on both the tragic and the comic sides of life simultaneously. The characters of the play meet in the darkness of a forest at midnight, but nobody knows for sure who the other is. In this mysterious and fearful situation the music gives a parallel description of the two different moods: the superficiality of the light, gay play on the one hand, and the oppressiveness of the ghostly forest on the other.

As far as his music-dramas are concerned, *La Finta Giardiniera* was a milestone in the development of the young composer. Christian Friedrich Daniel Schubart, a sharp-eyed, wise contemporary – poet, composer, aesthete, journalist, director of a theatre, and a courageous free-thinker who later had to pay for his principles with a ten-year imprisonment – in his *Teutsche Chronik* characterised the nineteen-year-old Mozart with the following beautiful and prophetic words: 'I also heard an opera buffa by this prodigy, Mozart; its title is *La Finta Giardiniera*. At times I felt the flame of genius glowing in it. However, it is not yet the quiet altar-flame that – like a cloud of incense – floats into the sky to please the gods. If Mozart is not a hot-house plant, he must become eventually one of the greatest composers the world has ever known.'

A few weeks after the success of *La Finta Giardiniera* Mozart received another opera commission. The town of Salzburg was expecting a visit from Archduke Maximilian, the youngest son of the Empress, and the town intended to crown the celebrations with a new opera by its famous young citizen. In less than six weeks Mozart composed the two-act opera *Il Rè Pastore,* in which he gave sparkling evidence of his virtuoso buoyancy, confidence and the experience gained in the course of the composition of eleven music-dramas — but scarcely more than that.

This was not only due to the ridiculously short period of time at his disposal. Mozart, as we have seen, composed easily and quickly: he did not tussle with words, but instinctively translated the message of the libretto in musical terms, often with more insight than the librettist had shown. More than once he had formed definite musical ideas before he actually received the text.[2] So the shortness of time and the fact that it was written for one particular occasion does not explain why *Il Rè Pastore* is of a relatively lower musical and dramatic standard than Mozart's earlier works (particularly *Bastien, Lucio Silla* and *La Finta Giardiniera*). There were other reasons. One of these was Metastasio's schematic, stiff text[3] which could hardly satisfy Mozart's ever higher demands for the artistic portrayal of life in the fullest possible way. The other reason was connected with the rude interference of the patrons in what had promised to be a *carte blanche* commission.

One of the typical features of baroque dramaturgy was the so-called chiusetta. Taken from the commedia dell'arte, it was a traditional manner of bringing to an end a role, character or situation, and comprised one, two or three characteristic final lines, or sometimes quotations taken from the classics — Dante, Petrarch or Tasso. These condensed into an epigram the essence of the message and mood of a scene. Metastasio liked using the chiusetta, and in his libretti the expressive concluding lines built into the play usually produced a dramatic effect. However, the noblemen of Salzburg, and especially the archbishop, were extremely anxious that the aristocratic listener should feel no insinuations in Metastasio's scholarly and, here and there, emphatic chiusettas. Therefore they mercilessly removed from the text anything that might be interpreted as a comparison between the relationships of the shepherd and his flock and the king and his people, as well as any allusions to the rights of the people, and especially the duties of the king towards them. And there was to be no appeal against the order of the patrons: the scissors of narrow-minded censors cut with cold indifference into the very flesh of the creation of the twenty-year-old musician and the nearly eighty-year-old poet. They closed their eyes to the fact that this crippled the work, distorted its proportions, and upset the finely calculated balance of the baroque drama; and this balance was not simply a formality, but the very essence of the genre.

Dramaturgically, *Il Rè Pastore* was built upon the traditional contrast between the recitative and the aria, with richly-coloured singing parts. Among the arias there appeared a new form, the aria-rondo and — unlike previous serenatas — this work contained no chorus (there was none available). But the most outstanding musical features of *Il Rè Pastore* are not provided on the stage, but by the orchestra, through the virtuoso technique of baroque tone-painting which gives a foretaste of *Idomeneo* and *The Abduction,* and also through the string and wind instruments' solicitous accompaniment to the singing.

Notes

(1) Mozart came across melodrama, this new genre of musical drama, during his stay in Mannheim in 1777-8, and in addition to the part in *Thamos*, he also devoted a complete work to it, *Semiramis,* which unfortunately has not come down to us.

(2) See the letters dated 26 September and 13 October 1781.

(3) Before Mozart used it, this text was set to music by no fewer than eight composers, including Gluck.

31

Semiramis, Zaïde VI

DURING the four years after *Il Rè Pastore,* with the exception of *Les Petits Riens* and one melodrama, Mozart wrote no new stage work. His journeys to Munich, Mannheim and Paris brought him towards maturity as he accumulated impressions and experiences, and, in fact, summoned the strength he needed to embark upon the great dramatic works of his last decade. But that opera was the genre closest to his heart, and that he was giving it much thought during this period, is proved not only by odd remarks found in his letters,[1] but also by those ten Italian concert arias with orchestral accompaniment that Mozart wrote between 1775 and 1779. In these he experimented with various combinations of instruments, and the blending of these with soprano, alto and tenor voices.[2]

But it was not only in the handling of singing voices and of the orchestra that Mozart took a considerable step forward in these years. The operas and theatrical performances he saw in Munich, Mannheim and Paris, as well as his friendship and work with Noverre, helped him to come to terms with a problem that had only been in the back of his mind so far: a problem raised and to some extent solved in *Lucio Silla.* It was that of creating realistic and individual characters within the framework of the operatic medium, and the ensuing difficulty of relating singing and acting on the operatic stage. We have already discussed Noverre's ballet reforms. Gluck followed the same path with his reform operas, first with *Orfeo ed Euridice* and *Alceste,* then with *Iphigénie en Aulide* in which he set himself the target of realistic characterisation, a unity of action and music and the expression of dramatic truth — in fact the creation of an integral work of art.

32

Mozart, primarily endeavouring to represent life in full, also tried to find means of expressing deeper dramatic truth: and in the period between *Idomeneo* and *The Marriage of Figaro* we can follow an extraordinary development in dramaturgical quality.

Realism in stage performance now became essential. As soon as the dull baroque characters were supplanted on the stage by credible people, shown in psychological depth and with individual personalities, all baroque methods of character-portrayal became obsolete. The letter Mozart wrote (in Italian) from Paris on 30 July 1778 to Aloysia Weber shows that his mind was occupied by this problem. Mozart helped the young soprano singer he had met in Mannheim in embarking on her musical career, and also in her theatrical training, with all the warmth of feeling a young man of twenty can shower upon his first love. In this letter Mozart called Aloysia Weber's attention to his concert aria '*Ah, lo previdi!*' with orchestral accompaniment[3] composed in Salzburg just before he set out on his long journey: 'It will suit you admirably and will bring you great success. I would advise you to lay the greatest emphasis on expression, to consider deeply the meaning and power of the words, to seriously imagine yourself in Andromeda's situation, and to try to identify yourself with her personality!'

During his six months' stay in Paris, Mozart was influenced, not only by Gluck and Noverre, but also by Grétry and Rousseau. Grétry's influence on Mozart was primarily in scene-construction, in the finale technique he used in his opéra comique, and in his use of the chorus to carry the action forward. Grétry's acts were constructed with outstanding dramatic sense, arias, duets and smaller ensembles building up to a large-scale choral finale; and this represents another variation of the opera buffa, one which reaches a higher level than was ever achieved by Italian opera buffa.

When Mozart met Rousseau he came under the influence of the philosopher's theories on the aesthetics of music and opera dramaturgy. This was the time when Rousseau's *Dictionnaire de Musique* was published in Paris, the progressive and often revolutionary principles and definitions of which greatly influenced the development of music and musical drama in the second half of the eighteenth century.

We do not know if Mozart studied the *Dictionnaire*; he must have had it in his hands, but Mozart's personality being what it was, it is very unlikely he studied it intensively. At any rate, it is interesting to compare Mozart's letter to Aloysia Weber, and also what he actually created in the field of opera dramaturgy during the last decade of his life, with the following quotation from the *Dictionnaire* which appears under the heading 'Acteur': 'The orchestra does not interpret sentiments which would not emanate from the soul (of the singer); his steps, every blink of the eye and every movement have to be incessantly in harmony with the music, but all this should be done in such a way that no one could notice the special effort on the actor's part. The singer must always fascinate, even when silent on the stage, or when he finds the performance of a role tiresome; if only for one moment the singer forgets the character he or she is playing then there is only a musician on the stage and not a performing artist.'

Rousseau's indirect influence was also reflected in a new genre, the melodrama, the ancestor of which was the one-act scène-lyrique, *Pygmalion,* Rousseau's monodrama.[4] The melodrama – particularly Georg Benda's two monodramas, *Medea* and *Ariadne auf Naxos,* both of which Mozart had heard during his previous stay at Mannheim – caught his creative imagination just when he was trying to discover new means of dramatic expression. On his way home from Paris he stopped again at Mannheim, that musically bustling town on the river Rhine – Aloysia Weber being one of the attractions – and there he was pleased to accept a commission offered by Wolfgang von Dalberg, director of a Mannheim theatre, to compose a duodrama on a script entitled *Semiramis* by Otto von Gemmingen, the German translator of Diderot, Rousseau and Shakespeare, and author of several dramas, as well as of an essay entitled 'Mannheimian Dramaturgy'. Mozart's letter to his father reveals how tremendously enthusiastic Mozart was when undertaking this job — a new, unusual and exciting assignment. He soon completed the work in spite of the fact that von Dalberg, who was now to be appointed intendant of the National Theatre in Mannheim, in the meantime withdrew the commission.[5] Before this happened Mozart wrote to his father: '[Dalberg] refuses to let me leave until I have composed a duodrama for him, and in fact I did not hesitate for long, for I have always wanted to write a drama of this kind . . . I watched the performance of such a piece twice . . . and really, nothing has ever surprised me more! For I always used to think that this kind of work can have no effect on people at all! I expect you know that there is no singing in these works, only declamations, and the music is a kind of recitativo obbligato. From time to time the actors speak in between pieces of music, and this creates the most wonderful effect. What I actually saw was Benda's *Medea*; Benda wrote one more work of this nature, *Ariadne auf Naxos* — both pieces are excellent indeed . . . I like them so much that I always carry the two scripts with me. And I think you can realise how happy I am now when I can at last compose the kind of work I have so much wanted to compose! Do you want to know what I think? This ought to be the way of handling most of the recitatives in opera, and they should only be sung at certain moments of the opera, where words can best be expressed in music.' And later: 'As for the monodrama or duodrama, no singing is required at all, since not a single musical sound is uttered; there is only speech; in a nutshell, this is the instrumental recitative with the difference that the words are spoken and not sung by the actor. I am sure you would like it, even if you heard it on the piano; but if you could hear it performed you would be delighted, that I can guarantee; what one needs is only a good actor or a good actress.'*

Semiramis was written at a greatly significant stage in the development of Mozart's dramaturgy. The genre of melodrama drives the composer to follow sensitively with his music the slightest shades of emotion and mood in the text,

---

* Letters dated 12 November and 18 December 1778.

while the less formal character of the medium urges the composer to express his subject matter more flexibly than could ever be achieved by words alone. In addition, the music of melodrama not only follows, but also prepares for the emotional changes in the poetic script, thereby forming a unity achieved through creative insight. Hence the orchestra takes on an equally important role in the drama.

The genre of melodrama requires creativity from the artist too. The performer has to have as much insight into the music as into the words, and has to express not only the obvious meaning of the text, but at the same time the latent message of the music. 'A melodrama can only be performed in a really satisfactory way if poet, actor and composer all fully understand, almost absorb one another, as if they were living one anothers' lives' is how a theatrical magazine of the period expressed it. Mozart needed to encounter melodrama so that he could, by learning from it, achieve the most convincing psychological portrayal of character, reach a high level of dramatic expression in music, and make a unique marriage of music and drama – exactly what in fact he did achieve in his later great operas, *The Marriage of Figaro* and *Don Giovanni*. But of course the genre was no more than a brief transitional stage for him: this kind of co-ordination of word and sound could never give rise to homogeneous music-drama.

Although we do not know the music of *Semiramis,* since the score has been lost, we do know that Mozart completed the work and it was performed at least on one occasion, probably in Mannheim. The 1779 volume of the *Taschenbuch für die Schaubühne* (Pocket Book of the Theatre), published at Gotha, mentioned it only as 'planned', but in 1782 the same yearbook mentions Mozart's *Semiramis* – in addition to *La Finta Giardiniera* – as a completed work.

Mozart's experiment in melodrama has a particular significance in his own life. The composition of musical works for the stage was his 'favourite job', and he was prepared to embark upon such a work without the guarantee of a fee, or even of an actual performance. This was another step in Mozart's progress away from the position of 'servant-musician' and towards artistic freedom.

The decisive turn was the final break with Archbishop Colloredo in May 1781. Only a few months before that, in a letter dated 27 December 1780, Mozart related to his father as the most natural thing in the world how he had humbly kissed the hand of the Prince-Elector who had praised his *Idomeneo* at a dress rehearsal in a superciliously patronising way. Now, however, he wrote: 'I don't want to know about Salzburg any more! I hate the archbishop!'

Naturally this turn of events did not occur out of the blue. A whole series of personal and artistic experiences had produced a state of mind ripe for rebellion: the servile mentality of the father still directing almost every move of his son, and the tyrannical haughtiness of the archbishop; the atmosphere of Mannheim, with its rich cultural life, simmering with the awakening German national consciousness; then pre-revolutionary Paris with the inspiring friendship of the encyclopaedists, especially Rousseau and Grimm. And I do not think it would be wrong to include among the immediate causes of Mozart's revolt his new and active association with the theatre. All the more so, since he began the composition of a German Singspiel, planned after *Semiramis,* without a commission or, indeed, the likelihood of a performance.

At any rate, the initiative to begin was definitely taken by Mozart. He also had a considerable share in the preparation of the text. Most probably he chose the theme himself, using the exotic Turkish background that had first captured his imagination during Noverre's first ballet, *Le Gelosie del Seraglio,* in 1771. Then a plan had formed in his imagination. Even now it wasn't completed. He only composed two acts and fifteen numbers; there is no overture and no last finale. It was published with a re-edited and partly rewritten text much later (the original libretto has been lost). It was entitled *Zaïde* after its heroine, and did not receive its première until seventy-five years after Mozart's death.

The music of *Zaïde* is a sort of resumé of the techniques

used in the stage works Mozart had written up till that time: it alternates Italian opera seria, German Lied and French comique numbers, replacing some of the recitatives with monodramas and duodramas, and re-introducing the rondo form among the arias. The musical characterisation, particularly in the larger ensembles, and the closely-related sympathetic handling of the orchestra, reaches a new and higher level. Here is a composer with the experience behind him, not only of many stage works, but of two dozen concert arias, thirty concertos, forty sacred works, an even greater number of symphonies, and various pieces of chamber music. In addition to the Turkish setting (and a minor character called Osmin), two features in *Zaïde* anticipate *The Abduction*: the orchestra is handled expertly, sometimes with dramatic passion, sometimes with a fine and lyrical touch; and the characterisation is free and real and abounding in contrasts.

Zaïde could be considered a summary of all Mozart's achievements in research and experiment into the composition of opera. Now he had at his finger-tips all the knowledge accumulated since the emergence of that art form two hundred years before. Mozart was thus equipped to enter the decade of his great creations in the field of musical drama.

Notes

(1) 'I have an indescribable desire to write operas again . . . I only have to hear an opera talked about, I have only to go to a theatre and hear the tuning up of the instruments — oh, then I am immediately overwhelmed.' (10 October 1777) 'You know, my deepest desire is to write operas . . . . Don't forget about my wish to write operas. I envy everyone who is now composing one.' (4 February 1778) 'I have asked him to get hold of something for me: I would be delighted to do it if

I was able to, particularly if it were an opera. Writing operas is an obsession with me.' (7 February).

(2) In the recitative and aria *'Alcandro, lo confesso'*, composed in Mannheim in February 1778 for Aloysia Weber, Mozart for the first time included clarinets in his orchestra.

(3) Recitative and aria, K.272.

(4) A melodrama with one character is called a monodrama, whereas a melodrama built round two characters is a duodrama.

(5) 'I am composing the first act of the declaimed opera, free of charge, and only to please Herr von Gemmingen and myself ... you see, I have such a great desire to compose things like this.' (3 December 1778).

Idomeneo *VII*

IN THE autumn of 1780 Mozart started composing *Idomeneo, Rè di Creta*, and within three months the three-act opera, consisting of thirty-three numbers, was ready for performance. The dress rehearsal took place on Mozart's twenty-fifth birthday, 27 January 1781, to be followed by the première two days later. It was a success, but an ephemeral one. *Idomeneo* did not long remain in the repertoire of the Munich Opera. Five years later an amateur Viennese opera group tried to revive it, but their well-intentioned efforts were frustrated by the indifference of the public and by the narrow-minded predilections of Emperor Joseph II. In spite of the fact that Mozart rewrote it several times, it received no other performance in his lifetime. Later efforts, including those by Wolf-Ferrari, Lothar Wallenstein and Richard Strauss, were met with as little success.

There are a number of reasons why *Idomeneo* did not become a 'repertory opera'. The libretto was written by Abbé Giambattista Varesco, court chaplain to the archbishop of Salzburg. It was a mediocre work, following the style of Metastasio but lacking his feeling for the theatre, his poetic imagination, and his dramatic economy. (The basis for the libretto was that of the French poet, Danchet, which had been set to music by André Campra, a French operatic composer of Italian origin, and first performed in Paris in 1712.) More than once Mozart had to suggest that Varesco make important changes and abridgements in the libretto. The letters[1] in which he wrote about the alterations he required, and those in which he discussed the problems that faced him in the composition of *Idomeneo*, show a remarkably well-developed sense of theatre. In earlier chapters we have seen how Mozart's artistic expression broadened in scope, how it grew richer with each new work, and how consequently his demands on himself, as well as on his librettists and performing artists, increased. Taking these factors into account, it now seems obvious that Varesco's schematic — though here and there poetic — baroque libretto could not possibly satisfy Mozart, and since he could not hope for any basic changes to be made he had to make up for the shortcomings of the text with his music.

Mozart's music frequently expresses more than the text it was written for, and his music sometimes expresses different things too. The all-sweeping, demoniacal passion of Elektra's first and last recitatives and arias, or the tender self-sacrificing, yet heroic determination of Ilia, for instance, could hardly be found in Varesco's classical lines. It is Varesco's lack of artistic vision that must be held responsible for the imbalance of quality between text and music. However, many aspects of the music itself aroused justified and understandable amazement: the romantic, unrestrained passion of the musical material; the artistic portrayal of characters in the subtlest shades of changing moods; the brilliance of musical invention sharply contrasted with the classically-balanced opera seria style, and the richness of style completely subordinated to and serving the artistic expression; and last but not least the diversity of musical language representing life in its entirety. As a contemporary wrote after the première: 'This is beautiful, but new, unusual and strange.' Naturally, it is not its 'new' aspect that is unusual and strange for later generations, but rather the old, negative characteristics of *Idomeneo*: the stilted relationship between text and music, the sober self-control, and lack of the wonderful economy of Mozart's later works. Nevertheless, *Idomeneo* carried the seeds of a new genre, dramma giocoso, which it helped to bring into the world.

At the time Mozart wrote *Mitridate* and *Lucio Silla,* his two successful works in the opera seria genre, he had not yet reached the degree of human and artistic maturity required by the performance of tragedy on the stage; in the last year of his life when he composed *La Clemenza di Tito* he had already got beyond this genre. After *The Marriage of Figaro* and *Don Giovanni* Mozart could no longer be satisfied with only one aspect of the fullness of life, expressed in wide-flowing terms, in themes and motives of wonderfully rich material, with beautiful vocal and instrumental music taking first place, and a balanced drama being of only secondary importance. Despite this, in my opinion the German aesthetic concept of the last twenty-five years[2] is wrong in considering *Idomeneo* as 'art for art's sake', as 'pure music' in the disparaging sense of the term. As we shall see later, although Mozart did not find new forms in which to present new subject matter in every part of *Idomeneo*, basically his music is still dramatic music, with adaptable, realistic character-drawing and a tremendous feeling for atmosphere.

Mozart's letters written during the two and a half months that passed between the beginning of the composition of *Idomeneo* and the completion of the preparations for the actual performance show how consistently he fought for the realisation of his own artistic principles; with what unusually strong, though diplomatic, determination he refused to accept any meddling on the part of the vain librettist and the conceited singers; how conscientiously he worked at achieving the co-ordination of all the components of the work, and with what absorbing care he tried to find the untrodden path of theatrical realism. It is worth quoting a few excerpts from these letters.

'I am in a hurry ... to see Cannabich [director of the Munich Opera], Quaglio [stage designer of *Idomeneo*], and ballet maestro Le Grand [art director of *Idomeneo*] to discuss all that there is to be done in connection with the opera.... Quaglio has put forward the objection we voiced at the very beginning, namely, that the king is completely alone on the ship .... He should be accompanied by at least one or two of his generals and faithful followers who he can dismiss ... with a few words ... which would be quite natural in this sad situation.' 'An aria or a duet would make the scene entirely weak and cool, in addition to making the rest of the actors feel uneasy as they would have to stand there without doing anything.' 'Instead, there should be a recitative here, during which the musical instruments can work in this scene which — due to the playing and grouping, as discussed with Le Grand — will be the most beautiful in the whole opera; there will be such noise and disorder on the stage that an aria would not come off at all here; and in addition there is the storm which, obviously, would not die down for the sake of Herr Raff's aria.' 'For the marches heard from a distance . . . I'll need sordinos for the trumpets and horns.' 'Panzacchi's recitative will have to be enlarged: this will be very effective because of the chiaroscuro, but also because he is a good actor . . . . The scenes . . . with father and son, and the one of Idomeneo and Arbaces are too long . . . particularly since in the first of these scenes there are two, and in the second there is one bad actor; and anyway, there is nothing but a description of what the audience has already seen.' 'With the arias I tried to do my best for them . . . but as far as trios and quartets are concerned, *carte blanche* should be given to the composer.' 'It looks so awkward when everybody leaves the stage here to let Madame Elektra remain alone.'

Varesco was deeply offended by the changes Mozart suggested in the text — and the fact that he stubbornly demanded that the libretto of *Idomeneo* be published in the first and original version shows how little he accepted the final form as his own. Therefore I feel we are entitled to regard *Idomeneo* as entirely Mozart's work which we should analyse accordingly: in the dramatic unity of text and music. Let us then forget about the pious abbé, who after all did nothing more than put a traditional tragedy into rhymed and rhythmic words, and let us see how the twenty-five-year-old composer built up his drama and created his heroes.

Returning from the Trojan War, the ships belonging to the King of Crete, Idomeneo, run into a storm. To save his own life, Idomeneo offers as a sacrifice to Poseidon[3] the first man he meets on the island. He reaches the shore; but the first man to greet him there happens to be his own son,

Idamantes. The King offers himself as sacrifice instead of his son, but the offended god will not accept such a violation of an oath, and sends a horrible sea monster to terrorize the islanders. The suffering people prevail upon the King to name the person to be sacrificed and thus avert the revenge of the god, and Idomeneo reveals the secret. Idamantes kills the monster. With that he has saved the people, yet at the same time, by killing the 'god's own monster', he has committed another sacrilege. The King is just raising his knife to sacrifice his son, when the statue of the god at the temple of Poseidon suddenly begins to speak and pardons the sinners.

The basic conflict is, then, that of promise and fatherly love, drawn out to its fullest extent by the oath having been made to a god, and by the sacrifice being a human one. As a supplementary conflict, the double love imbroglio runs parallel: on the one hand Ilia's requited love for Idamantes (the conflict of love and patriotism, for Ilia is the daughter of Idomeneo's enemy), and on the other Elektra's unreturned passion and jealous intrigues. Both these are woven into the basic conflict, and they promote or withhold the development of the drama, changing and evolving according to the progress of the action.

At the same time the basic conflict itself undergoes a considerable change in the course of the drama. The conflict (oath to the god/fatherly love) exposed at the dramatic meeting of father and son, changes when, in the middle of the third act, the chief priest presents the alternatives to the King, not only on Poseidon's behalf, but also in the name of the people of Crete: if Idomeneo wants to save his people, he must sacrifice his son. Here, fatherly feeling clashes not only with the abstract oath made to the god, but with the real duties of the King, with his responsibility for the safety of his people. In this conflict unequivocal victory is won by the latter force, the interests of the people. The usual and schematic *deus ex machina* solution does not appear until after the moral decision has been taken, and then only to prevent the physical execution of the verdict. Simplified, the message of the opera is this: even the socially most powerful (king), and the most justified individual interests of human beings (parental love + love between man and woman + innocent victim), shrink into insignificance when compared with the interests of the community.

As we have said, although *Idomeneo* is a beautiful combination of vocal and instrumental music beyond anything else it is still — from the first to the very last note — basically *dramatic music*. The atmosphere of drama is created by the overture, composed in an irregular sonata form (the shortest of Mozart's opera overtures), the three characteristic motives (A, B and C) of which return with a significant dramatic function later in the opera.[4] The first of these motives is the opening theme in unison, of a heroic character, performed by the whole orchestra:

This is followed by the succinct motive jointly played by flute, oboe and bassoon:

After an alternating major tonality the melody modulates towards the dominant, where the second theme — which never returns (it is missing from the recapitulation) — appears in an unexpected A minor, and after a few bars in C major it transforms just as unexpectedly as before into the closing theme in A major. The twelve-bar development, as well as the big coda that grows from the incomplete recapitulation, elaborates the B motive with a bold chain of harmonies, and sharp, dramatic dissonances (simultaneously played B flat, C, D, E flat; C sharp, D, E flat, etc.).

In the closing bars of the overture a new idea appears, characterised by an imitation entry and a diminished fourth interval:

The first act opens with Ilia's plaintive recitativo accompagnato. The antagonistic feelings of hatred and love, revenge and gratitude, struggle in the heart of the sad, lonely girl taken as a prisoner from Troy. The orchestra, dramatically active and expressing sympathy with her grief, leads us, almost imperceptibly, into Ilia's G-minor aria (Mozart's 'tragic' key); the smoothness of transition is helped by the short, staccato orchestral introduction emerging from the closing chords of the recitative, as well as by a similar staccato melody from the irregular nine-bar first period. The painful, plaintive cry 'Grecia!' is followed by the B-flat B motive of the overture, appearing in the bass and extending into two bars:

The recapitulation is not identical (the traditional da capo form, taken from Italian opera seria, is put by Mozart to the service of dramatic expression): the B-major close of the first small cadenza preceding the recapitulation immediately undergoes further modulation into which the recapitulation slides almost unnoticed, and only returns to the basic key in the third bar. The closing of the period marks the beginning of another series of modulations, at the end of which the B motive of the overture returns, this time in the minor key. At the end of the aria Mozart describes the storm of antagonistic emotions by accumulating various musical means, all aimed at increasing tension: repeated intervals of diminished ninths, a Neapolitan sixth, an augmented second, the chromatic flow of a long cadenza, and then the abrupt, unexpected conclusion. As there were no preludes or interludes, there is no coda either: after the closing cadenza, with two thinly-orchestrated chords in G minor, the aria comes to a sudden end.

A few bars of recitativo accompagnato: Ilia sees Idamantes approaching. Here we find an ingeniously simple and expressive, purely musical idea:[5] Ilia's recitative ended in C minor; the secco sung by Idamantes — who is just entering and dismissing his entourage before addressing the girl — begins in a different key: B flat major. Only when he returns to Ilia does the previous C tonality return, now, however, in the major key: Idamantes enters into conversation in a polite, sociable, almost chatty way. With Ilia's answer the music turns again into the minor, and Idamantes also begins to strike a more serious tone. He makes some veiled allusions to the deep impact the girl's beauty has made on him. First Ilia is astonished (interrupted cadence), then she flatly rejects the advances of the 'enemy' (unison with hard, punctuated rhythm) while she can hardly conceal her love (caressing, soft, broken bass chords). Idamantes answers with a lengthy virtuoso aria, a typical 'castrato bravuro number', which – despite, or perhaps because, it is so conventional – faithfully reflects the various aspects of the prince's character as we have come to know him: he is elegant, balanced, somewhat stiff, and not particularly sharp-witted.

After the chorus in which the Trojan prisoners and the Cretan people sing to the glory of peace, Arbaces enters. He brings bad news: on its way home, the royal fleet was shipwrecked, and Idomeneo was drowned. It is worth stopping for a short while at one very characteristic melodic turn of the recitative. The melody to Idamantes's words, 'Horrible news . . . . My father is no longer alive? . . .'

will occur several times in the opera in similar situations:

Ec-coti, Si-re il mi-o, la vit-ti-ma io son.

This similarity is not pure coincidence, for years later, when composing *Don Giovanni* and *The Magic Flute,* Mozart used almost exactly the same musical thought to express the loss of a lover, grief, uncertainty, sorrow and death:

All the examples quoted above are either questions, or are question-like in their nature; in fact, each of them has identical cadences, and most of them are in the same key, D minor — Mozart's 'dramatic' key. Even amid the infinite melodic variations and the traditional 'stereotyped' turns of the recitative, Mozart created a dramatic language, a particular, individual world of expression entirely his own.

Idamantes is deeply shaken by the tragic news. The secco develops into accompagnato and it is for the first time that the sensitive human soul of Idamantes emerges from the lively roulades of the orchestra, the broken triads, sad chromatics, hard, sharp, dramatic unison chords, and the quick major-minor-major alternations.

Elektra remains alone on the stage. An ill omen gnaws at her heart. Her recitativo accompagnato starts with a one-bar motive, developed from the A motive of the overture and repeated several times, and then, an augmented second lower, the whole of the first phrase is repeated. With the death of the king her secret hope to become Idamantes's wife has vanished. The threatening A motive of the overture is again played by the orchestra — first in C, then in D major, to be followed by a new, dramatic motive in D and E minor: Elektra seeks revenge with passionate jealousy. After excited string tremolos a tense chromatic sequence leads into the aria which starts on an A organ-point; and only after a triple staccato sequence of an indefinite tonality and with an augmented second cadence do we realise that in fact it is in D minor: Mozart's 'dramatic' key. In the thirteenth bar of the orchestral introduction the stubborn bass organ-point suddenly stops; for a moment the balance is completely upset, and the regular 4/4 rhythm, hitherto considered to be such solid ground, slips dangerously away. The false forte-piano accents reflect Elektra's hysterical jealousy, and blind thirst for revenge. In the fifth bar of the vocal part a new sequence starts, consisting of a descending triad and an almost howling leap of a tenth: Elektra appeals to the furies of hell to help her in her revenge. The orchestra is in a frantic storm of emotions: after a seven-bar iambic phrase in F minor a chromatic scale leads into an F-major phrase in contrary motion, full of accents and sforzatos into which two more bars in F minor are wedged. Above the permanently alternating major-minor tonality there is a gulping vocal part of punctuated rhythm. The recapitulation starts one note lower, in C minor; and by the end of the aria the dramatic tension is increased to an almost unbearable degree by a darker tone-colour, the leap of a seventh (that is linked to the two leaps of a tenth and leads back to D minor), the even more condensed major-minor alternations, the syncopated rhythm, the Neapolitan sixths and diminished sevenths, as well as the repeatedly upset metre of the coda.

With the inverted A motive of the overture the attacca aria leads into the four-part male chorus of the next scene. The storm in Elektra's soul now turns into a genuine storm, and the people of Crete, assembled along the sea-shore, are praying for the mercy of the gods, while snatches of distant sounds, voices of the shipwrecked, are carried on the wind. The orchestral accompaniment to the two choruses is different: while the people are singing on the shore there is a terrified, helpless flurry of strings; the off-stage chorus of the sailors is accompanied by the tense calm of the woodwinds, symbolising the instinctive self-discipline of seamen in trouble. From the A motive of the overture proceeds a threatening danger-motive in the violins; later, in a different form, this is extended to the basses as well. The sea gradually quietens and, having survived the storm, King Idomeneo lands with his entourage.[6] He thanks the gods for his survival, while the B motive of the overture radiates an atmosphere of calm (two-bar polyphony). But he will pay a high price for his escape (basses with punctuated rhythm): he has sworn by oath to sacrifice the first man he meets. The mood is also reflected in his aria which, quite unexpectedly, merges into another recitative: a man is coming along the shore. The secco is replaced by a dramatic accompagnato when father and son recognise each other. There follows a soothing piano theme in quavers from the C motive of the overture: Idamantes realises with relief and joy that his father is alive. But Idomeneo pushes aside his son's embracing arms in horror. Idamantes does not understand why, and his bewilderment is represented by the previous motive in forte and in diminution; then from the A motive of the overture arise the two shocked outcries from the orchestra which are continued in a doubled form above dominant and diminished seventh tremolos with half tone cadences, as an accompaniment to Idamantes's recitative. He has at last found his father whom he believed to be dead, yet his father runs away from him in terror! What can be the explanation? He decides to follow and ask him (a soothing thought from the C motive of the overture). His aria makes his character even better defined: the attractively simple melody and the rapid major-minor alternations reflect a youthful, perhaps a bit unrestrained, but undoubtedly bold and honest personality. The earlier outcry motive and the repeatedly performed identical bars demonstrate that the thoughts of Idamantes are centred on one problem. In the choral scene that closes the act, the B motive of the overture reappears; the return is introduced by a painting in sound of the waves of the sea.

A lengthy recitative from Idomeneo and Arbaces opens the second act.[7] Once again we hear about the oath and its terrible consequences (a five-bar series of dissonances starting with E major and leading to G minor). After Arbaces's well-shaped, but dramaturgically uninteresting bravura aria, and a recitative from Ilia and Idomeneo, comes Ilia's beautiful E-flat-major aria, accompanied by a woodwind quartet.[8] The four concertante solo instruments (flute, oboe, horn and bassoon), with their long prelude, interlude and postlude, suggest to our imaginations a sweet and charming girl; and one or two aspects foreshadow Constanze's C-major aria in *The Abduction*.

Idomeneo is left alone on the stage. His recitativo accompagnato, 'in tempo dell'aria', is introduced by the second theme of the previous aria, originating from the B motive of the overture; but while Ilia's thoughts were expressed through the clear dolce sounds of the four woodwind instruments, bringing an atmosphere of brightness and harmony,

Andante ma sostenuto

the dark colour and lower register of the strings now create a mood of sadness and fear.

The motive recalls one of the variants of the B motive in the overture, i.e. the second theme of Ilia's first aria (even the keys are identical). The King is tormented. Does Ilia really love Idamantes? If so, Poseidoń will have not two, but three victims; the son will be killed by the sword, while the father and the girl die of grief. The next great aria, *'Fuor del mar'*, ('the mośt wonderful aria in the whole opera', according to Mozart himself) is – within the confines of baroque virtuosity and allegorical description of mood – a forerunner of the great character arias of the later operas: turbulent sea and turbulent soul; four-part imitations on the name *'Nettuno'*, eight-bar coloratura roulades on the word *'minacciar'*, etc.[9]

Its form structure is A – B – A, opening with a large orchestral introduction which is followed by a three-theme A part resembling an exposition in character and size. The ensuing central passage starts on the mediant, but wanders away and gathers new musical ideas. After the orchestral transition – formed from the A motive of the overture – comes a full reprise with a traditional fermata and a cadenza before the coda. An old form is filled here with new material: we have a large-scale, attractive Italian bravura aria together with psychologically accurate musical characterisation. In addition, it is very realistic in texture: above the transparent orchestration prevails a tenor part which can be sung well and easily despite its virtuosity. (At least in Mozart's time, when coloratura was not the technical privilege of a particular register but any reasonable singer's means of expression, it could be sung well and easily. Raff, for whom Mozart moulded the role of Idomeneo, was sixty-five when he sang at the première!)

Elektra's second scene shows the Greek princess from a

different point of view than before: her hopes regarding Idamantes are flying high again. The theme which begins the recitative foreshadows the character of the dolce aria; and this is stressed by the mezza voce string accompaniment and the tenderly caressing third and sixth parallels. The motive appearing with the words, *'l'amante cor'*, comes from an inversion of the B motive of the overture; the analogy is confirmed by the mirror-inversion of the recapitulation:

The recapitulation itself is even larger and richer: the melodic line is somewhat changed, one more bar is added to the cadenza, after which another four-bar phrase is inserted. Thereby the coda becomes a full period, the second half of which — developing from the opening thought of the aria — gives the feeling of another, second reprise, as if Elektra, in her over-whelming happiness, longs to tell the world for the third time what she has already said twice.

But she is interrupted by the distant sounds of a march. This C-major march starts in the middle (played now by sordinoed brass as contrasted to the previous string intonation)[10] as if we could not hear the beginning on account of the distance. It starts on the dominant corresponding to the G major of the previous aria. It is only later, as the march approaches and becomes louder, that we hear the beginning of the returning A — B — A form.[11] In the meantime the scene has changed and once again we are in port, where Elektra and the people of Crete sing about the peaceful sea and a favourable wind (E major, so called 'Venetian 6/8', in the dolce mood of the previous aria, with tender third and sixth parallels). The next trio, in which Elektra, Idamantes and Idomeneo take part, clearly indicates the different natures and sentiments of the characters. The chromatics and frequent harmonic alterations of the two-bar orchestral introduction project a mood of ominous uncertainty. To

Idamantes's ten-bar phrase, Elektra adds another variant with richer accompaniment, more colourful harmonies and interrupted cadences that tend towards the parallel minor, while she also adds one more bar to the second half of the period; her premonitory feelings are not revealed by her words but by the music. After Idomeneo's words – which appear as a new variant – the three voices are interwoven, but at the same time each of them meditates on his or her own troubles, and the orchestra's chromatic and scale passages indicate that danger threatens.

After a sudden change in tempo, metre and mood, a threatening motive appears, formed from the A motive of the overture, and the gradually increasing tension culminates in a sudden storm. A horrible monster rises from the sea: the gods must indeed be angry! There is a dramatic C-minor chorus with excited trills, ominous chromatics, threatening roulades, shuddering tremolos and sinister orchestral syncopated passages. At the words 'the anger of god', the four parts merge into shrieking unison. During bold modulations a new variant of the overture's motive A is heard in a three-octave unison of basses and flutes, a variant that returns later in a condensed form on violins and flutes:

'Who is the culprit?' the people ask, and the three woodwind chords repeat the question. Amid the hard chords and rushing scales of the orchestra stands Idomeneo, facing the revenge of the offended god and singing his great recitative: 'Cruel god, be satisfied with my own death; don't be unjust, do not punish the innocent!'[12] A dramatic D-minor chorus follows: 'Let us escape!' The orchestral unison, growing from the A motive of the overture, flares into a horrifying roar of triplets, after which the sopranos begin an excited scale sequence in which all the other parts join, one by one. We hear bold dissonances, and between the

A-B-F-G, A-G-D-E chords the four parts now and then meet in startling unison. When the bass, held on the organ-point so far, also joins the imitation, a new sequence appears, taken from the B motive of the overture:

After diminished seventh passages and major-minor changes the people escape, and Idomeneo stands alone in the raging storm.

Ilia's recitative that opens the third act anticipates the first theme of the following aria. The aria is one of the most expressive, fascinating and exquisite musical numbers of the opera. In the E-major key of the already-mentioned Venetian 6/8 chorus, Ilia sings about the zephyr, and sends a message to her lover with the gentle breeze. The enthusiastic orchestra repeats, accompanies and, indeed, often supplements Ilia's words – adding new colour to every returning musical thought. The painfully tender minor phrase of the middle passage, the movingly refined chromatics of the bars preceding the reprise, the sustained notes of the closing period holding out against despair and every obstacle – all these show facets of the character of a girl who is not only charming, but also strong-willed and ready to fight for those she loves.

The aria melts into a recitative: Idamantes is coming and Ilia does not know what to do. Should she confess her love, or keep it a secret? Should she stay, or go away? The diminished sevenths of the accompanying broken harmonies demonstrate Ilia's bewilderment. Idamantes wishes to say good-bye before he leaves to fight the monster. Ilia is unable to master her feelings any longer and confesses her love. The secco merges into accompagnato and the orchestra interprets the emotional states of the two people: Idamantes's astonished, happy excitement (wavering, broken harmonies), and

Ilia's calm above a sea of deep inner tension (standing chords and a motive with punctuated rhythm that rises higher and higher). The shy, innocent love confession, '*t'amo*', is accompanied by a tender third parallel which leads into an attacca duet. Idamantes hardly dares to believe Ilia's words (broken half-sentences above the large swell of the orchestra's murmuring thirds). Ilia's answer is in the minor key. Hers is the heavier burden, but of the two she is the stronger and the more determined. While the young man keeps repeating his earlier, hesitant phrases, the girl carries the new musical thoughts forward. The orchestra plays the same variant of the overture's B motive that we heard in Ilia's first aria:

And now at last the A-major key, heard at the beginning, returns: the girl's strength lends courage to the young man too, and the singing of the two lovers blends into happy thirds. However, Ilia remains the leader and initiator: she opens the following imitation, with Idamantes obediently singing it note by note two bars later.

The duet is interrupted by the appearance of Idomeneo and Elektra. The heavy chords of the recitative (a series of dissonances with a chromatically descending bass sequence) reminiscent of Bach's monumental tragedy-intonations, the Passions, lead into the quartet which starts with an inversion of the A motive of the overture. For characterisation the music uses sharp outlines again. A wonderfully constructed musical fresco is formed by Idamantes's chromatic counter-motion, syncopated chords, and his peculiar subdominant with its *sixte ajoutée*; Ilia's calm, balanced octave accompaniment and minor-bound melody; the lovers' intertwined third and sixth parallels which turn into minor at Idomeneo's and Elektra's entrance in identical rhythm but with counter-motion; and finally the common suffering uniting the four people at the word, 'soffrir'. In the reprise the broken major chord of the opening theme is distorted into a·chord of a diminished seventh by Idamantes's outburst of despair, but Ilia's self-sacrificing courage lends him strength again. There is a four-part imitation on the repeated word 'soffrir', a declining C motive of the overture in the orchestra, and once again – as if it were a second reprise – comes the opening theme. But Idamantes is unable to finish the sentence; his voice falters and the quartet ends with the soft, broken sighs of the orchestra.[13] As far as the depth and intensity of emotional and dramatic expression are concerned, this quartet is peerless even when compared with Mozart's later works.

Arbaces's ensuing recitative develops from the last of Idamantes's motives from the quartet. This continuous, linked method of dramaturgical construction goes far beyond all operatic conventions of the age. However, despite all its precise musical beauty and power of expression, the aria is a regrettable anti-climax after the dramatic character of the quartet. With the faltering queries of the orchestra, the meditative four-part imitations, the thematically returning hopeful syncopated passages, and the hard punctuated rhythm, the recitative still manages to keep up the earlier high level of tension. In the aria, however, the action grinds to a halt. Mozart was aware of it, but he had to abide by the wishes of the singers who were only interested that their own virtuoso aria should show off their talents to the best advantage, and who cared much less about the ensembles that required a lot of preparatory work and were, from a selfish point of view, less rewarding.[14]

The next scene starts with an augmented form of the motive A variant that we heard in the trio of the second act; developing from the second part of this, a new motive accompanies the high priest's recitative. This recitative moves from parlando into broad cantabile when the danger threatening the people with utter destruction is described. The orchestra plays decisive scales and broken triads in strong, punctuated rhythm in unison when the high priest calls upon the King to fulfil his oath and offer up the sacrifice he had voluntarily pledged (two-bar polyphony as during the prayer in the first act). A G-minor tremolo: 'So let it be!' A sad, painful C-minor motive in a diminished fourth modulates into D minor with a diminished second: the victim is Idamantes. Chromatic chords, a series of dissonances, and the declining C motive of the overture in F minor: 'You will see how a father kills his own son!' The great funeral chorus in C minor contains a bold chromatic link-up of harmonies with a four-part imitation by the participating Cretan people, another returning chromatic motive at the word *'morte'*, and the threatening A motive of the overture in the middle passage. In the coda there seems to be a ray of sunshine, a faint flicker of hope: C major. But it is too early to be hopeful: the function of the C major is not to give relief, but to create new tension; i.e. instead of being a tonic it is a dominant that prepares the way for the following F-major march. The march was exclusively Mozart's idea, and he attached a significant dramaturgical role to it.[15] Incidentally, not only its tonality, but also its melodic line, rhythmic construction, harmony, mood and dramatic function remind us of the march that opens the second act of *The Magic Flute*. The close is almost identical.

The King, on his knees, prays to the god of the sea. The priests reply to his beautiful, floating melody in a monotonous, rhythmic song. And suddenly, from off-stage, comes a victorious D-major flourish of trumpets and a chorus: Idamantes has killed the monster. (Remember again *The Magic Flute*: 'Long live Sarastro!') The young man, relaxed and almost happy, awaits death at the hands of his father. The beautiful one-and-a-half-bar opening idea of the recitative returns several times later; the sonority of the orchestra is melodic and descriptive. He is content that his life should be taken away by the person who gave it to him. The B motive of the overture is heard three times, played simultaneously with its mirror-inversion:

With the thought that Idamantes's death is approaching, Idomeneo suffers helplessly for his own sin (an F-major phrase is followed without any transition by D major). Idamantes now proves to be stronger than his father (allegro risoluto passage): he warns the King of his duty towards his people (with rhythmic pizzicatos above and below the string tremolos) and requests him with the opening theme of the recitative to adopt Ilia as his daughter. In these grave moments Idamantes rises to the situation and we realise he could grow to be a courageous, strong, honest man.

These features are again reflected in his next aria which begins with a theme formed from the A motive of the overture; in its sixth bar the previously-mentioned opening theme of the last recitative appears again (later it is omitted from the recapitulation). The beautiful, although rather lengthy aria[16] melts into a recitative. At last Idomeneo determines to offer up the sacrifice (a short, decisive, simple motive). A quick farewell, and he is about to lift his sword when — with a horrified and startled scale of uncertain major-minor tonality —

Ilia rushes onto the stage and casts herself into the arms of the King. She implores him to kill her instead of his son (desperate prayerful and tearful broken motive above the tremolos). The rich orchestral sounds express in a thousand different, colourful ways a gradually growing tension while the various characters, faithful to their own personalities, react in different ways.

With a D-minor passage in unison of succinct rhythm, and with two sharp, hard chords, the drama reaches its peak. Ilia already kneels before the sacrificial altar. At this tense moment, at the culmination of the conflict, we hear three forte chords of a strange and unusual colour — at least, unusual in Mozart's time — played by three trombones and two horns. At that time the trombone did not enjoy equality with other instruments and in fact was not yet really accepted in the orchestra; its use was always linked with something extraordinary and transcendent. Mozart used the trombones as Gluck did in *Alceste* and in *Iphigènie,* as an accompaniment to the god's voice. Later, too, in *Don Giovanni* and *The Magic Flute* Mozart expressed power that is 'not of this world' by using trombones. The scene, by the way, is strongly reminiscent of the churchyard scene in *Don Giovanni.*

Both from a musical and even more from a dramaturgical point of view, Mozart was vividly interested in the problem presented by the *'unterirdische Stimme'* (the voice from below).[17] He knew (he had learnt it from Shakespeare!) that it is easier to make the audience accept the impossible than the improbable provided it is kept in harmony with the laws of the stage and in the atmosphere of true operatic stylisation. That is why he wanted the accompanying instruments to be put on the stage, right beside the singer (out of sight of course), and that is also why he rewrote the whole scene at least twice.[18] 'Don't you think that the speech of the voice from below is too long?' he asked his father in one of his letters.* 'Think it over carefully. Just try to imagine the theatre; and remember that the voice should be horrifying . . . . The audience must believe it is real . . . . How can that effect be achieved if the text is too long, for this would convince the audience of superfluousness? . . . If in *Hamlet* the ghost's speech were not so long, it would achieve an even greater impact . . . . The speech of the voice from below can be shortened without any difficulty; one would gain rather than lose by it.'

The three versions of the scene of the Voice do not differ only in their extent. In the second version, only the beginning and the end of the first one, a bare half-period, remain. The third, and most concise, version has a melodic bass motive, accompanying harmonies in punctuated rhythm instead of sustained chords, shorter values in its more cantabile vocal passages and an unexpectedly lyrical cadenza.

* Letter dated 29 November 1780.

It is not only shorter, but it creates a recitative-like, more human effect. The god we hear now is not invisible and intangible, but one of ourselves, only a wiser, fairer judge.

After the massive C major of the brass comes an ethereal dolce D major from the woodwinds: the sound of happy relief from tension. Only Elektra is dissatisfied with the decision. In her passionately dramatic recitative the A motive of the overture is compressed to an almost hysterical degree. The wildly-shrieking scales of her first recitative and the tough, striking, broken triads of her first aria are the ruling elements. Her rage increases violently. After a moment of horrible quiet, the raging storm of passions explodes with tremendous force. As in the first aria where the tonality could only be identified later (reflecting the depths of her inscrutable soul), it is here only in the fifth bar that it reaches the basic key of C minor with the furious and compressed repetitions of the A motive that broaden into a tritone. The vocal part is of Spartan simplicity both in melody and rhythm: this is not the time for bel canto and coloratura. Another fragment of the A motive appears on the violins – a shriek – and then a four-bar trill motive introduces the recapitulation. From time to time Elektra's voice falters, and then her message is taken over by the orchestra. The coda is packed with various musical means aimed at creating tension: two-bar syncopated melodies are followed by spurting chromatics and descending scales in orchestral unison. The declining tremolo of the closing bars of the aria is rooted in the C motive of the overture, but this time it is performed in unison and without imitation, and the diminished fourth now widens into a diminished seventh. The hard chords bid a final farewell to the impassioned Elektra.

The last scene of the opera begins with a string canon in four parts. In the second bar of the canon, we hear again like counterpoint the B motive that has run through the whole of the opera:

Idomeneo's recitative is accompanied by the motive fragments from the introduction, including the sequence of the
canon theme. The conclusion is also composed from this
(with the mirror-inversion of the theme in the last words of
the recitative) and – now with various rhythmic changes –
this also runs through Idomeneo's aria, the three-bar phrases
of the 3/8 middle passage which reflect the revival of his
soul. The concluding chorus, in praise of matrimonial love,
casts two familiar musical thoughts into new forms. Right at
the beginning is the opening motive from Idomeneo's aria,
'*Fuor del mar*'; and in the middle emerges the main theme of
Idomeneo's recitative and aria from the third act.

The dramatic action and sublime message of *Idomeneo* are
projected by richly portrayed characters – personalities who
undergo considerable development in the course of the play.
The most artistic musical interpretations are those of the two
women characters where the music reflects in truly Shakespearean depth the contradictions in character, the fundamental ties between society and the individual, between the
human soul and the external circumstances affecting it. The
characterisation of the two male figures is more conventional
and what one might call 'more operatic'.

The first recitative and aria of the captive Trojan princess,
Ilia, reflect a lonely, sad soul struggling between hatred and
love, revenge and gratitude. During her conversations with
Idamantes, her character is enriched by her noble conduct –
while her second aria shows the sweet, charming aspects of a
girl worthy of love and pity. The opening recitative and aria

63

of the third act sum up what we know of Ilia's personality, so paving the way for her further development and the decisive role she is to play later in the drama. In her next scene with Idamantes, her character is portrayed in greater depth; and when in the quartet Idamantes staggers for a moment under the weight of the task ahead, it is Ilia's self-sacrificing, heroic courage which fills him with the strength he needs to fight the monster. And finally, Ilia's behaviour at the climax of the drama crowns the progress she has made in the course of the three acts. She is ready to sacrifice herself for the people of Crete in order to save the life of her lover. Hers is a charming yet heroic character. She has the courage and skill to direct her own life bravely and wisely, as well as the lives of those she loves. She is the direct predecessor of two great Mozartian heroines, Constanze of *The Abduction* and Pamina of *The Magic Flute*: women ready to risk their lives for love.

While the development of Ilia's character is straight-forward, that of Elektra could be said to come full circle during the course of the opera. When she first appears on the scene to hold Idamantes (whom she secretly loves) respon-sible for the release of the Trojan prisoners, in the depths of her soul there is the same wild, cruel thirst for revenge that is shown in her last scene, at the end of which she rushes madly off the stage, filled with rage and frenzy, and disappears for ever. However, had circumstances taken a different turn, Elektra could have become a faithful wife and loving mother at Idamantes's side – at least, Mozart did suggest this possibility in the characterisation. She is not a kind of female Iago: she was not born evil, nor is she wicked for wickedness' sake; it is simply that love has driven her out of her mind and makes her want to destroy everything around her.

This is revealed in her first recitative in which the typical egotism of the jealous woman is expressed. News of the death of the king interests her only because her secret desire to marry Idamantes may be frustrated. The second act shows a completely different Elektra, hardly the same person. Due to the changed circumstances her desire to marry Idamantes has some chance of fulfilment, and now she prepares to return to her native country in the company of the man she loves. The aria, in dolce mood, shows us the pleasant aspects of the many-sided character of the Greek princess. Her dark emotions have vanished, and the mild harmony of regained happiness fills her soul. With a contented heart Elektra bids farewell to the shores of Crete. By the trio, however, ill omens have already made her uneasy: will she succeed in winning Idamantes's love? We almost feel pity for her; she is not evil, but unhappy, and deserves a better lot. But this better lot could never be hers. Events are overtaking her and Elektra, overwhelmed with jealousy, is a helpless witness of Ilia's heroic deed and of the union of the two lovers. She loses Idamantes once and for all, not as a consequence of the god's order, but because in the decisive moment she was too weak and did not prove to be worthy of the man she loved; for even her love was conquered by her grinding, hysterical selfishness and jealousy. When the Voice cuts the by now inextricable knot of the conflict everyone is happy and relieved, except Elektra, who rages with frantic anger. She would rather the lovers were dead than happy together. So, the circle has closed, and we are back to where we first met Elektra. In the meantime, however, Mozart has shown us that in one heart there is room for good and evil, the beautiful and the ugly, the human being and the demon.

Prince Idamantes had a long way to go before the easy-going, elegant and somewhat shallow-minded young man, in the fire of passion and love, became a hero and a worthy king of his people. His development begins when the false news of his father's death reaches him, and it continues with the dramatic meeting on the sea-shore. Idamantes's second aria presents his character at a new, more mature level. The decisive push is provided by his unexpectedly found happiness; in love and through love Idamantes becomes a true man. For him Ilia is not only an object of passion, but also a companion and friend, wiser and stronger than he; he would follow her advice and abide by her judgement for a lifetime. He conquers not only the monster, but also his own fear and weakness. He peacefully waits for his inevitable death. And it is precisely when Idomeneo is floundering hopelessly as a consequence of his own sin that

Idamantes finds himself. After this transformation, Poseidon's verdict entrusting Idamantes with the government of the island and its people is perfectly justified. The passage in which the Voice declares that 'Idamantes should be the King and Ilia be his wife' is worthy of attention. Even the most shortened version of the scene includes this condition, to show that Idamantes alone cannot worthily fulfil this position, but only with the help of Ilia, the better half of his soul.

The leading character of the play, King Idomeneo, appears for the first time on the stage in the eighth scene. However, we have heard about him from the other characters, so we recognise him when he enters. Thus he is able to present the basic conflict, without any introduction, in the first words of his recitative. His aria reflects the antagonistic emotions of doubt and relief. The first recitative of the second act, and then the *'Fuor del mar'* aria, show the King's whole character: heroic, magnanimous and honest; but weak and easily influenced. He cannot avoid the serious consequences of his folly. Trying to outwit Poseidon by sending Idamantes to Greece in Elektra's company only makes matters worse: the anger of the god strikes the island. At the dramatic moment when he is held responsible for what he has done, Idomeneo shows his noblest qualities in shouldering full responsibility, and this moment represents the zenith of the role. As a tragic victim of an unfortunate chain of accidents and of his own lack of fore-thought, he stands alone in the storm, like Lear, abandoned by everyone. From this crest he can only descend: no one can violate godly and human laws without punishment. First he is alienated from his people, and then from his son: and finally comes the verdict of the god which, although it absolves the father, condemns the king. He was weighed in the scales and was found wanting; he proved to be unworthy of rule. And it is now, in the moment of defeat, that Idomeneo's true greatness is revealed: he hands over the throne to his son with relief, in peace and with a reviving soul, acknowledging without bitterness the natural order of things: that old people have to be replaced by younger ones.

As we have seen, the characters of the opera undergo considerable development in the course of the drama. Partly due to events and partly because of the effect they have upon each other, they transform before our eyes. But beyond that they have their own past and future as well. They were not born in the first act, and do not disappear into thin air with the last notes of the finale, but continue living in our souls after the curtain falls. They are emotions and feelings personified. They belong to eternally human types, but are at the same time entirely individual people who we like and feel close to despite their shortcomings, because in their unbridled or shyly restrained outbursts we recognise ourselves. We experience again our own joy in their happiness, our sadness in their grief.

Perhaps Arbaces is the only character who does not give the impression of being a real living person, but merely seems to be a cog in the dramaturgical wheel. His role is that of the trusted friend who draws out Idomeneo's narratives and meditations. His two arias fail to carry the play forward, in plot or psychology, and anyway the second aria is undoubtedly an anti-climax after the greatness of the quartet. On the other hand, the part of the high priest, who is given clear musical characterisation and considerable importance in the progress of the drama, is much more significant. It is he who, in his great recitative, sums up the catastrophe, and, as spokesman for Poseidon, forces the King to come to a decision. However, he could not do all this were he not the representative of the people as well. The chorus takes an active, indeed, a decisively important part in the drama, particularly during the final unfolding of the plot. It is not just a homogeneous, faceless crowd, but a group of individuals, portrayed in various ways. The dramatic double-chorus at the shipwreck in the first act, the chorus heard at the appearance of the sea-monster, and that in the temple scene of the third act, all recall Gluck; the Venetian 6/8 sailors' chorus of the second act, impressing us with its shining Mediterranean brightness, already anticipates *Così fan tutte*.

Mozart assigned an equally active role to the orchestra

67

which, throughout the entire opera from the overture
onwards, carries the drama, and mirrors the action and the
parallel psychological developments. The sweet singing and
rushing roulades of the violins, the dark sonority of the violas
(in Elektra's recitatives and arias), the solidity of the bass
instruments, the flexible, tender singing of the concertante
woodwinds, the peculiar effects of the sordinoed brasses — all
give evidence of an advance in Mozart's co-ordinated vocal-
symphonic method of construction. And in the third act,
which in itself 'took more trouble than a whole opera,
because there is hardly a single scene in it that is not
extremely interesting',* there is hardly a secco. The great
majority of the recitatives — especially later, with the tension
becoming more and more concentrated — are richly and
colourfully accompanied by a dramatically active orchestra.

Three of the musical means Mozart uses in order to achieve
Idomeneo's dramatic effects are worthy of particular
mention here. The first one is what Lert [19] calls the *'Prinzip
der fallenden Pointe',* and what we might loosely translate as
the 'principle of the dropped hint'. Mozart does not set to
music great words or poignant stage situations. He writes
drama and presents living human beings with psychological
depths. He does not exploit situations to their extremes, or
squeeze the last drop from them, but, adhering to Shakespeare's 'moderation amidst the whirlwind of passion', he
creates the necessary tension and achieves the effect he wants
to achieve by moderation — indeed, by restraint. One of his
letters shows how deliberate and conscious this technique
was: '. . . during a conversation one can often just drop a
hint, and this produces a much greater effect than if one had
announced the same thing dictatorially.'† Several dramatic
moments in *Idomeneo* and in the later operas illustrate the
conscious application of this truly Mozartian principle of
understatement.
    The second new feature in Mozart's operatic thinking is

* Letter dated 3 January 1781.
† Letter dated 17 August 1782.

continuity: a continuous blending in construction. Almost unnoticed, secco melts into accompagnato, and this into aria or ensemble. And the reverse is also true. The majority of 'complete' numbers merge into recitative, ensemble, chorus or musical interlude. The smallest unit is not the musical item, not even the scene, but the 'picture' (*'Bild'*). However, there are occasions when even two pictures are linked with music by Mozart. He does not achieve this with decorative interludes, but with functional music which carries the action forward, growing naturally from the closing scene of the first picture, and from which the opening scene of the second picture grows just as naturally. At the same time, the recitatives often recall themes and motives from pieces already heard, and allude to ones to come.

The third characteristic of Mozart's musical construction is the conscious use of recurring musical thoughts. The three most important themes of the overture, as well as several other musical motives appearing later which illustrate various emotions, moods and relationships, return regularly in the course of the opera and contribute to the flow of the drama. Neither earlier nor later in Mozart's dramatic works do we come across such a thorough application of this technique.

Mozart assesses and experiments with every method and form which might promote dramatic expression, and anything unsuitable is tossed aside for once and for all.

The musical language of *Idomeneo,* the forerunner of *Don Giovanni* and *The Magic Flute,* is to a certain extent not yet the language of the later dramma giocoso genre, but is no longer that of the Italian opera seria either. This opera represents Mozart's transitional period, illustrated by the broadness of its musical expression, diverse characterisation, ceaselessly evolving dramatisation, and the colourful rendering of mood and emotion by purely musical means. Under the burdens of love and death, and the almost unbearable pressure of many years' servitude, Mozart has grown into manhood. Having learnt, developed and acquired an abundance of musical experience, he has reached a turning-point in his life and in his art. 1781 is the year of conclusion and recommencement, the turning-point where Mozart summarises, and takes account of, his achievements as a human being and as a creator of works of art.

Notes

(1) Letters dated 8, 13, 15, 29 November; 5, 19, 27 December 1780; 3, 18 January 1781.

(2) A. Heuss, O. Schumann, B. Paumgartner *et al.*

(3) Varesco used the name of the Roman god, Neptune, rather than that of the Greek god, Poseidon — presumably because the text of the opera is in Italian. However, as the setting and the other names are Greek, he should have chosen the Greek name for the sake of consistency. I use the Greek name, Poseidon, here so as to correct this anachronism.

(4) The analysis of *Idomeneo,* as all further analyses in this volume, examines the work from a single viewpoint: that of dramatic means of expression through the language of music.

(5) See letters dated 8 November 1777 and 26 September 1781.

(6) See Mozart's letter of 13 November 1780 for remarks on dramaturgy.

(7) See Mozart's letter dated 19 December 1780.

(8) See letter dated 8 December 1780.

(9) See letter dated 27 December 1780.

(10) See letter dated 29 November 1780.

(11) Mozart applies this same solution to the problem of representing an approaching march in *The Marriage of Figaro.*

(12) See letter dated 15 November 1780.

(13) 'The more often I imagine the quartet on the stage, the greater the impact it has on me . . . . If I found just a single note in the quartet that required alteration, I would do it at once; but in this opera there is nothing which satisfies me so much.' (from letter dated 27 December 1780)

(14) See letter dated 5 December 1780.

(15) 'After the funeral chorus the king, the people, and all

those present leave the stage, and in the following scene the directions state that we should see Idomeneo kneeling in front of the temple. This is simply impossible: he must come in with his whole entourage. A march must be introduced here, and therefore I have composed a simple one, for two violins, viola, 'cello and two oboes to be played a mezza voce. Meanwhile the king enters, and all the things required for the sacrifice can be prepared by the priests. Only then can the king kneel down and begin the prayer.' (from letter dated 3 January 1781)

(16) See letter dated 18 January 1781.

(17) See letters dated 29 November 1780; 3, 18 January 1781.

(18) 'The oracle's speech is still too long, and I have shortened it; but Varesco need not know about it — the text will be printed just as he wrote it.' (from letter dated 18 January 1781)

(19) Ernst Lert, *Mozart auf dem Theater,* Berlin, 1918.

The Abduction from the Seraglio

IN THE autumn of 1782 the following announcement was published in one of the Leipzig papers: 'A person called Mozart abused my drama, entitled *Belmonte and Constanze*, and had the audacity to use it as a libretto for an operetta in Vienna. I wish to take advantage of this opportunity to solemnly protest against this illegal interference, and at the same time announce my intention of taking further measures regarding this matter. Christoph Friedrich Bretzner, author of *Tipsiness*.'

The first offspring of lasting value of the German Singspiel – the newest stage musical genre which had been in existence for less than a decade and a half – *The Abduction from the Seraglio (Die Entführung aus dem Serail)*, has roots delving deep into tradition. The creator of the new genre, Johann Adam Hiller of Leipzig, in his dozen or so musical dramas, united the century-old traditions of the Italian opera buffa, the French opéra comique, the Austrian Stegreifposse, the English operetta, the German Lied, and last but not least that English parody of Italian opera seria, *The Beggar's Opera*. The direct sources of the libretto of *The Abduction* are a type of opera semi-seria by Martinelli and Jomelli entitled *The Liberated Slave-girl*, an English operetta, *The Sultan, or a Peep into the Harem*, and a Singspiel by Bretzner and André, *Belmonte and Constanze, or the Abduction from the Seraglio*, performed in Berlin in 1781. The well-to-do Leipzig merchant, the proud author of *Tipsiness*, however, thought twice before 'taking further measures', since his *Belmonte and Constanze* was not what one might call a very original work of art, but a fairly exact copy of an old English pastiche compiled from the works of several English and Italian composers.

This rich, formal conglomeration is filled with new life, human feeling and a deeply humanist message by Mozart in his opera, *The Abduction from the Seraglio.*

'I long to rush to my desk and I am always delighted to remain there,'* Mozart wrote thirty-six hours after he received the first draft of the libretto from his friend, Stephanie junior, the intendant of the new Vienna Opera House. During that day and a half, he had composed Belmonte's second aria and Constanze's first, as well as the trio finale of the first act, and within another week the entire first act — with the exception of the introductory aria and duet — was completed.

So far everything had gone smoothly; but now trouble began for poor Stephanie. Mozart demanded basic changes in the libretto. '. . . and Stephanie is up to the eyes in work; . . . perhaps he is only friendly to me when we meet face to face, but the only thing that matters is that he will still make the text exactly as I want it, and, by heaven, I do not expect anything more from him!'†

The very beginning of the opera undergoes a change: Belmonte's monologue in prose is changed into an aria, while the ensuing dialogue becomes a duet, closely linked to the first song.[1]

Osmin, who in the original version was only meant to have a small part, is now given, in addition to the single little song Stephanie allotted to him, two arias and three duets. Thereby the role grows in importance and it also gains a significant dramaturgical function. Osmin, by representing the darker side of life, forms a contrast with the pasha, who personifies a high ideal of dignity and greatness, and with the socially-limited but in themselves well-intentioned Europeans.

Osmin is entirely Mozart's creation (he wrote the first aria long before a word of the text was written);[2] he is the most profoundly individual of the characters in *The Abduction,* and was hitherto unprecedented in operatic literature. Even

* Letter dated 1 August 1781.

† Letter dated 26 September 1781.

his first appearance, with the seemingly innocent little folk-song and the ensuing duet, reveals something of the barely-restrained, instinctive cruelty and sensuality — demoniacal features even in a comic context. The beginning of his first aria (number 3) with its obstinate circling around a single musical note,

its primitively monotonous repetitions,

its stereotyped rhythms and stupid scales,

are reflections of Osmin's stubbornness and arrogance. The aria moves into a stretta 'in identical tempo but with quick notes. But as his anger gradually increases, there comes (just when we think the aria has come to an end) the allegro assai, in a completely different metre and in another key. This will create the best effect. For a person so full of raging emotions violates every order and entirely forgets himself; and similarly, it is necessary for the music to forget itself too.'* In order to express this without offending the ear, Mozart chose a related rather than a strange key: but instead of the nearest, D minor, a more remote one, A minor. Again we notice the moderate means: the thirty bars of the allegro assai represent a slightly ironic and understated, but still very accurate musical sketch of monomaniac anger.

The stupid sequences and stereotyped repetitions of the aria govern Osmin in the trio closing the first act too. The two duets of the second act expose the savage's vulnerable spot: as a helpless victim of his own sensuality, he is outwitted by clever Blonde and cunning Pedrillo. And here I have to argue with such distinguished Mozartian scholars as Jahn, Lert and Cohen. They hold the view that Osmin's drunkenness and sleep were not described by Mozart's music in the 'Saufduett' (number 14). True, he could not describe the latter one, since that only occurred in the dialogue after the duet. But Mozart did demonstrate musically the effect of the wine very clearly in the duet's few minutes' duration. After the first draughts, Osmin sings in counter-motion with Pedrillo:

* Letter dated 26 September 1781.

After a few bars, however, the dizziness can be felt: the two voices blend first in parallel thirds:

and shortly afterwards even in octave unison:

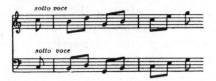

In Mozart's works (and in music in general) the parallel, as a means of expression, always symbolises some kind of bond – love, friendship or family relationship. Here this link is created by the wine which usually stimulates drunken people to hobnob with those around them; and here it suddenly sweeps away Osmin's earlier aversion to Pedrillo. By the end of the duet, Osmin is completely drunk, 'he entirely forgets himself'. One bar is omitted from the Turkish military music of 'Vivat Bacchus!' and so the period narrows down to seven bars, while the orchestral postlude turns into a five-bar phrase: the music has forgotten itself too!

This is how in his disciplined way Mozart describes Osmin's drunkenness. And he also shows with purely musical means this basically comic character's blind, fanatical cruelty[3] in the gallows aria of the third act (number 19) that in parts has an almost evil atmosphere. The form he applies with ingenious dramatic sense is the rondo A-B-A-C-A-D-B-A, with tone-painting taken from baroque music but developed and psychologically strengthened. The blood-thirsty plan for revenge returns with the obsession of a maniac in the ritornello, as do the already familiar stereotyped repetitions in the extended coda. In the concluding vaudeville-style finale, after the four Europeans have expressed their gratitude for Selim's magnanimity with roughly identical melodies, Osmin cannot restrain himself any longer and, having been enraged by Blonde's teasing, interrupts the latter's closing words. He begins as if he would continue the song of gratitude with the others, but with the tempo getting quicker and quicker Osmin's anger becomes less and less restrained, the accompanying bass instruments intensify the atmosphere, and after a strong, tense modulation with a sudden change of metre the music passes on to the coda of the first aria. Osmin can only give vent to his unsatisfied viciousness in his imagination. As with Elektra in *Idomeneo*, the circle is complete; only Osmin is shown even more profoundly as an individual. He is Revenge personified.

Belmonte is the least revealing character in *The Abduction*. Yet from one point of view, his is a revolutionarily new part. Belmonte is the first tenor heroic lover after the almost two-centuries-old unnatural monopoly of castrati, and women singers dressed up as men. Perhaps the weakness of the role is due to its pioneering character. This tenor part — which of course means not only a different register, but a different personality as well! — was without predecessors in operatic literature. Belmonte is not a particularly sharp-witted young man (Pedrillo is rather more cunning), nor can he boast a great deal of imagination (he mostly thinks in the patterns of his social class); indeed, he is not a very great hero either (Constanze is definitely more courageous). But Belmonte is kind, good and honest: he is Love. His intellectual outlook is straightforward; he is a dreaming, emotional, even sentimental soul. His character remains the same throughout the opera; some slight development can be found only in the duet of the third act. But we will discuss this later when we speak about Constanze; because — like Idamantes before him — only in love and through love does Belmonte become truly a man.

Constanze is a womanly character from the start. As a type, she is Faithfulness. True that of her three arias, two fall victim to the 'skilful larynx of Mademoiselle Cavalieri';* however, we should not forget that it is Mozart who makes concessions here – Mozart who is at home in every form, every genre, and every style, and who finds the means of dramatic expression and true characterisation even within the confines of the virtuoso bravura aria. Constanze's first and third arias display to us the active, courageous heroine who can fight, suffer, even die for her faith, honour and love. The heart-stirring recitative-like main theme of the first aria and particularly the touchingly beautiful second aria, reflect the girl's tender, warm soul.

Let us pause for a moment at this G-minor recitative and aria (number 10). It is common knowledge that for Mozart, who was vitally conscious of tonality, G minor expressed lonely grief, resignation and hopelessness. Among his symphonic and chamber music compositions there are relatively few works in G minor, and it is particularly significant in this light that all Mozart's three young heroines of his later operas, Ilia, Constanze and Pamina (*The Magic Flute*) – who show many similarities in type, personality and, indeed, fate – have one G-minor aria each at the most tragic moment of their role.

Dent's view that Constanze fails to be an individual personality, and is simply a prima donna, would be proved wrong even if Constanze sang nothing other than that single recitative and aria. I have a feeling that Dent, and a number of other critics as well, completely misunderstand *The Abduction*; particularly as a few lines later he says: '. . . there is the strangest suggestion of Bach in the arioso of Constanze . . . . The words might have come from a church cantata; how they ever came into the libretto of a Viennese comic opera is beyond guessing. But the notes which Mozart writes for them might have come from Bach too.'† The misunderstanding lies in the fact that *The Abduction* is not a comic opera, but is, in certain ways, a forerunner of the genre of dramma giocoso – of course still within the more modest framework of the Singspiel. And as far as the virtuoso

* Letter dated 26 September 1781.

† E.J. Dent, *Mozart's Operas*, Oxford University Press, first published 1913.

roulades and cadenzas in Constanze's great C-major aria are concerned:

1. coloratura is not employed for its own sake, but is in character and is dramatically linked with the text ('I only *laugh* at pain and suffering', 'the sky gives its *blessings*', 'death provides *redemption*', and so on);
2. why should we deny the singer the use of the cadenza as a means of expression when it is almost compulsory in a concerto?

Constanze's character develops further in the large quartet finale of the second act. Belmonte now recognises her faithfulness and innocence, after his having just held her – in G minor! – under unjust suspicion. The peak of her part is the recitative and duet preceding the last finale in which she first plays the leading role (as Ilia did in her duet with Idamantes in the third act of *Idomeneo*). She is the stronger of the two, and it is her calm integrity, wisdom and gaiety which time and again dissolve the young man's self-reproach and despair. Constanze's great spiritual strength is at last triumphant and (this is where the male Belmonte outgrows the limits imposed upon the castrato Idamantes and his predecessors) the coda of the duet is now begun by the man, and it is the girl who follows obediently, note by note. In a happily intertwined parallel of thirds, they await death fearlessly together.

Pedrillo plays an important role in the development of the plot: it is he who takes Belmonte to the pasha's residence where, due to his skill, he has managed to ensure freedom of movement for himself, and it is he who conceives and executes the whole plan of elopement. Pedrillo, Belmonte's faithful servant, is somewhat cowardly, but very honest. He is a child of the people, an example of sober peasant cunning. He is a more colourful, richer and more individual character than his immediate predecessor, the servant of the commedia dell'arte and of the opera buffa – just as Blonde is considerably more than an offspring of tradition. Blonde is a courageous and self-assured girl who can preserve her independence even during imprisonment – free of any kind of sentimentality (English!) – and has her own definite

principles of life: a strong personality indeed. She accepts life
as it is, and makes the best of every situation. She looks at
people — including her own mistress — with mild, supercilious irony. The words of her second aria *'ihrem schwachen,
schwachen, kranken Herzen'* ('her weak, weak, sick heart')
ironically recall the melody of the line *'haucht sie alle meine
Klagen'* of Constanze's G-minor aria with a similar meaning.
The dramaturgical justification of this reference is the fact
that Blonde had secretly overheard Constanze's aria:

Mozart does not deny Blonde the right of coloratura either;
however, Blonde has altogether three smooth scales and
broken triads, instead of Constanze's richly complicated
passages:

The girl's personality and background do not allow more
intellectual and musical ornamentation. [4]

Even before we become personally acquainted with Pasha
Selim, we learn from Pedrillo that he has principles. This
aspect of his character is not enlarged upon later in the
libretto: obviously it was necessary in order to provide basis
and opportunity for Constanze's faithfulness. An everyday
Turk of the period would hardly care about the inner
sentiments of his lawfully-acquired odalisque. At the same

time, Selim's principles are the cause of the unexpected turn in the last dialogue, the magnanimous pardon that puts Belmonte and any European audience to shame with its epigram-like, whimsical, yet wise, concluding sentence: 'He whom you cannot win over with goodness, would be better got rid of.'

The only thing we learn about Selim's part from Mozart's correspondence is that it was originally supposed to be a singing part.[5] We have no accurate information as to why this idea was modified in due course, and why Selim became a passive listener to Constanze's arias. Or, more important, why Selim – who embodies the ethics and carries the message of the opera – has been placed dramaturgically lower than all the other characters. According to Lert, in the end Mozart 'wrote Selim's part – very tactfully – to be a prose part. Mozart did not want to and could not thunder arias of tyrants, and love-songs did not become the personality of that Moslem who approached love from a practical point of view and finally gave up.'* Schurig, who approached Mozart in a fairly critical way, found a much more prosaic explanation: there was no singer capable of carrying the weight and significance of the character.[6] Both reasons are possible; the latter seems to be the more probable.

The essence of the Selim-concept is revealed most satisfactorily in a remark made, unintentionally, by Dent: 'One of the serious shortcomings of the opera is that Selim pasha does not sing at all . . . . However, if we say that music is the most important way of expressing sentiments and emotions then a person who only speaks and does not sing, could as well be dumb.'† But this is the key to the whole part! For Selim's emotions are inessential to the play. What is essential is only the principle he represents: the ideal of enlightened humanism. Personality and the emotional expression it requires are, without music and without musical characterisation, inconceivable in a musical genre. However, Selim is worth more, and at the same time less, than the other characters in the play. He is in fact merely a walking moral

* Lert, q.v.
† Dent, q.v.

concept. The fragile framework of the young genre of Singspiel was only capable of bearing this burden in the easier and more airy form of prose. The individual version of the type, and the musical formulation of humanist ideals, will not come for another ten years, in *The Magic Flute*.

Fantasy and reality are interwoven in the musical texture of *The Abduction*. The overture, which flows naturally into Belmonte's first aria, sets the mood by contrasting the C-major presto of a Turkish atmosphere with a languishing C-minor andante.[7] Apart from this, Mozart applies the colourful elements of Turkish orchestration only in the janissary choruses of the first and third acts, in the '*Saufduett*' of the second act, and in Osmin's two arias.[8] It is a funny sort of 'comic opera overture': almost the entire middle passage of the three-part song-form, and nearly a half of the two outside passages are in minor keys – in fact Mozart's three 'tragic' minor keys: G, C, and F minor. The subito forte and piano passages, as well as the sharply marked off major and minor sections, and the exotic colour of the clarinets and percussion instruments (bass drum, cymbal and triangle); introduce a novelty in orchestral sound, creating the oriental atmosphere of a conventional fairyland. The sentimental lyrical sound and 'irregular' periods of the thinly-veiled anticipation in minor key of Belmonte's first aria (five-, seven-, and nine-bar units, with just one regular eight-bar period) show the deep currents of human conflict beneath the smooth surface of the colourful, playful Singspiel.

In Belmonte's A-major second aria (number 4)[9] Mozart applies the baroque Tonmalerei technique[10] as in Blonde's first and Osmin's last arias. But *The Abduction* is incomparably more developed than the earlier operas as far as tone-painting, psychological motivation, and quality of music are concerned; and the Tonmalerei technique is not an aim, but just a means: one of the many and not even the most important means. Much more important is the intonation of Belmonte's arias, the slightly sentimental and melancholy, tender and shy melodic line and link-up of harmonies. This scale-melody, with its characteristic two augmented seconds in the rising sigh of the line, *'Es hebt sich die schwellende Brust'*

will return in one of the few tragic situations in *The Marriage of Figaro* (see examples on pages 124 to 126). The heart-stirring major-minor play of the recapitulation (five-bar minor cadence) in Belmonte's second aria recalls similar moments of the overture. Perhaps it is not an accident, but a musical symbol of the spiritual contact between the two lovers and of the fate-conquering feeling of belonging to one another, that the recapitulation of Constanze's following aria also begins with a similar five-bar minor turn slipped casually into the end of the tiny 'development' of the miniature sonata form.

When speaking about Ilia's first aria in *Idomeneo*, we mentioned that Mozart developed the traditional da capo aria form, taken from the opera seria. In Constanze's first B-flat major aria (number 6) the da capo form of the Italian bravura aria reflects certain unmistakable marks of the significantly higher standard sonata form. In *The Marriage of Figaro*, as we shall see, Mozart composes whole scenes and ensembles in regular sonata form. The adagio opening theme of Constanze's aria dreams of past happiness; in the following allegro, after a few thematic and modulating transitional bars reflecting the sorrow of departure, the second theme appears in F minor describing the sadness of the present; and this is followed by the two-part closing subject in F major. The ten-bar development above the new, imitative motive of the orchestra further develops in the minor key the first half of the main subject in the vocal part. Into this slides the

83

recapitulation theme which, although somewhat varied and extended, still quite accurately repeats the exposition in the original key. As in Idomeneo's *'Fuor del mar'*, the improved form of the Italian bravura aria fulfils a dramatic function, and flexibly serves the musical characterisation. Indeed, not only does Mozart improve the musical form, but the text as well. 'I have tried to express the lines starting with the words *"Trennung war mein banges Los"* in the music, as far as the Italian bravura aria permits. I have changed the word *"hui"* for *"schnell"*, so it becomes: *"Doch wie schnell schwand meine Freude"*. I do not know what these German poets of ours are thinking of; even if they have no idea of theatre — or at any rate opera — they should at least not make their characters sound as though they were addressing a herd of pigs.'*

It is only because of its potential power that the trio concluding the first act serves as a finale. Musical characterisation sharply separates Osmin from the two tenor voices which move, either parallel or in canonic imitation, together throughout the trio.

After Blonde's aria of folk-song simplicity that opens the second act, we are again made to realise by Blonde's and Osmin's duet (number 9) how Mozart carved each of his characters from one block, and how the musical characterisation of each figure is uniform throughout the opera. A single phrase from Osmin, for instance, contains in a condensed form almost every constituent of the musical material of the character: the primitive sequences, the silly scales, and the conceited triads:

* Letter dated 26 September 1781.

The following bars, sung by Blonde, ridicule Osmin's arrogance by purely musical means, by imitating his melody in a comically deep register for a soprano. A bent for ridiculing others seems to be part of Blonde's character: she ridicules Constanze with fine irony in her second aria, and then in the quartet. In the middle passage of the duet Osmin's blockheaded triads are again characteristically separated from Blonde's easy, playful roulades.

This duet is an example of a development in relationship expressed in musical terms. The allegro that opens the duet is begun by Osmin: he has the upper hand. In the andante, however, the two voices are set against each other with contrapuntal equality. The concluding allegro assai is commenced by Blonde, while her melody is respectfully imitated by Osmin, who has been beaten in the battle of words.

Constanze's two arias (numbers 10 and 11) have already been partly discussed; the only thing we might add is that while the heroic concertante character of the Italian bravura aria is supported by the virtuoso performances of four solo instruments (flute, oboe, violin and 'cello), the wonderful 'Traurigkeit' aria that attains Paminian heights (one of the most beautiful musical expressions of grief) is given a strange, plaintive, tragic flavour by the dark tone of the basset horn. The basset horn was the youngest offspring of the clarinet family, and had only been in existence for a few years at the time The Abduction was composed. Mozart first exployed it in a serenade for wind instruments composed at the beginning of 1781. Afterwards he experimented with it in two smaller chamber music compositions, and then, combined with a voice, in Constanze's G-minor aria. In later years we find the instrument in his six trios written for two sopranos and bass, as well as in an aria for soprano, and it appears in all three great works of his last year: *The Magic Flute, Titus* and the *Requiem.*

The action, which had drawn to a halt, now continues with Blonde's second aria (number 12); the colourfully-orchestrated little song reflects the healthy optimism of the clever young girl who takes all dangers in her stride. The patchwork of rhythm and harmony in Pedrillo's aria (number 13), the fragments of melody coming in fits and starts, the excited accompanying triplets and restless bass sequences, give a psychologically perfect characterisation of the *malgré lui* hero, the little lad who tries to overcome his fear of the dark by singing and whistling. After the *'Saufduett'*, Belmonte's aria (number 15) interrupts the action. Despite all its musical beauty it does not add one jot to his characterisation.

The quartet which concludes the second act (number 16) does not really carry the action forward. However, with fine psychological insight, Mozart shows two versions of a single incident: a lovers' quarrel. The aristocratic couple and the servant couple each react in their own ways. During Constanze's and Belmonte's somewhat pathetic effusions, the practical Blonde and Pedrillo discuss the arrangements for the elopement. Constanze reacts with tears to the storm in a tea-cup, while Blonde solves her misunderstanding with Pedrillo with a slap on the face. The trouble starts in G minor: the suspicion is very grave, even though it lacks dramaturgical significance. The accusations and also the apologies are started by Pedrillo whose lack of inhibitions enables him to overcome social conventions. In the musical texture of the quartet, the effusively sentimental tone of the aristocratic couple again sharply contrasts with the staccato speech of the servant couple. (The parallel quarrels and simultaneous reconciliations of the two couples recall a similar situation in *The Merchant of Venice*.) The musical representation of forgiveness is a brilliant trouvaille: with artifical elegance Blonde imitates — in a canonic sequence — Constanze's slightly bombastic phrases. The line Mozart chose in the *Idomeneo* quartet is continued in the quartet of *The Abduction*: from these seeds the ensembles and finales of the later operas will grow. There we shall find various characters simultaneously carrying the story onwards, and reacting to events in their own ways. The possibilities of parallel action made opera a mirror reflecting life and nature in a more complete way than any other theatrical genre.

The third act starts with a long dialogue during which the practical Pedrillo begins to put his careful plans for the abduction from the seraglio into operation. Perhaps it is not by accident that now, when there is greater need for quick decisions and actions than at any other time, the brave Belmonte stands rooted to the centre of the stage, and in another (his fourth, number 17) lengthy aria tells the world about his excitement and happiness, and leaves the work, with an elegant gesture, to his servant. Incidentally, this aria is one of the most beautiful pearls of operatic, Mozartian or, indeed, tenor music: a single wonderful, endless melody, the relieved singing of a happy soul; there is not a dissonant chord or even a minor key harmony throughout. It is a pity that this lovely aria is often omitted from performances of the opera, with the excuse that it stops the flow of action. I have a feeling that the reason is really that both musically and technically it presents an extremely difficult task for the tenor.

Pedrillo's romance (number 18) has an exotic air, although it is in different style from the Turkish pieces. It is a little Italian or Spanish type of song with a slight Arabic tang, and it has a pizzicato accompaniment that imitates guitar-playing. But it has not been inserted arbitrarily; it has a dramatic function (it is a signal), and moreover its simple serenade-like character suits the situation. (Subdued fear, and barely-disguised excitement at the prospect of the great adventure lurk behind the strange harmonies of the fading guitar accompaniment.)

The duet (number 20) following Osmin's gallows aria is the

twin of Ilia's and Idamantes's duet of *Idomeneo*. The
introductory recitative starts with Belmonte's 'defeatist'
words; the frightened heart-beating of the syncopated accompaniment, and the gasping, faltering, declining broken
chords of the violins

demonstrate Belmonte's fear. The intonation suddenly
changes with Constanze's calm, almost heroic sentences.
Lengthy, sustained string harmonies denote her peace of
mind that defies even the prospect of death. The first
andante part of the duet also starts with these two elements
of intonation; then, as a result of Constanze's great strength
of character, Belmonte also comes to terms with himself. He
faithfully imitates his lover's melodies, and follows her in
tender thirds. Yet there are still one or two desperate
exclamations, above the shrieking violin triads (the inversion
of the figuration of the introductory recitative),

and above the orchestra's chords of punctuated rhythm, to
demonstrate the man's hidden fear. However, he finally
overcomes his weakness: it is he who starts the allegro that
concludes the duet. At death's door, and beside the woman
he loves, Belmonte has grown into manhood.

To what we said before about the vaudeville finale

(number 21) that concludes the opera, we may add that the character-drawing is finely differentiated even within the four similar stanzas. In keeping with their more prosaic, down-to-earth personalities, Blonde and Pedrillo sing Belmonte's and Constanze's melody in a less elegant, simplified and more earthbound way:

It is due to the faults of the text, and especially to the inherent weaknesses of the Singspiel, that the structure and dramaturgical unity of *The Abduction* are of a lower standard than those of *Idomeneo*. With a few exceptions, the vocal numbers are completely without action — they only describe the characters and their feelings. The most important active parts of the opera — among them the final resolution, and the elopement scene itself — are mostly described in prose, without music. Even the three finales only fulfil a finale's function in so far as they close an act. Their character is rather that of a fresco-like, lyrical ensemble which suspends the action at a high point of the opera; they are still a far cry from the true Mozartian finales of the later years which are characterised by great tension, increasing dramatic compression, leading to a climactic resolution. Take, for instance, the quartet of the second act: at the moment of crisis, when the long-awaited first meeting between Belmonte and Constanze takes place, the action stops, and the music describes lengthily — though very beautifully — the spiritual states of the four people. Although the jealousy scene has a serious message, and with its résumé already foreshadows *The Magic Flute,* it does not carry the action forward any more successfully. One tends to feel it has been added later since the conflict is completely solved within the framework of the number.

Mozart saw the dramaturgical faults of the libretto very clearly, and did his best to correct them. 'Now the whole story has to be turned upside down ... at my own request. The third act starts with a charming quintet, or rather a finale, but I would like to put that at the end of the second act. The realisation of this, however, requires significant alterations – indeed, a completely new plot.'* 'The text is very good at showing Osmin's stupid, rude and wicked character. I know the verse is not of the highest standard, but it fitted in so well with my musical ideas (already whirling in my head) that I could not help but like it . . . . Why are Italian comic operas so popular, despite their miserable libretti, even in Paris where I have personally witnessed their success? Because in them the music is entirely dominant, and this makes one forget about everything else. An opera will be even more of a success if the play is based upon a well-constructed plot, but the text only serves the music and the meaning is not sacrificed for the sake of a few miserable rhymes ... or even complete stanzas which destroy the composer's whole idea. Of course music cannot exist without verses; but rhymes for their own sake are only harmful . . . . Therefore the most fortunate solution is if a good composer, who also understands the stage, and can himself take part in writing the libretto, works with a skilful poet.'†

Stephanie, however, was unable to invent a new 'plot', or perhaps was not keen to find one, and consequently his libretto is dramaturgically of a lower standard than Bretzner's. Ethically, however, with Mozart's own idea for the final solution, it rises well above Bretzner's libretto. In Bretzner's version, Selim recognises Belmonte as his own son, and this *deus ex machina* motive makes the pardon understandable and therefore weightless. In Mozart's story, however, when the pasha sets Belmonte free, he is not only

* Letter dated 26 September 1781.
† Letter dated 13 October 1781.

freeing the would-be kidnapper of the woman he loves, but also the son of his most hated enemy.

It is interesting to compare Mozart's concept with two other dramatic versions of the kidnapping theme: those by Euripides and Goethe. The Euripidean conflict in *Iphigenia Among the Tauri* has a *deus ex machina* solution: at the order of the goddess Athena, King Thoas is compelled to release his prisoners. Goethe, on the other hand – who started writing the prose version of his *Iphigenie auf Tauris* a few years before *The Abduction*, but completed and published the verse-drama only half a decade after the first performance of the opera – allowed the barbaric king to be convinced by Iphigenie's and Orestes's arguments in the great monologues of the last scene.

Mozart's deep humanism, however, takes him even one step further than Goethe. He does not convince by argument – on the contrary, he even accumulates difficulties to obstruct the way to a favourable solution. Selim had been banished from his native land by Belmonte's father, the Spanish governor of Oran; it was also Belmonte's father who separated the pasha from his lover, and deprived him of his honour, power and wealth. There could hardly be any greater reason for revenge. Yet in spite of all this, of his own will, Selim extends his pardon, and releases his prisoners. 'I despise your father so much that I could do nothing resembling his actions. You are free, take your Constanze, return to your native country, and tell your father that you have been my prisoner, but I set you free so that you could inform him. It is a much greater joy to pay for injustice with good than to repay old crimes with more crimes . . . . Be more humane than your father used to be: that would be a worthy reward for my deed.' So, according to Mozart's idea, it is not due to alien intervention, and not even to convincing argument, that a favourable solution is achieved. Here the solution is provided by Selim voluntarily obeying an instinctive human-ism by which he conquers his own self, and then even turns his enemies into more noble people.

The Abduction is another significant step in Mozart's

development towards the Shakespearean ideal of portraying life in its completeness. Love and death, fiction and reality, irony and pathos, lyricism and drama, tragedy and comedy, an endless scale of moods, emotions and passions, are all strung like beads on the single thread of the action. It is not only the *first* German opera, but (despite its Turkish, Spanish and English characters) from the first to the last note it is *entirely* a German opera.

Notes

(1) 'The original text began with a monologue, but I asked Herr Stephanie to turn it into a small arietta, and then to put in a duet to replace the dialogue after Osmin's song.' (letter dated 26 September 1781)

(2) 'I have given an aria to Herr Stephanie: and the majority of the music was completed before Stephanie knew anything about it all.' (letter dated 26 September 1781)

(3) 'Osmin's anger becomes comic by the fact that I have accompanied it with Turkish music,' wrote Mozart in connection with Osmin's first aria (number 3). (letter dated 26 September 1781)

(4) In contrast to all earlier practice that left such 'secondary additions' to the mercy of the singers, Mozart wrote down every single ornament, cadenza and coloratura passage in *The Abduction*.

(5) See letter dated 1 August 1781.

(6) A. Schurig, *W.A. Mozart,* 1913.

(7) 'The overture . . . is quite short; forte and piano passages alternate in it, the Turkish music coming in at the forte passages.' (letter dated 26 September 1781)

(8) On the day Mozart composed the first janissary chorus he visited the military camp near Vienna. 'The janissary chorus is exactly what is required: it is short and gay, and written to please the Viennese,' he wrote later. (letter dated 26 September 1781)

(9) Mozart's favourite aria. (see letter dated 26 September 1781)

(10) '. . . even the beating of the loving heart can be felt . . .' (letter dated 26 September 1781)

L'Oca del Cairo, Der Schauspieldirektor, IX
The Marriage of Figaro (1)

DURING the four years following the première of *The Abduction,* Mozart took an interest in the genre of comic opera. What he wanted to write was not opéra comique, or opera buffa, but 'komishe Oper': German comic opera. 'Each nation has its own opera; why should not we, Germans, have our own too? Can't one sing in German just as well as in French or English? Isn't German better for singing than Russian? Well, now I am going to write a German opera for myself: I have selected Goldoni's comedy, *The Servant of Two Masters.'** This plan, however, was never realized, and Mozart continued to search for a libretto. 'I have looked through about a hundred or even more libretti, but there was hardly one to satisfy me,' he wrote to his father.† Reluctantly he ordered another libretto from Varesco: 'The essential thing is that it should be very funny.'

After *Idomeneo,* Mozart did not expect much from Varesco; he tried to make him understand, by stressing once more, that in an opera the main thing is the music, and therefore the librettist should make as many alterations as the composer required. By December, *L'Oca del Cairo* (The Cairo Goose) was progressing, and Mozart gave detailed instruction as to the actual construction of the second act.[1] However, the old abbé failed once again, and in the end *L'Oca del Cairo* remained unfinished. But the significance of this fragment – consisting of only a few arias, two duets, one quartet and a finale – is that the finale was Mozart's first buffo finale with action, with a properly composed gradation

---

* Letter dated 5 February 1783.
† Letter dated 7 May 1783.

throughout, a contrast of two groups of people, and sharply outlined musical characterisation of the various figures within the different groups. Clearly we are approaching *The Marriage of Figaro*!

After another experiment with Italian comic opera,[2] and a pantomime which was completed, but most of which has since been lost,[3] a plan for a German komische Oper came up again.[4] The libretto of the one-act composition, entitled *Der Schauspieldirektor* (The Impresario), was based on an idea by Emperor Joseph II, and was written by Stephanie junior, the librettist of *The Abduction*. Mozart found a new kind of wit in this light, funny play, written for four singers, and consisting of only five numbers. Whether it is due to the German text, to the theatrical atmosphere, or to the six Haydn quartets completed but a short time earlier, one doesn't know; but *Der Schauspieldirektor* reflects an enrichment of Mozart's buffo language, characterisation, and dramatic means of expression, especially in the high standard of the counterpoint. This is seen better than anywhere else in the wittily and wonderfully constructed quarrel trio which – along with the brilliant comic-opera overture – is the most valuable number of the play.

Understandably enough, Mozart showed little interest in this 'comedy with music', that was anecdotal and parodic, but lacking in deeper dramatic possibilities (in modern terminology, it would be classed as a kind of musical comedy). After all, such an assignment was unworthy of him: at that time he had entirely different and more ambitious plans.

1783: Mozart made the acquaintance of Lorenzo da Ponte, the newly appointed 'official theatre poet' of the Italian opera company in Vienna.

1784: After eight years' delay, Beaumarchais's comedy, *The Marriage of Figaro, or A Crazy Day* – banned until then by royal order – was at last performed in Paris.

1785: Mozart became a member of one of the masonic lodges in Vienna.

These three completely unrelated events made a decisive impact on the further development of Mozartian music-drama. *The Marriage of Figaro* was the first character-comedy of operatic literature, and – together with its original prose version – it effectively contributed to the intellectual preparation for the French revolution. The friendship and prolific creative relationship with da Ponte resulted in three giant operas which at the same time gave the world a new musical genre. And affected by masonic ideas, Mozart was 'at that stage of intellectual development when he might well begin to realise that the religion of his fathers did not provide him with so complete a philosophy of life as he had hitherto been taught to believe.'* Approaching the summit of artistic maturity, Mozart fully understood the completeness of life, and the perfect artistic reflection of it.

Mozart discovered da Ponte for himself, finding in him, perhaps, his first suitable creative partner. Beaumarchais's comedy was still banned in Vienna when da Ponte was granted permission for the performance of the opera – after he had persuaded the Emperor that, with the poison fangs of *The Marriage of Figaro* removed, only the basic action of the play had been retained.

Unfortunately, Mozart's correspondence provides no information as to the development of the *Figaro* libretto: composer and librettist lived in the same town, and worked together on it. It is certain that the actual idea originated from Mozart himself (he was acquainted with Paisiello's *Barbiere di Siviglia* as well as with Beaumarchais's own incidental music for his comedy); and a letter of his father's confirms as well that he played a significant part in the reshaping of the text. 'In all certainty it has to be translated from the French very freely, so that it can be effective also as an opera,' Leopold Mozart wrote about Beaumarchais's play,† and with this half-sentence he indicated one of the eternal laws of the genre. For if it is true – and no doubt it is – that in opera the main thing is the music, then a good

* Dent, q.v.
†Letter dated 11 November 1785.

96

prose drama in its original form cannot be a suitable opera libretto because it is already a complete stage work in itself. Thus music could only play a secondary role, that of accompaniment, and could never be a master of the text, or even its equal partner. It is not accidental that those few literary stage works set to music in their original form, without being rewritten into libretti, were all book-dramas, that is to say, dramas which in their own right were hardly worthy of the stage. In vain would one look for Heine's *Ratcliff*, Maeterlinck's *Pelléas*, or Wilde's *Salome* on theatre play-bills for they were only taken off the book shelves and placed on the stage as a result of Mascagni's, Debussy's, and Richard Strauss's music. Boito *recreated* Shakespeare when he wrote the libretti of *Othello* and *Falstaff*. And da Ponte recreated Beaumarchais: the conception, action and construction remained essentially the same, but da Ponte's adaptation made the work suitable for use in the operatic medium.

In the course of his adventurous life, that bore many resemblances to that of da Ponte, Beaumarchais (watchmaker, spy, arms-smuggler, publisher and playwright) tried his hand at opera-libretti as well. One of them, entitled *Tarare,* was written for Gluck who, however, left the uninteresting, pseudo-historical horror drama to be used by his student, Salieri. In addition, Beaumarchais experimented with composition. For instance, in the original version, *The Barber of Seville* was meant to be a comic opera, with music compiled by himself from Spanish folk-songs and dances. And although the second work of the trilogy, *The Marriage of Figaro,* is a more serious work of art as far as its message is concerned, still, its song and dance interludes, its pantomime and vaudeville finale almost cry out for a composer of opera. So da Ponte safely adopted the formal construction of Beaumarchais's comedy since its original version already contained certain features characteristic of opera.

Da Ponte prefaced the original libretto with the following comments:

'The usual duration of a theatre performance, as well as the limited number of characters to be used; then the setting, costumes and other items expected by an opera audience — these are the reasons why I did not simply translate this excellent comedy, but rather made some kind of transcript . . . .

'Therefore I found it necessary to reduce the original number of sixteen characters to eleven, of whom two can be played by the same actor; and I was also compelled to leave out not only a whole act, but a number of other effective scenes, and a lot of the witty lines in which the play abounded. I had to make up for their absence with canzonettas, arias and choruses which seemed appropriate for setting to music, and also I had to add such thoughts as can be expressed with the help of poetry but never with prose. However, despite all attempts by the composer and myself to condense it, the opera is not a short stage work. We hope to be excused by the artistic handling . . . as well as by the multitude of essential musical numbers which reduce the superfluous movement of the characters, as well as the monotony of long recitatives. We hope that we have succeeded in rendering the emotional content imaginatively, and in realising our main aim: to present a virtually new kind of play to the stage, for an audience of refined taste and sure artistic sense.'

Da Ponte's libretto is 'an obedient daughter of the music'; it gives an opportunity to express in its own language the action of the work, to draw the characters, and communicate its own ideas. In accordance with the specific character of the opera genre, Figaro's monologues, the social, political and ethical allusions made by Figaro and Marcellina, as well as some of the parallel threads of the action, are left out; so the roles of the subordinate characters become even less significant, and the five leading characters themselves, as well as their interrelationship, also undergo certain changes. Beaumarchais, who adopted the well-known characters of *The Barber of Seville* and continued its story, could afford the luxury of having a plot with many side lines, but without an exposition. However, Mozart and da Ponte had to single out a main theme from the complicated details, and this naturally resulted in altering the personalities of the characters and, more than once, even in their almost complete recreation.

However, the basic conflict — the open clash between the aristocracy and the lower classes — remained unchanged. And the solution of the conflict also remained the same: the inevitable withdrawal of feudalism, and a certain gaining of ground by the underprivileged class. (A common feature of Mozart's three 'Italian' operas is that he censures and to a certain extent even ridicules the aristocracy.) The basic tone, that of irony and satire, remains; and love and class conflict are the driving forces of both works. Beaumarchais, Mozart and da Ponte all knew the ups and downs of life from personal experience since all three of them had lower-class backgrounds, and so they understood the situation of the oppressed classes. On the other hand, due to their talents, all three attained some degree of acceptance in the highest social circles, indeed, in the court itself. And so the castle of Aguasfrescas, near Seville, becomes a battlefield for opposing forces: the people and the court.

The overture of revolution: that is what Beaumarchais's play was called in its own time; while, according to Napoleon's description, 'The Marriage of Figaro is revolution in full swing.' 'I make people laugh and thus change the world,' was the epithet Beaumarchais gave to his comedy.

In Mozart's opera, too, action is the ruling element. At this stage of his development in musical drama, an increasing importance is attached to the role of the ensemble where two or more characters act simultaneously while the story develops and the situation often changes significantly. In the ensembles Mozart recognised enormous opportunities for movement, development, and varied musical rendering. One of the results of this was that, compared with previous works, *The Marriage of Figaro* contains a much larger proportion of ensembles. In contrast to the fifteen arias and three ensembles of *Idomeneo,* and the thirteen arias and seven ensembles of *The Abduction,* here we have twelve ensembles and fourteen arias (not counting the two choral numbers), and if — in accordance with their dramaturgical functions — Figaro's aria of the first act and Susanna's of the second are also regarded as ensemble numbers, then the shift in proportion is even greater: twelve arias — fourteen ensembles!

Even the arias are dramaturgically justified, and serve the action; indeed, Mozart and da Ponte ingeniously made use of their obligation to compose traditional solo numbers for each singer. Let us take, for instance, the beginning of the fourth act. Barbarina's small cavatina in folk-song mood with muted string accompaniment (number 23) in F minor — the key which in Mozart's tonality system expressed pretended sorrow, pseudo-tragedy, or subjectively real grief due to an objectively unimportant reason — plays a decisive role in the action. Had she not lost the pin, Figaro would never have discovered Susanna's 'unfaithfulness', and would not have learnt of the place selected for her meeting with the count. However, when Figaro and Marcellina take Barbarina by surprise as she is trying to find the lost pin (the cavatina stops in the middle, on the dominant: she did not find the pin) the girl gives away the secret and the action can continue. Nevertheless, for the time being Figaro is helpless: he has to wait until Susanna and the count arrive at the chestnut grove. Beaumarchais's solution is simple: an intermission followed by the great Figaro monologue. But Mozart and da Ponte make a virtue of necessity, and use this enforced break in the flow of the action, dictated by the time factor, for the inclusion of two 'compulsory' and two 'functional' arias.

Among these, Marcellina's coloratura aria of a baroque character (number 24) gives a rather conventional rendering of the type, and has a somewhat awkward melody line, moving in a small circle, with some unexpected and unjustified leaps. Overwhelmingly feminine cadences, artificial, heavy coloratura passages and conventional cadenzas with excited, indeed, nervous accompaniment, show a spinster in her 'dangerous years', full of inhibitions and suppressed emotions.

Basilio's ensuing donkey-hide aria (number 25) is also a 'compulsory number': a musical portrait of the bootlicking

courtier, the social climber. The musical characterisation and
the allegorical manner of expression reveal a narrow-minded
but dangerous back-biter, with flexible manners and plenty
of smooth talk, bred in the court's miasmic atmosphere of
intrigue.

Figaro's next recitative and aria (number 26) takes the
place of the original great monologue. Nothing is left of the
political allusions, the sharp social comment, or the bitter
sarcasm of the monologue (that was the price of permission
to perform!): instead, male emotion rages here against female
'unfaithfulness'. The changing moods of the recitativo accompagnato reflect Figaro's mental state, wavering between
doubt and love. With its passionate, almost unrestrained
turbulence, the aria is a psychologically perfect musical
diagnosis of jealousy. But how different this jealousy is from
that shown by the count in his recitative and aria in a similar
situation in the third act! Figaro's is sober, sincere and
natural — one could almost say modern in tone; the count's
baroque and hypocritical. Each character in *Figaro* is an
individual: personalities are outlined with music that is not
only psychologically suitable, but is of the same texture
throughout the opera. Figaro's jealousy aria presents to us
the man of contrasts we met earlier, playfully buoyant and
hard as steel, living in serfdom but with courageous self-
confidence, and capable of passionate love. The three horn
fanfares at the end of the number are a witty expression of
what is never uttered in the text — the Italian word *'corni'*
and the German word *'Hörner'* both mean 'cuckold' as well!

In Susanna's next recitative and aria (number 27) the
tension created by the suspended action is drawing to a
climax — indeed, the action that had been stopped at the
beginning of the act swings forward with the secco preceding
her accompagnato. The characters are in their places: Figaro
eavesdropping behind the bushes, the countess waiting for
her cue in the pavilion, the count on his way to be trapped.
The play can begin. Susanna's recitative and aria are
apparently out of character with what we have already learnt
about her. They lift her with wonderful psychological feeling
to the highest spheres of poetry. The situation — the exploit-

ation of which was completely Mozart's and da Ponte's invention – is this: Figaro believes that Susanna is waiting for the count to appear by mutually accepted appointment; on the other hand, Susanna knows for sure that at the appointment the count will actually be met by the countess, disguised in her (i.e. Susanna's) clothes; and Susanna has also learnt from Marcellina that Figaro is hiding among the bushes. Figaro cannot but think that the depth of feeling behind her aria is for the count – while Susanna is absolutely certain that, provided the events of the night take place according to her plan, nobody will be able to prevent her future happiness with Figaro. Her sincere emotion glowing through her acted role is really soaring towards her fiancé.

In earlier delicate situations which took place during that crazy day we saw what a good comedian Susanna is. So, this time, too, it is no difficulty for her to put on, not only the clothes of her mistress, but also her refined, day-dreaming sophistication, and give her own mood expression in the rather sentimental voice of the countess. Susanna acts in this way partly because she actually identifies herself with the role she is performing, but also to confuse jealous Figaro and punish him for his lack of trust. This explains why the wonderful dolce sound of the recitative and aria contradicts Susanna's coquettish, face-slapping, glib-tongued, 'staccato' personality. It only bears resemblance to the way she sang in the letter duet – but there the countess was dictating the words! The tender string theme of the accompagnato, and the serenely fine melodic line of the whole recitative, with the motionless, almost spellbound, sustained string harmonies; the chaste tone of the aria free from any sensuality (there are no clarinets); the lovingly intertwined third and sixth parallels, and mild counterpoint of the three woodwind instruments – oboe, flute and bassoon – above the string pizzicatos, represent a wonderful and (even among Mozart's works) unparalleled blending of character-drawing; description of place, time and mood; absolute music; and the creation of a complex dramatic situation.[5]

With Susanna's aria, the tension, sustained since Barbarina's cavatina, reaches its climax: now the page can come and the last finale, the comedy of errors, can begin.

It was much less of a task to find a functional place for the rest of the arias. Figaro's first cavatina (number 3) is in fact 'revolution in full swing': he swears to teach the count a lesson! In the violent, almost aggressive bass-sequences of the recitative that preceeds the cavatina (with the mention of Susanna's name it is overcome with emotion for a moment), and then in the tense, quick minuet – borrowed from the reserved court dance of the aristocracy: characteristically the first triple metre in the opera! – Figaro declares war on the count who is trying to seduce his fiancée. (Later on, in the finale of the second act, Susanna, too, ridicules her ashamed lord in an ironical minuet rhythm.) And in the ensuing stretta, from which the previous dance-rhythm has disappeared, we hear the voice of the bold servant who rebels against his master. As for the dramatic function: the cavatina is the beginning of the counter-plot that crosses the plans of the count.

Bartolo's revenge aria (number 4) is only loosely linked with the main thread of the action. Rather, it provides a contrast to Figaro's aria. There, too, the dominating element was the desire for revenge, but while Figaro's reserved, taciturn and moderate rendering filled the transparently-orchestrated minuet form with dramatic force, here Bartolo's bragging and empty threats depict a basically comic character. The musical means of expression recall Osmin's character – but Bartolo is a more civilised, more inhibited, and consequently less dangerous intriguer: a bumptious boaster.

According to Beaumarchais's analysis of the part of the little page: 'He is like the dream every mother forms about her son, no matter what great suffering this dream will bring her later on.' *Cherubino d'amore* is adolescence personified. He absorbs Woman with-open eyes, and as soon as he catches sight of a skirt, his blood boils; all his thoughts are centred around girls, women and love. He is a young Don Giovanni who regards every woman as the great She: indeed, he is not in love with women, but with love itself. Even if he has no object for his affections, he sings about love – to himself. All this is expressed in his first aria (number 6), in the ceaseless quaver motion of which there already glows the demoniacal passion of the champagne aria of *Don Giovanni,* yet still suffused with the bloom of youth. (For the first time since the curtain went up, the clarinet appears with its finely erotic chromatics.) Other means of character-drawing here are the irregular rondo form, and the surprising ending.

Cherubino's arietta – or canzonetta – (number 11) of the second act, with its conventional guitar accompaniment (the theme is introduced by the clarinet!), is a seemingly obvious and dramaturgically justified number, since at this point in Beaumarchais's comedy there was a guitar-accompanied romance too. However, the principle of 'music in the music' – in other words, when the music, breaking away from the natural language of the genre, steps on the stage demanding an independent existence for itself – can easily upset the precarious balance of the genre. It can break the basic principle accepted by the audience, namely that the language of opera is music. Yet Mozart is not afraid of such dangerous obstacles; he deliberately seeks them out, and in every case overcomes them. The simple melody line, the naïvely rhythmic, richly refined orchestration, the unexpected romantic harmonies of the arietta, all reflect the awakening eroticism of the boy who is 'no more a child, but not yet a man',[6] and also represent a sharp contrast to the disciplined richness of emotion expressed in the countess's previous cavatina.

The countess's personality is markedly different from that in the original comedy. Beaumarchais's countess is a more down-to-earth character: she is Rosina, the slightly coquettish, skilfully hypocritical, and passionate girl, who has become somewhat lofty and reserved as a result of her aristocratic marriage, and rather resigned because of the way her husband has treated her. But, despite this, she does not remain entirely insensible to Cherubino's outburst of adoration, and does not feel it beyond her honour to be jealous of her own chambermaid – and indeed not even because of the count, but because of the young page! Mozart's countess is alone on the stage when we first see her; her cavatina (number 10) in E flat major, Mozart's 'solemn' key, with its richly-orchestrated and unusually long introduction is nobly reserved and disciplined, but reflects sincere emotions in a finely tender and hardly recognisably sensual tone (two clarinets in thirds).

Her second aria (number 19) is also sung behind closed doors, without witnesses. The personality and social position of the countess do not allow her to indulge in what is a necessity for Cherubino: a public revelation of the heart. She can only reveal the depths of her reserved soul when she is alone. She is beyond suspicion: even in the most delicate situations of the 'crazy day' she has the upper hand; her relationship with Cherubino – in contrast to Beaumarchais's countess – is free of any kind of sensuality on her part. Her two arias are destined to create a picture of her character; they have no other function in the play. From a dramaturgical point of view the cavatina is more or less justified: it is there that we make the acquaintance of the countess. However, the recitative and aria of the third act (in Mozart's 'heroic' key, C major) sound rather as though they were inserted later. This is particularly so since the seventh and ninth scenes (i.e., the dialogue before and after the recitative and aria) are not naturally linked to the recitatives that follow the sextet and introduce the letter·duet. The original court scene has been shortened and the third and fourth acts condensed, and da Ponte's easy pen is obviously stalling. There are occasional bumps and jolts in the otherwise faultless libretto.[7]

While the countess only expresses tragedy in a mild glow of sadness, the count reveals it in wildly passionate and dramatic emotions. He does not need a solo in which to introduce himself: his character is unmistakably outlined by the two trios of the first and second acts, and by the finale of the second act. His only aria (number 17) gives more evidence of Mozart's and da Ponte's congenial dramatic sense, and lifts his character high above Beaumarchais's petticoat-chasing, basically comic little count, always nosing and fussing around, and even plotting with his own employees. In

Beaumarchais's comedy there was only a monologue of a couple of lines, that carried little weight, where Mozart and da Ponte place the count's aria. With the count's self-revelation timed at the most dramatic moment of the role, Mozart and da Ponte expose not only a type, but a whole social class. The count's aria is also one of revenge (the third in the opera), but it is not sung with a comically thundering voice, like Bartolo's, or in a tense and restrained dance rhythm, like Figaro's, but with unbridled, unrestrained, violently raging emotions. The count had already felt his sweet prey, Susanna, in his arms – but not for the first time she had slipped away. The haughty aristocrat's disappointment, the heated masculine emotion and the violent, crude hatred towards 'the damned bunch of servants', break forth in this recitative and aria of almost demoniacal passion, presenting to us a complete picture of Figaro's adversary. Through this, their struggle is raised to a much higher dramatic level than Beaumarchais achieved. Beaumarchais's Figaro plays cat and mouse with his master, and the outcome of the struggle is not for a moment in doubt. Mozart's count is a more worthy and more dangerous character: one may say, an opponent of equal strength. The balance of forces brought about by the aria, as well as the higher emotional and intellectual heat, make his defeat even more grave, just as they make Figaro's victory even more significant.

So, what Mozart and da Ponte lost by leaving out the topical political allusions, they made up by placing the dramaturgical emphasis on the social message, mainly by means of the arias, sung by the representatives of the two opposing camps, at constructionally identical spots in the play. Structurally, the four-act opera is divided into two parts as only the second and the fourth acts have regularly-constructed finales. The first part starts with Susanna's and Figaro's divided duet and recitative. In this scene Figaro learns about the count's plan, and immediately launches into his first cavatina: the war cry of one of the camps. The second part (third act) starts with the recitative and duet of Susanna and the count (Susanna is the prize – the personified object of the struggle between the two camps). It is after this that the count is informed about the strategic plan of Figaro and the others, and his aria follows: the war cry of the other camp. Thereby the duel between Figaro and the count for Susanna widens into a struggle of two forces for the possession of power: one demands rights and freedom, and the other fights tooth and nail to defend its privileges. The contrast is sharper than it was in Beaumarchais's work. The forces involved are greater. The fight is a matter of life and death. The conflict is increased by the force of the music. The struggle between two men represents the battle to the last of two ideas, two classes and two worlds.

The result of this superior intellectual and ethical material is the dramatic and aesthetic superiority of the values of genre as well: the unity of comedy and tragedy, these two sides of life, in one single work — indeed, in one single character — raise the opera to the great heights of Shakespearean drama. Although in an (incomplete) list of compositions written by Mozart himself and published by the Berlin Mozartgemeinde, *The Marriage of Figaro* is referred to as opera buffa, I do not think there can be any doubt about the work being much more than that. In the Peters piano score* a playbill of the first performance is published, and here the opera is clearly defined as dramma giocoso. I do not know whether this is authentic or not (nowhere else could I find confirming data), but from a certain point of view it undoubtedly provides a better approach to the genre.[8]

Subsequently we shall see the seriousness behind Mozart's sense of humour which is mostly underlined by irony, but never by parody; and we shall also witness the simultaneous presence of comedy and tragedy, the double roots of drama, in the ensembles of *The Marriage of Figaro*.

* Berlin, 1939.

Notes

(1) See letters dated 6 and 24 December 1783.

(2) *Lo Sposo Deluso.*

(3) 'I think we shall soon perform a pantomime,' Mozart wrote to his father on 15 February 1783, and a month later (12 March) he reported on the success of the play, a small commedia dell'arte. The choreography was by Mozart himself. Only fragments of the music have come down to us.

(4) 'If once we Germans would seriously start thinking as Germans, acting as Germans, speaking in German and, indeed, even singing in German!!!' (letter dated 21 March 1785)

(5) In his classic short story, Mörike appositely describes the music of this scene: 'She began to sing Susanna's aria from that garden scene which spreads the breeze of sweet passion, as a spicy summer evening spreads its scents.' Eduard Mörike, *Mozart's Journey to Prague*; Budapest 1856; London 1964

(6) 'Not yet old enough for a man, or young enough for a boy; as a squash is before 'tis a peascod, or a codling when 'tis almost an apple: with him in standing water between boy and man. He is very wellfavoured and he speaks very shrewishly; one would think his mother's milk were scarce out of him.' Malvolio's lucid description of Viola disguised as a boy (*Twelfth Night,* act I, scene 5) could pass for an apt character-study of the young Count Cherubino too.

(7) At his revival in Vienna of *Figaro,* Gustav Mahler tried to bridge the break in the libretto by restoring the original trial scene with a secco composed by himself.

(8) In the libretto da Ponte defines *The Marriage of Figaro* as 'commedia per musica'.

The Marriage of Figaro (2)   X

IDOMENEO and *The Abduction* started with the traditional aria; *The Marriage of Figaro* and each of Mozart's subsequent operas begin with an ensemble — indeed, more than once with a whole series of ensembles. And in an ensemble the performers have to speak as much as sing. Susanna's and Figaro's two duets that open the first act tell us a number of important things right away. One of these is that the hero is not Figaro himself — as in Beaumarchais's play — but Figaro and Susanna together. We also learn that the two of them are united and will always remain so: this guarantees their superiority over the rest of the characters in the opera. The natural and sincere warmth of their love creates the potential energy that can ultimately conquer every obstacle. Even if they quarrel sometimes — and at such times one or two slaps on the face may occur — it does not last for more than a few minutes, a few bars. Peace is restored between them within the same scene, within the same musical unit (for instance, in the sextet of the third act, or in the finale of the fourth act). Figaro will be the master of the house — Susanna is the mistress of his heart, and with her cunning feminine tactics she can be sure that the last word is always hers, even if Figaro does not always realise it. As Shakespeare's Iago says: 'Our general's wife is now the general.'

The first duettino (number 1) is a summary of what their whole future married life will be like: Figaro does a lot of serious, useful work, while Susanna struts in front of the mirror, trying on her new hat. Both of them are acting and expressing their thoughts separately, and the two musical ideas never come into contact with one another. Figaro's melody, stretching farther and farther (to a fifth, a sixth, a seventh, and finally to an octave), illustrates what is going on on the stage: the slow, leisurely process of measuring:

Here we see the sober, practical side of Figaro's character, his stubborn firmness. Once he makes up his mind to do something, it is difficult to dissuade him from it. However, Susanna knows how to treat menfolk; she can twist Figaro round her little finger. Hardly have a few bars passed than Figaro has adopted Susanna's melody, and he then goes on to imitate her next musical thought as well.

The first duettino (in cheerful G major) presents the chief characters of the opera; the second (number 2), in gloomy B flat major, exposes the conflict. The consonant harmonies of the parallel third and sixth are disturbed by the dissonant notes of the count. We have not yet actually seen him, yet we feel his influence. The form, now and throughout the whole opera, adjusts itself with a wonderful flexibility to the requirements of dramatic expression. The first theme of the duettino is presented by Figaro who is still in a state of happy ignorance. This is varied in the middle passage by Susanna; she knows more than the naïve Figaro, and so views the whole ominous bedroom question from another aspect, expressed by her minor key. These twelve bars – the first appearance of a minor key (G minor!) in the opera – prophesy tragic moments. Thereby the recapitulation of the duettino, which the suspicious Figaro interrupts, gains a new, latent meaning. For a moment Susanna is forced to go on the defensive, and with classic feminine cunning she embarks upon a new thought. Yet although Figaro takes this over from her, he does not let himself be diverted from the subject. The seriousness of the conflict is shown by the consistently different rhythms and counter-motions of the two melodies.

The duettino remains open: the tension is only resolved in the recitative that follows the number. By the way, in the scene there is no trace of the erotic flavour of Beaumarchais's work. Like the countess, Susanna and Figaro are more reserved, one could almost say more innocent, than their counterparts in the comedy. Erotic tendencies in the opera can only be found in the count's and the page's characters.

Susanna's and Marcellina's duettino (number 5) is essentially similar to the corresponding scene in Beaumarchais's comedy. However, Mozart and da Ponte delve deeper to exploit the comic possibilities provided by the situation and characters. Since in the opera (as opposed to the play) Bartolo is not present during the duel of politeness, the two women can use their tongues freely, stinging each other with poisonous compliments. First, Marcellina is in the lead. With delicate sarcasm she wraps her offensive words in courteous conversation. Susanna, who is less experienced in this field, is first forced to defend herself, breaking out only in one or two short forte explosions – until she finds Marcellina's weak point: her greater age. And from this moment Susanna has the upper hand. In the recapitulation, it is Marcellina who cannot master her sentiments, while her helpless anger is laughed at with characteristic staccato triplets by the triumphant Susanna.

The trio (number 7) is the climax of the first act. The heavy tension of the eventful recitative culminates in the interference of the count, eavesdropping behind a chair. The scene faithfully follows the original action, and the farce is raised to the level of drama by the use of the 'dropped hint'. The first musical characterisation of the count provides a basic description of him: he is an aggressive grand seigneur, accustomed to command and demanding absolute obedience.

Basilio's smooth and superficial, but shrewdly harmonised, creeping melody presents a picture of a courtier ready to carry out any dirty piece of work,

and Susanna's four bars reflect her sincere, and far from groundless fear.

The situation is delicate, indeed it is dangerous; and the F-minor music seems to consider it as such. Of course we, being aware of the psychological and dramaturgical function of F minor in Mozart's tonality system, know that the apparently embarrassing situation is not in fact as serious as it seems to be. The count has the greatest reason to be afraid of scandal, since at this moment he is in Susanna's room.

For the time being, however, there is an unexpected turn of events for Cherubino has been hiding in the chair. The situation is rather awkward; Susanna even faints with a declining scale when his discovery seems imminent. The music does not reveal whether the faint is a genuine or a tactical one, but the latter is more likely, for immediately they want her to sit in that particular chair, she recovers, in tragic G minor. It would be terrible if the page should be discovered! Far from innocently the two men feel (in solemn E flat major) Susanna's violently beating little heart (ironically laughing violin syncopations comment on the two men's enthusiasm):

With his earlier smooth, hypocritical melody, Basilio assures the count that what he said about the page was only suspicion; however, Susanna's nervous outbreak rising to a forte, reveals that the suspicion was not entirely without foundation.

After a few bars of recitative the count explains how he took Cherubino and Barbarina by surprise. If the first act culminated in the trio, then these eighteen bars would be the climax of the whole scene. The count's narration begins with Basilio's melody and string accompaniment, since the count, this time, instead of using his own commanding attitude, adopts Basilio's spying, sneaking manner. When the count in his story – and in reality too – lifts the table-cloth and notices the page in the chair, the string melody suddenly reverses, and with a long sustained note the woodwinds enter. The consternation is complete, and the impact – reached by extremely simple means – is enormous.

During the general astonishment, it is the count who first finds his tongue, and with his pianissimo motive he quickly takes charge of the situation. Susanna is nervous, while Basilio giggles maliciously: he enjoys scandal.

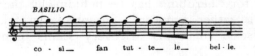

He even adds a little fat to the fire by sarcastically repeating his earlier statement: that what he said about the page was mere suspicion. As in Susanna's and Figaro's duettino, here too a satirical tone is added to the original text by the changed circumstances. There could be no better stage instructions than those given by the music. Timed in seconds, it denotes every action, gesture and even facial expression.

Figaro's aria (number 9) that closes the act does not primarily add to Figaro's character (although it does that too, through its irony), but it shows us more of Cherubino's — through Figaro's eyes. So far we have seen Cherubino as a woman-crazy page, a young Don Giovanni. Now in Figaro's aria we meet the little lord, a 'young Almaviva', the future despot. Although placed at the end of the act, the aria is not intended to fulfil the function of a finale. It is different in quality and superior to the static endings of acts in *The Abduction* which were characterised by the principle: the greater the noise, the better; the shorter, the better.

The situation is similar to that of Susanna's aria (number 12) in the second act. Just as Figaro commanded the page, and made him march to and fro a short while ago, now Susanna tugs Cherubino about while dressing him in her own clothes. Although the aria is sung by Susanna, the larger part of the musical material is performed by the orchestra, and the action is primarily allotted to Cherubino. We can observe one more significant element which proves that Mozart 'thinks in terms of the stage': the decisive role of the time factor. Repeated parts of the aria's text and its small orchestral interludes allow exactly the time required for the page to be dressed. He is just ready when Susanna reaches the coda, and while she enthusiastically praises the appearance of the handsome young lad, Cherubino walks around the room in his new clothes. The slight atmosphere of erotism in the scene is illustrated by Susanna's closing words (not in Beaumarchais's play): 'Women know very well why they like this boy.' She herself knows it very well, and perhaps, just a tiny bit, so does the countess!

The trio (number 13) of the second act is in a regular,

miniature sonata form: first theme, modulation to the dominant, second theme, closing theme, a ten-bar miniature development, a full recapitulation in the tonic and an extended coda. It is like a Japanese garden with tiny waterfalls and inch-high rocks – or perhaps more like a storm in a tea-cup. The perfect form, however, takes the comic situation completely seriously. For it is only comic for the audience, and not for the three participants. Susanna's helplessness, the countess's fright and the count's anger are genuine.

Mozart's ingenious idea of employing the sonata form – rather rare in an operatic ensemble – ideally fits the dramatic situation. The setting is a clash of two conflicting wills (the count orders, the countess forbids), and the reactions of Susanna, hiding in the background. The short development that introduces a new theme only increases the tension, and prepares for the recapitulation which, through another dramatic motive, deepens the conflict: the count orders that if 'Susanna' cannot come out since she is dressing, she should at least say something. The countess cannot find any logical argument with which to counter this, so she simply bids – with an almost hysterical, quick crescendo and roulade – the person hiding in the room to remain silent:

Originally the three excited chromatic scales of the closing theme were also in the countess's part (Susanna could hardly remain unobserved in the background if she started to sing high Cs!). It was only in later theatre practice that the two parts were to a certain extent changed. The metre of the trio is worth considering: it is a 3/4 quick minuet rhythm. The great dramatic scene of jealousy between the count and countess takes place in an elegant conversational tone, in the stiff form of court ceremonial!

While the sonata form was the most suitable framework for the complex action of the trio, the straightforward dramatic force of the ensuing duettino (number 14) by Susanna and Cherubino – how can the page escape from the locked room? – is expressed in a single musical idea. This syncopated and slightly polyphonic four-bar motive runs through the duet in constant octave motion, ceaselessly modulating hither and thither; rising in panic-stricken sequences at Cherubino's saving idea and at Susanna's terrified protest, then turning into a tragi-comic G minor at the pathetic farewell of the page. Again, the situation is only comic for the audience – it is very serious for the characters. The G minor persists to increase the suspense following Cherubino's jump (Susanna and the audience do not yet know if he landed safely). The little scherzo is accompanied by the strings; again, Mozart moulds the form like wax to serve his theatrical purpose.

The huge, almost thousand-bar long finale (number 15) of the second act – this 'independent little comedy, a drama within the drama', as da Ponte called it – advances in an unbroken sequence from the first note to the very last.[1] The action is continuous, and the increasing number of characters appearing on the stage also results in an increase in tension. Again and again new complications arise, evolve, and reach their solution – or remain suspended to reach their conclusion in the following act. Mozart and da Ponte built up the finale much more successfully than Beaumarchais, whose ending was not at the climax. He removed his characters gradually from the stage, and not even always in the most convincing way. He let the fire die down before the act came to an end (scenes 23-26). Mozart and da Ponte bring the end of the act forward, and, from the first E flat major which returns in a large curve to the opening key, break the action at the point where the conflict of the two camps reaches its climax.

117

Mozart's feeling for tonality has already been discussed, but I would like to add that the finales — indeed, the operas in their entirety — are characterised by a closed circle of tonality. The basic key of *Idomeneo, The Marriage of Figaro* and *Don Giovanni* (the tonality opening the overture and closing the last finale) is D; while that of *The Abduction, Così* and *Titus* is C; and that of *The Magic Flute* is E flat. Without any endeavour to draw conclusions, it is worth mentioning that all the numbers of decisive significance, and those implying basic spiritual moral or philosophical messages, are in every case in the basic key; e.g., the great dramatic arias of Idomeneo, Elektra, Constanze and the count; Anna's and Octavio's oath, and Anna's aria following her recognition of Don Giovanni; the duel, and the whole of the scene involving Don Giovanni and the Commendatore in the last act; the sextet, and Alfonso's maxims in both acts of *Così*; the friendship duet and Sextus's dramatic recitative in the first act of *Titus*; Tamino's aria, and Pamina's and Papageno's duet in *The Magic Flute*; and very many others. And the finales form a complete little circle in themselves within the big circle of the play.

I would like to call special attention to a few particularly characteristic elements in the finale of the second act. The first of these is Susanna's entry. Beaumarchais's stage directions are: 'she enters laughing gaily', etc. Again, Mozart takes the comic situation seriously: the count is standing in front of the door with his sword drawn — if Cherubino were really coming out of the room, he would certainly kill him! At Susanna's appearance, there is a modulation with simple string unison (the 'hint' again), and after an astounded pause a simple four-part piano chord of strings marks the beginning of a new tempo and metre. And this new metre is again the measured 3/4 of the minuet: like Figaro in the first cavatina, or the count and countess in the trio of the second act, Susanna now uses the 'aristocratic' tone of the court dance in order to mock with fine irony the count's awkward situation as he stands dumbly with his drawn sword.

The rhythm, melody line, and simple tonic-dominant/dominant-tonic harmonisation of the music at Susanna's entry is perfectly concise. Deprived of any superfluous decoration, the elegant mannerism of distinguished society is stripped to the bone.

Susanna is not playful and frivolous as in Beaumarchais's play, but supercilious, yet calm and dignified. The orchestra laughs all through the allegro, and Susanna, too, can hardly restrain her laughter while she and the countess scold the count in thirds. Just as the third and sixth parallels at the end of Susanna's and Figaro's first duet expressed the perfect harmony of their love, here too the parallel expresses the common front of the two women against the count.

The eight bars at the end of the typically buffo scene — soft, velvety woodwind chords above the bass organ-point, and the caressing, dreamy triads of the violins with the transparent homophony of the unexpectedly intertwined three singing parts — veil the basically comic situation with brightness and poetry.

A new conflict, a new, remote key; after the B flat major, a subito cheerful G major; after the four-beat, a lightly dancing 3/4 rhythm, while completely new musical material is introduced as Figaro appears, absolutely ignorant of what is happening. The count's questions are polite but full of sarcasm: during the gallant dance melody we hear the bassoon giggling in staccato semi-quavers. There is another wonderfully poetic turn as the malicious giggling of the bassoon stops for eight bars, and it seems as if the count begins to be moved by the countess's, Susanna's and Figaro's fine polyphonic entreaties. In an 'aside' we learn that he is waiting for Marcellina; his melody, however, imitates Susanna's apologising tune.

Da Ponte left out Antonio's gags. Instead, the drunken gardener is characterised by Mozart's music. The speedy sequence of events is followed by a duel of words (andante 6/8 with sustained tension): the count tries to catch Figaro in the net of his own lies, but Figaro always evades him. The bellicose appearance — accompanied by timpani and trumpets — of Marcellina, Basilio and Bartolo brings the count a fresh supply of ammunition (it is now that we again reach the opening key of the finale) and the second act culminates in a dramatic contrast between the antagonistic plans and emotions of the two hostile camps, sharply separated musically from one another.

New features strengthen the characterisation of the count in the duettino (number 16) of the third act, and also show differences in personality from the count in the original comedy. Beaumarchais's count — even in this scene, where he can hope that the much entreated Susanna may yield to him at last — behaves in a very frivolous manner, and wants nothing more than to add Susanna to his list of conquests. Mozart's count is moved by genuine passion. The one and a half-bar orchestral introduction of the duettino

121

reminds us of Constanze's deeply tragic G-minor aria:

This melody returns once again in the count's ensuing aria at the moment when he speaks of Susanna. He says, 'She heats my passion, but feels nothing similar for me':

The atmosphere of the first ten bars of the duet is definitely tragic with strong harmonic and rhythmic tension (sforzato at the weak beat of the bar, subito piano at the strong one), and with its violin figurations suggesting muffled heart-beats:

With the descending inversion of the count's rising chromatic accompaniment, Susanna modulates from a pathetic A minor into a calm C major. She is another character moulded from one piece. Here she employs the eternal feminine trick of 'changing the subject', just as she did against Figaro in the duettino of the first act. She cools the count's glowing passion with a slightly ironical commonplace. He, however, does not give in by letting himself be diverted from the subject, and above the heart-beat motive he stubbornly returns to the initial tonality. Finally Susanna accepts the appointment and now the count is relieved: with a compromise between the two keys (A minor and C major), he continues to court the girl in A major. Above his almost romantically flowing melody we again hear Susanna's characteristic staccato quavers, begging for forgiveness for her white lie:

In the meantime, however, she has had two rather narrow escapes, when – confused by the quick succession of questions – she said 'yes' instead of 'no', and then 'no' instead of 'yes'. But she finds her feet quickly, and she willingly imitates the count's melody musing on love; at the end of the duettino – with contradictory words – her voice is even temporarily united with that of the count in a long third parallel.

Beaumarchais's trial scene is omitted from the opera, the

123

whole scene précied in a single recitative. In the following sextet (Mozart's favourite, number 18), however, the original action continues. The musical character-drawing reflects the changed situation: Marcellina is singing a flowing melody; Bartolo and Figaro are now in the same camp and the long organ-point seems to represent a sound basis for the new, solid relationship between them; as for the other camp, the dissatisfaction of the count and the judge erupts in short, angry quavers. Susanna appears with the money with which to pay Figaro's debt. Here, unfortunately, some obscurity is caused by the fact that da Ponte never divulges how Susanna could have raised such a large sum so quickly, whereas the explanation is simple: she has just received her dowry from the countess. Now she finds her fiancé happily embracing Marcellina. The gay buffo atmosphere is again replaced here by the sombre tone of tragedy. Susanna's painful four bars (above the string tremolo broken by fortepiano beats)

are in both melody and key identical to the ascending and sadly declining melody of a little song entitled 'Als Luise die Briefe ihres ungetreuen Liebhabers verbrannte', composed one year after *Figaro,* in which a lonely young girl, abandoned by her lover, burns his letters in despair:

The mood of the song is that of absolute hopelessness – and Susanna's situation (at least as she herself sees it at that moment) is no better. The key is C minor, Mozart's other 'tragic' tonality. While G minor is the key for tragic resignation, C minor is the key for tragedy with undercurrents of greater activity and passion, where the character is unwilling to accept the tragic fate meekly (Elektra). This C-minor attitude is in harmony with the courageous optimism of Susanna's self-assured, energetic personality. It is hardly by accident that Belmonte's feeble sorrow with a similar melodic line (see example on page 83) appears in the relatively weaker lyrical B minor: he is definitely more

womanish than either the demoniacal Elektra or the eman-
cipated Susanna!

Accompanied by the gentle melody of the violins, Figaro
tries to explain the misunderstandings, but Susanna does not
listen to him. She even slaps his face, and blinded by her
jealous anger she now takes sides with the count and the
judge. The two groups, Marcellina/Bartolo/Figaro and
Susanna/Don Curzio/the count, are sharply separated by the
music, which – for a moment – even seems to indicate
Susanna's desperate idea to take revenge on Figaro by really
fulfilling her promise to the count (the imitation of bars
51-52):

The situation is saved by Marcellina who briefly puts Susanna
in the picture. Her six-bar phrase (a lengthened variant of the
opening theme of the sextet)

recalls the musical thought with which her duettino with
Susanna in the first act began:

It seems that Marcellina has not completely forgotten the events of the morning: Susanna won't have an easy time with her mother-in-law! There is an irresistably amusing scene when Susanna incredulously – but at the same time on the alert – asks all those present, *'Sua madre? Suo padre?'* (the invention of Mozart and da Ponte). The question is justified, for the theme of the 'lost and recovered child' is undoubtedly burlesque in its improbability. Mozart, however, is not at all embarrassed by it and, by playing upon the repeated questions and answers, he builds the musically most amusing scene of *The Marriage of Figaro*.

The greatest obstacle in the way of their marriage – Marcellina's claim for Figaro – having been removed, Susanna is given for the first time, instead of her quick staccato passages, a flowing cantilena:

Relationships have changed: Susanna has joined Figaro's group, while Marcellina's and Bartolo's embittered souls have been reborn in the light of newly-found happiness. The tender, dolce harmonies, however, are interrupted by the count's angry chromatics in punctuated rhythm, which – in the manner of a good courtier – are duly aped in unison by Don Curzio, the stuttering judge. It is not only the wit that Mozart takes quite seriously, but he fills even the cheapest comedy clichés with lyrical beauty and dramatic tension.

The rise in the proportion of ensembles to arias in *The Marriage of Figaro* implies a step forward in opera technique. And this has an effect upon the recitatives, about fifty per cent of which blend attacca into the ensuing number. Although they keep the characteristics that distinguish them from the closed numbers, nevertheless the border begins to blur. This is proved many times in *Figaro,* for instance, in the recitative following the sextet in the third act, and in the second scene of the second act where Figaro, in his recitative, quotes twice from his own earlier cavatina. And in the same scene even the continuo steps beyond its traditional role of impersonal accompaniment, and with the help of a melodic and legato harmonic link illustrates that Figaro now has a new plan:

Susanna's and the countess's letter duet (number 20) also grows naturally from the previous recitative, and here too the continuo has an independent dramatic role: the text dictated by the countess starts with the harpsichord motive:

and the orchestra only enters when Susanna starts writing. The form again flexibly serves the material. The first half of the two-part lied form is taken up with the dictation and writing of the letter. After the simple, two-part string accompaniment to the dictation, the oboe and bassoon always appear during the actual writing, as if they musically illustrate Susanna's carefully drawn letters. The second half of the lied form is the perusal of the finished letter. Thus the formal requirement of a complete recapitulation becomes justified dramaturgically as well. However, while in the first half the small orchestral interludes have been wedged between the fragments of sentence dictated by the countess and the final words repeated by Susanna, during the perusal of the letter this is no longer necessary, and the two women cut into each other's words as they read the lines of the letter. Note the time factor again in the first half: Susanna is given the precise length of musical interlude she requires to write down the dictated text! There is a fine example of the poetry of everyday life here: during the dictation Susanna does not understand a word — the diminutive form of *bosco* (forest): *boschetto* — and she asks her mistress to repeat it. Originally da Ponte planned the letter duet to be a recitative; the closed form and its congenial solution is completely Mozart's creation. In Beaumarchais's play the whole writing scene consists of altogether four lines, adopted word for word by da Ponte.

The finale of the third act (number 22) appears to be an exception to the rule of the closed circle of tonality: it begins in C major and ends in G major. However, this C major is in fact only the dominant middle passage of the G-major march, gradually approaching from a distance – we do not hear its beginning until later, when the crowd appears on the stage (the same solution as in the march in *Idomeneo*). The finale is not so regular as those of the second and fourth acts, obviously because of the traditional two-part construction of the opera buffa genre. The march is followed by a soprano duet combined with a chorus, and then comes a fandango, the only piece of music of genuinely Spanish origin in the opera (Mozart found the melody in Gluck's *Don Juan* ballet). This forms part of the action not only through its wedding-dance character, but because it contains a very important incident as well: it is during the dance that Susanna hands the letter about the assignation to the count. Figaro sees but does not realise its significance until the beginning of the fourth act. The dramatic use of the count's and Figaro's recitative – above the transparent, light dance music into which it is built – paves the way for the finales of the next opera, *Don Giovanni*. It is worth noting how – even in this rather complex musical situation – Mozart sharply contrasts the voices of the two men: the affectedly supercilious manner of the count with a smooth dance melody underneath, and Figaro's suspicious, mocking words backed by the increasingly compressed melody in dactylic rhythm. After the count's short monologue, the previous chorus number is repeated in a slightly ironical tone: 'Praised be the good master who returns the bride to her groom untouched.'

The finale of the second act entangled the threads of the action to an extent when they became almost indistinguishable, and the finale of the fourth act disentangles them one by one again. The last finale (number 28) starts with the scene of the countess and the page. In his character-study, Beaumarchais wrote of Cherubino: 'In the presence of the countess he is extremely timid, but otherwise a charming and naughty child; there is restless and inconceivable desire in the depths of this character. He matures into a young man without any definite plan, or special ability, and he throws his whole personality into each of his new adventures.' This was the character presented in Cherubino's first aria, and it is this young gentleman, a budding Don Giovanni, who steps onto the stage in the finale, too, eager to court every woman under the sun, and inquisitively adding to the confusion that already exists. From here onwards — with certain abbreviations — the action follows the original precisely, and in spite of the lyrical episodes (Figaro's short monologue, his reconciliation with Susanna), it preserves the comedy mood of Beaumarchais's play.

But only, however, until the countess appears at the door of the right-hand pavilion. Within a few seconds, the mood completely changes as the character of the music undergoes a complete transformation. The change takes place unobserved: the count's four-bar final outburst at the peak of the finale, strengthened by a sforzato tutti in unison, is followed by the countess's short, but in its tone already perfectly new cantilena:

and this prepares the way for the supressed tension of the following tenor/baritone/bass trio.[2] Beginning in the G-minor (!) basic tonality, the nineteen-bar episode returns to its starting point after having modulated into all the related keys (D minor, E flat major, C minor, B flat major) – as if it drew the large circle of concept/judgement/conclusion, as well as expressing the abundance of emotions revealed by those who have been in the dark so far when they face the unexpected situation. The excessively modulating scales of the violins, knocking with merciless regularity; the broken heart-beats of the accompanying harmonies of the woodwinds; the sotto voce male voices with their short, broken, faint breathing – all these create a dispirited, almost terrifying mood that cannot be expressed in words. It is an atmosphere of human tragedy in the middle of an essentially comic situation, at the climax of the whole drama.

The count's words begging for forgiveness

introduce a theme heard earlier. In Susanna's and Figaro's second duettino this was the new motive that followed the exposition of the conflict, the count's first musical (though not actual) appearance in the opera, and it was to this melody that Susanna sang the first half of the text: 'If you want to hear more, stop this hurtful suspicion.'

dis - cac - cia i so - spet ti, che tor - to mi fan.

cresc.

Otto Schumann's conclusion – that Susanna might after all have had an affair with the count – would perhaps sound quite plausible in this light. But if this were the case, we would be at a loss with the second part of Susanna's sentence ('stop this hurtful suspicion') which, on the other hand, is identical with the countess's previous entry. This is one of the many places in Mozart's oeuvre where it is impossible to express in words the nuances of concepts and relationships shown by the music.

The countess answers in a tone of happy devotion, and, raising the music almost to the level of a hymn, the whole ensemble repeats the resolving, calming words. One should note that the three sections – the countess's interference, the count's entreaties, and finally his reprieve by the countess – are performed with almost identical instrumentation, which not only gives a unity to the three musical thoughts, but at the same time fills them with a special meaning. These fifty bars – the catharsis – represent the spiritual and emotional centre of the whole composition. With this Mozart steps far beyond Beaumarchais's ending, where the count, landed in a pretty fix, can do nothing but apologise, and is thereupon pardoned by the countess in an easy, laughing manner. Da Ponte hardly changed the text – the sincere message of the fifty-bar episode comes exclusively from Mozart, and can be epitomised in the following sentence taken from a letter of his written a short while later: 'Are not the delights of insecure, fickle infatuation and the joy of genuine, deep love, as far removed as earth from heaven?'*

* Letter dated 4 November 1787.

Just as the construction of the peak was gradual, the brightness of the closing stretta is prepared and introduced step by step. The andante – with a strange, wavering string motive – modulates into the allegro assai coda which, after one bar of uncertain, undefined major-minor tonality followed by an unexpected two-bar outbreak, sets out in suppressed D-minor piano (the memory of the 'crazy day') to find the happy, freeing D major only in the tenth bar (the all-conquering strength of love). The voices of the five women and six men melt into one harmony, and even when the two groups are separated they speak and sing the same. It is only the count who – with the individual rhythm of his singing – is at first at odds with the others, but, later on, he is also forced to yield.

The finale, built for eleven solo voices, retains the transparent chamber character of the opera: the chorus – the role of which is not much more than that of the crowd in the play – does not participate in it.

Action and ceaseless motion are the ruling elements of the overture of the opera – the only overture among the great Mozart operas that has no thematic connection with the play. It anticipates the whirling of coming events, with all their problems. The 'action' of the overture does not stop for a second: presto sonata form (which according to Mozart 'cannot be fast enough'), with a sixteen-bar, tiny development and comparatively enormous coda. The overture – like Mozart's overtures in general – does not tell a story but creates an atmosphere, and – like a prologue – prepares the audience for what they are going to see and hear in the course of the play. Arousing but not satisfying the curiosity of the audience, it puts into music, as it were, the sub-title of the play: 'a crazy day'. Its atmosphere is not that of light comedy: it does not have the buffo character of Italian comic opera. The ironical, but at the same time threatening, dark sound of the bassoon mingles with the undefined whispering of the strings, and the sharp contrasts of piano followed by subito fortissimo and then again by subito piano are once more replaced by the previous mysterious whirling.

This merciless, and far from comic setting of sharp contrasts persists throughout the overture – indeed, throughout the whole opera. There is hardly another opera, or for that matter any other composition by Mozart, with so many decrescendo rising and crescendo falling melodic lines, fortepiano accents, sforzato accents, subito piano, subito forte and fortissimo dynamics as *The Marriage of Figaro*; and this is especially true of the overture, the quintessence of the play, in which there is only one short six-bar crescendo at the beginning of the coda, and all the other dynamic changes are subito, without any transition! Under the seemingly smooth surface of buffa terrifyingly important events develop in the woodwinds' small counterpoints on the first theme, in the unexpected forte chords of the second theme, in the ill-omened chromatics and excited accompanying figures of the closing theme, in the series of dissonances in the delayed sequence of the recapitulation, and in the characteristic rhythm of the coda.

It is primarily the music that carries the message of *The Marriage of Figaro,* and the orchestra's role and participation in the drama is both in quality and quantity much greater than it was in all previous operas. 'The union of text and music is perfect: the musical instruments complete the sentence started by the text, or develop the ideas that remain hidden in the action,' says Henri de Curzon in his study of Mozart. The same idea is expressed by Wagner who wrote this of *Figaro*: 'On the basis laid down by the Italian opera buffa [Mozart] erected a building of such infinite perfection, that he was absolutely right in refusing to sacrifice even one note when the emperor demanded abbreviations . . . . Here the dialogue fully becomes music and the music itself becomes the dialogue; and this could only be achieved by the Maestro through such an extensive use and development of the orchestra that people of that time – or perhaps even of our time – would never have dreamed of.' Schurig completely misunderstands Mozart's music when he states that in the opera 'Figaro is only and exclusively a lackey who hasn't a trace of the spirit of revolt in him'.[3] On the contrary: Mozart, for whom 'music always remains music' expressed in music all that could not yet be expressed in words at that time.[4]

Paul Bekker aptly defines *The Marriage of Figaro* as 'the opera of critical realism'.

Notes

(1) Da Ponte who, like Noverre and unlike Mozart, defined his principles on music-drama and libretto-construction in categories, outlined his theory concerning the correct construction of the buffo finale as follows: 'The finale, which has to be closely related to the whole of the opera, is nothing but a self-contained little comedy, and therefore has to have an individual action and conflict of its own. This is the best opportunity to reveal the composer's genius, the various abilities of the singers, and the most effective situations of the drama. There can be no recitative in it: everything is sung, and room must be found for all kinds of singing: adagio, andante, . . . strepitoso, . . . strepitosissimo. As theatrical theology has it, one of the basic doctrines of the finale is to allow every character to appear on the stage — even if their number amounts to three hundred — one by one, two by two, three by three, six by six . . . singing solos, duets, trios, sextets . . . . Even if the action of the play does not make it possible — the poet has to find a way . . . if necessary, despite his own judgement, taste, and all the Aristotles of the world; and if after all these he finds that the play reaches a dead end — well, he should do all that he can to get out of it again.'

(2) In the manuscript: Basilio/the count/Bartolo. However, in some editions — obviously with the original prose play in mind — the two extreme parts are doubled with Don Curzio and Antonio. Beaumarchais does not 'double', but in the finale gives a separate role — and a rather significant one too — to the stuttering judge and the out-spoken gardener.

(3) Schurig, q.v. This author also commits a serious mistake in his analysis of the finale when he overlooks, or simply ignores, the fact that Figaro recognises his fiancée disguised in the clothes of the countess, and that his 'violent' courting of the 'countess' is only play-acting. According to Schurig, Figaro here seriously courts the 'countess' and so 'degenerates to the moral level of his master. This faithlessness finally defines the fate of his love. If not now, in the course of this crazy day, then sooner or later Susanna will certainly yield to the count . . . .'

(4) In 1829, Vincent Novello and his wife Mary visited Mozart's widow Constanze in Salzburg. They asked her what Mozart had mostly enjoyed reading, and Mary Novello noted Constanze's comments: 'Mozart liked reading, and from translations he knew Shakespeare well. A work by one of his favourite authors is at present in her [Constanze's] possession and she often reads from it; this is a nine-volume book, but since it is banned in the Austrian Empire, Constanze refused to name it — I [Mary Novello] am of the opinion that it must be one of the literary works of the French revolution.'

Don Giovanni

THE MARRIAGE OF FIGARO was Mozart's idea – *Don Giovanni* was suggested by da Ponte. After the numerous prose, verse, operatic and balletic versions of the legend, this is the first true dramatic interpretation in music which also gives life to a new stage genre: dramma giocoso, a comedy with a serious message. Since Mozart first fluttered his wings, and particularly since *La Finta Giardiniera,* we have been following the steady development of his dramaturgy towards the eternal dramatic ideal, the description of complete life. On this ascending road – which we have followed from *La Finta Giardiniera,* through *The Abduction,* to *Figaro* – we have now reached another significant stage. In *Don Giovanni* both faces of life, comedy and tragedy, are simultaneously reflected. And the commonplace and the intangible are united.

In examining *Don Giovanni* it is interesting to see to what extent Mozart and da Ponte made use of the century-and-a-half-old legend. What alterations did they make to the characters and conflicts of earlier dramatic interpretations? And did they make any note-worthy additions – or omissions?

Whether Don Juan Tenorio, the hero of the legend, ever actually lived is a much-debated and still unsettled question. However, I don't think it really matters to us whether he did or not. The important fact is that such a character has appeared quite frequently in literature and art during the past three hundred years. He has been called Don Juan Tenorio, Don Giovanni, Eugene Onegin and even John Tanner. But whoever he is, this man looking for truth and then fleeing from the actual realisation of it is a tragic character, because single-handed he takes up arms against his own society and the ruling outlook of his age, and he necessarily has to be defeated in the ensuing struggle. This character has provided a splendid opportunity for every nation and epoch to raise its own problems and present its own topical moral, philosophical, social and political messages. Our aim is to discover what Don Juan's character meant to Mozart; and what Mozart expressed through the character of Don Juan.

According to Schurig, the historical basis of the legend is rooted in the first struggles between the Spanish knights and the invading Christians. Schurig argues logically that perhaps the Jesuits, who were not too scrupulous in their means of evangelism, killed two birds with one stone by attributing the suspicious death of a Spanish knight they had murdered for 'reasons of principle' to just and well-deserved punishment by supernatural forces.

The first stage adaptation of the Don Juan legend to come down to us is a drama by Tirso de Molina entitled *The Seducer of Seville, or the Stone Guest,* first performed in 1613 and published in 1630. It presented a bold, broad-minded attitude for that age, not only as regards the delicate issues of the possibility of heavenly redemption and the opposing doctrines of predestination and free will, but also for its disguised but unmistakable social criticism. It shows up the perfidious young playboy of noble birth of the early fourteenth century, yet it also condemns the depraved, cruel feudal aristocracy of de Molina's time. Because of the nature of Don Juan's crimes, which were practised widely by the Spanish aristocracy, it was necessary for him to receive supernatural punishment for his violation of morality rather than punishment at the hands of his own people.

There are three aspects in de Molina's drama of decisive importance as regards the further development of the subject. The first is that it is here for the first time that the two roots of the legend and the two sides of the character are united: the womaniser, and the desecrator of the dead. The second aspect is that, in spite of the tautology, in the outlines of the characters, the progress of the action and, indeed, in the whole construction of the play, we find the germs of almost all the essential themes of the later dramatic adaptations. The third is Donna Anna's character (though she is of but secondary importance as yet, and only speaks a few words).

Incidentally, de Molina's Don Juan is the renaissance ideal of a hero, with manly beauty and knightly courage, who — with enviable charm — stabs every man who gets in his way, and conquers every woman he happens to come across, yet can still spare the time to save his faithful shipwrecked servant. And all this is done at the risk of his own life! As far as de Molina is concerned, no earthly power could thwart Don Juan's plans. This story of a free intellect rebelling against social conventions and disregarding them too, after existing as a myth for many thousands of years, develops for the first time into a theatre drama in politically, religiously, and morally stiff baroque Spain. In addition to the rebellious side of the character is the aspect of the seducer in him which makes the theme so international as to doom Don Juan to become one of the most frequently adapted heroes of the literature and art of every country and race.

Having turned into a 'best-seller', de Molina's theme continued its career in various commedia dell'arte adaptations in the middle of the seventeenth century. In accordance with the rules of the genre, by emphasising the character of the servant as well as the burlesque motives in general, Italian and French plays bring the comic aspect of the theme to the fore. Although it is not one of the author's most successful works, the first adaptation of a good literary standard of that period is Molière's five-act comedy, *Don Juan, or the Stone Guest* (1665).

Like that of de Molina, Molière's hero is anti-social — only he is a *l'art pour l'art* villain driven by his wild instincts. He is a cynical, selfish intellectual, a shrewd and crafty diplomat, a conscious atheist, a cold rationalist who does not believe in anything but the rule of two and two making four. He has no human feelings at all.

Molière's satirical, and very often sharp, social criticism, required a new form of presentation. In his *Don Juan* he remoulded the personality of the hero and developed him further psychologically, as well as the other characters, and even developed the action. Don Juan's servant is a more warm-hearted and poetic soul than his master, to whom — time and again — he gives a piece of his mind. As for Donna Elvira, Mozart and da Ponte were inspired by Molière's expertly-drawn woman torn by conflicting emotions. On the other hand Molière left out Donna Anna altogether.

Stage versions of the story abounded all over Europe during the next hundred years, and Don Juan, the dissolute blasphemer, was known far and wide. The first musical connection with the legend was probably Purcell's accompaniment to the English playwright Shadwell's tragedy in 1676. Among the numerous seventeenth-century versions of the Don Juan theme was a ballet composed by Gluck based on a very simplified form of the story, and this made some impression upon Mozart — musically rather than dramaturgically — for he saw a performance of it in Salzburg.

Da Ponte was somewhat influenced by Goldoni's tragicomedy, *Don Giovanni Tenorio, or the Profligate,* as far as the creation of some of the characters and stage-effects are concerned. However, Goldoni, in an effort to bring the theme up to date, removed all supernatural phenomena from the play, and left the theme rather thin and bloodless.

Of the incredible amount of Don Juan material written and composed between 1770 and 1780 the most significant from our point of view is probably the one-act comic opera by Bertati and Gazzaniga, *Don Giovanni Tenorio, or the Stone Guest.* In this, the supernatural was reinstated to its ancient rightful position — built into the structure of the play. The brevity required by the one-act form probably helped to keep this work lively and credible, and to present the two sides of life, tragedy and comedy, that Mozart and da Ponte would soon present so successfully. Bertati's libretto served as a direct source for da Ponte.

Now let us see how Mozart and da Ponte tackled the much-used Don Juan theme.

Like that of *Figaro,* the overture to *Don Giovanni* is the quintessence of the play, and prepares the audience emotionally for it. Its form is that of the French overture, divided into a slow and a fast part; and from this time onwards all Mozart's opera overtures are constructed in this form, though containing different dramatic contents. The overture opens in D minor, Mozart's 'dramatic' key, to which in spite of a series of bold modulations it stubbornly returns time and again — and it starts with the harrowing statue-music, on sustained bass notes, of the later dramatic peak,

with broken period fragments, made from various materials, and laid side by side like pieces of a mosaic. In the threatening sforzato-piano violin motive, four times stubbornly repeated in bars 15-16,

we welcome an old acquaintance: the most important motive of *Idomeneo,* which returns on a number of occasions and always in a new form, the tragic musical symbol of happiness derived through love, yet threatened by the intrigues of earthly and heavenly powers.

The accumulation of musical means creates heavy tension suggesting the approach of a terrible storm: the syncopations of the first four bars which are later diminished to half their value on the violins; the merciless, threatening punctuated rhythm; the scales of flutes and violins rising higher and

142

higher in chromatic sequences; the two unexpectedly exploding, full-bar dissonant tutti chords; and so on. But the actual explosion does not yet take place: the overture (again like that of *Figaro*) outlines the conflict but does not solve it. From the suppressed piano passage at the end of the andante, the allegro molto emerges almost unnoticed. Its first bar does not reveal whether we have arrived at major or minor, just as in the last finale of *Figaro* it was only in the second bar of the dim transition from andante to allegro assai that the uncertain ground of undefined tonality became more or less solid under our feet. With its sharp contrasts, the allegro molto further increases the tension and then, modulating obscurely, it is left unfinished. The dynamic effects of the overture without the use of transition have already been experienced in *Figaro*. But there they appeared in one basic mood; here they serve to dramatise the contrast between two irreconcilable forces.

The introduction (number 1) following the overture attacca, as a contrast to the previous mood, starts in a buffo tone. It has a string and bassoon unison also familiar from *Figaro*, and even within the buffo character there is a sinister, threatening undertone. On the stage is Leporello, the chief comic character of the play. The situation is similar to that in Bertati's libretto; but by merging the characteristics of Bertati's two servants into one, da Ponte up-grades Leporello to the position of a leading character and gives him more concentrated dramatic significance. In this way Leporello outstrips all his predecessors, and even with his first appearance projects his full personality, which contrasts significantly with his master's. The tonality of the introduction sharply separates the four situations of the scene. Leporello's buffo monologue is in F major. The Anna/ Giovanni/Leporello trio is in B flat major. (Here Donna Anna is the initiator throughout; in this trio Don Giovanni consistently follows the rhythm and melody suggested by Anna, partly due to his defensive situation, and partly as a consequence of one of his basic characteristics — that he talks to every woman in her own tone and style.) The play is no longer a comedy, but it is not yet a drama, only the story of

143

one adventure (less successful than most) among many. Don Giovanni's and the Commendatore's duet, as well as the ensuing duel, are in G minor, and then proceed to D minor: the mood slowly changes into drama. The Don Giovanni/Commendatore/Leporello trio is in F minor, a suppressed tragic tone, in which the melody carrying Don Giovanni's frivolous words

recalls cynically Anna's melody of the B-flat-major trio:

he has to kill her father now because of the girl's stupid 'obstinacy'. Wavering chromatics lead into the recitative that closes the scene.

The introduction marks a new stage in Mozartian dramaturgy. In its construction and function it is closer to the finales than to the ensembles. It is a series of events with dramatic conflict, and succinct character-drawing (it seizes the essential features of the leading character at the very start, showing Don Giovanni engaged in trying to obtain by force both love and death), with scenic units that, though basically linked, have independent musical textures and different keys, and with a tonality that comes full circle. In contrast to his predecessors' works, Mozart shows the outcome of the Donna Anna episode as clearly and unambiguously negative: Don Giovanni has failed to seduce her. Neither the text nor the music leave any doubt about this. The various interpretations by the romantics (E.T.A. Hoffmann, Sören Kierkegaard, Wagner, etc.), in spite of being clever and thought-provoking, lack any actual musical found-
144

ation, and make nonsense of the original message of the drama. Their views have already been refuted by Jahn, and by others following in his tracks, especially Abert; so the only thing that should be added here is that some twentieth-century 'post-romantic' musicologists have also misunderstood the issue. Schurig and Cohen first of all claimed that Don Giovanni must have seduced Donna Anna, because he is the 'conqueror' to whom every woman yields despite herself. In their opinion the Don Giovanni type would not be perfectly represented if even one victim escaped.[1]

However, if we carefully follow the events of the two acts, we cannot but realise that it is the inevitable failure of the Donna Anna adventure that epitomises the theme of the opera. Mozart's Don Giovanni is pursued by misfortune throughout. When he tries to seduce her, Donna Anna calls for help. Don Giovanni is obliged to escape, and in self-defence he kills her father, the Commendatore. When he next catches sight of a beautiful woman he, of course, accosts her; but she turns out to be Donna Elvira, a woman with whom he had at one time had an affair. He had long since tired of her and deserted her. Meeting up with her again is a disaster, for she jealously proceeds to cause havoc. No sooner is he on the verge of seducing a pretty peasant girl than Donna Elvira whisks her away, out of his grasp. Then his bad luck throws him together with Donna Anna again. Before, he had worn disguise, and if he were to behave carefully now the odds are he would pass unrecognised by Anna; but Donna Elvira again causes complications, Don Giovanni acts in character, and Anna realises who he is. During the party scene, Don Giovanni succeeds in attracting the interest of Zerlina, but her fiancé, Masetto, interferes at an awkward moment, and the party that started so promisingly becomes a scandal, and Don Giovanni has to rely upon his sword in order to escape from his own house. Masetto puts paid to another promising relationship – with Donna Elvira's maid. His adventure with one of Leporello's girlfriends is the first and only adventure in the whole opera that seems to have been a success – but even this is only related by him, and to Leporello at that, which casts doubts upon the authenticity of his story (incidentally, even during this he was disturbed and forced to escape).

Where now is the conqueror who always succeeds? His failure to seduce Anna at the opening of the opera begins a two-act sequence of bad luck. It leads – through the pitifully tragi-comic series of accidents – to the inevitable fall of Don Giovanni. The introduction presented the 'hero' of the drama characteristically in action, and similarly the whole of the action emphasises that Don Giovanni's enormous success is quite superficial. His 1,003 (or, if we add all the figures on Leporello's list, 2,065) successful adventures were only apparent victories. The tragedy of his character is that each victory is also a defeat – and this is precisely what Mozart stresses in his opera. In every woman Don Giovanni searches for his Ideal – but he can never find it. His fate, his tragedy, is in his restlessness, in his demoniacal desire that cannot find fulfilment, in his ceaseless and hopeless search. Don Giovanni is not the Great Lover but the Great Beloved. He attracts every woman in a different way. At the time each one of them momentarily appears to be his Ideal. With an ingenious instinct he can adapt himself like a chameleon to her; one Don Giovanni stands before Anna, another meets Elvira, and a third courts Zerlina. If we can rely on Leporello's account, then there are 2,065 Don Giovannis! But the spiritual essence of Mozart's hero is that these 2,065 conquests are Pyrrhic victories. He is like a mountaineer who at last reaches the peak thought to be inaccessible – and finds that another, even higher peak rises before him.

The recitativo accompagnato (number 2) that follows the introduction separates in a characteristic way Anna's sad, wide-flowing and richly orchestrally accompanied sound from Ottavio's stiff words which move in a tight circle. At the beginning of the D-minor revenge duet Anna's harder and more dramatic intonation again differs sharply from Ottavio's lyrical singing. However, after the oath recitative by which the two-part form is divided, as a sort of compromise between the two kinds of sound the two parts merge into one long third parallel, in the tiny melodic imitations of which

Anna displays her stronger personality. In spite of its dramatic character, the duet is the elegant and mannerly dialogue of two aristocrats and does not go beyond the bounds of custom prescribed for the given situation, obeying the rules set out in the chapter in the Spanish book of etiquette entitled *How to Behave if We have Almost Been Raped, and Our Father is Stabbed into the Bargain*. Due to the personalities of the heroes in the play, this plan of revenge is considerably less dramatic than, say, that of Count Almaviva in *Figaro* – who is after all a Spanish nobleman, too, with a similar social position to that of Anna and Ottavio – and who has less justification for revenge than Donna Anna! The reason is that Almaviva fights with an opponent of dramatically equal rank and he is defeated in that struggle; on the other hand, Anna and Ottavio are dwarfs beside Don Giovanni. Human revenge simply bounces back from Don Giovanni's unrestrained passion – his Satanic power can only be conquered by a superhuman power!

Elvira's aria (number 3) is in fact a trio – another congenial dramatic trouvaille. It introduces in solemn E flat major this gentlewoman from Burgos who was once seduced and then deserted by Don Giovanni. The tone of the aria presents a somewhat aged, dignified, slightly hysterical lady who, however, loves and hates with sincere passion. She once thought she had found her own long-awaited Ideal in Don Giovanni, and is now, if necessary, ready to search the whole of Spain to find and regain him. For the first time since the overture the clarinets appear now in the formal baroque orchestral introduction to the aria. (In *The Marriage of Figaro* Mozart gave this new colour to Cherubino's introduction: his idol was Woman – that of Elvira is the One and Only Man.) During Don Giovanni's and Leporello's ironic interjections the character of the music changes: softly whispering violin syncopations and broken triads prepare for the first manoeuvre towards a conquest. In the recapitulation Don Giovanni's sarcastic words are already intoning the soft fourth interval of his seducing routine:

147

Later he uses the same tone to court the beautiful Zerlina:

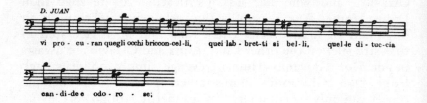

Elvira's repeated, passionate, almost eccentric cadenza is strengthened by an orchestral tutti:

and then Don Giovanni, augmenting the earlier, softly-whispering violin motive, leads us — attacca — into the next recitative:

Even in *Figaro* we could observe that the harpsichord accompaniment to the seccos had taken on a dramatic role. Now, the moment when Don Giovanni and Donna Elvira recognise one another is illustrated by a marked motive on the harpsichord.

A feature of Elvira's musical characterisation is the unusually long (fourteen-bar) recitative melody through which she gabbles almost in one breath, and about which Leporello is right to say: 'As if she was reading it from a book!' (The dramaturgical principle of Mozart's characters 'being moulded from one block' has by now become valid for the recitatives as well: even in the seccos each character speaks in his or her characteristic tone.)

So far we have seen our hero in his natural element: seducing women and killing men. He now leaves the stage for a while in order to let us see him through Leporello's eyes. Naturally, Leporello's picture of him is not complete, and therefore not entirely authentic either. Leporello forms a somewhat idealised image of his master, with whom he has mentally come to identify himself during the score of years spent with him and in the course of everyday adventures.

149

Although among all the characters of the opera he is the one closest to Don Giovanni and who knows him best, he still cannot see his full personality, and cannot really understand his master in all his demoniacal depth — despite the fact that in the catalogue aria, for instance, he almost gives himself his master's role. Leporello is a child of the people, Papageno's elder and more cynical brother. As servant and confidant he shares with his master good times and bad alike. He is a warm-hearted and gay fellow who sincerely likes his master, and likes this exciting, adventurous life. He sees Don Giovanni through the rosy spectacles of affection — in the gay D-major catalogue aria (number 4) in which the dark shadow of the true Don Giovanni appears only for a few seconds, in the three interrupted cadences, in the minuet-like second part of the two-part form. (As in *Figaro*, we hear the court dance again!)

Such an indirect characterisation of Don Giovanni, constructed from various perspectives, is one of the dramaturgical principles of the opera. (Later, in *The Magic Flute,* it is not only a type, a character, but indeed a vista of an entire world order that Mozart presents in such an indirect way, from Tamino's point of view.) This is the only way to musically define a character who expresses himself exclusively through his actions. Don Giovanni's indirect characterisation is another of Mozart's trouvailles: nothing happens in the course of the opera that is not closely associated with him; all the words and experiences of the rest of the characters reflect him; but each of these reflected images is only a part of the whole — and all of them together make up the complete picture.

As an excellent contrast, the peasant couple appear on the stage (number 5) in gay, dancing G major with irregular periods, and with bold modulation in Masetto's refrain.

'A simple, childish melody with good humour sparkling in every part of it,' wrote Mörike. This rusticity is also characteristic of Masetto's next aria (number 6), in the first episode of which the augmented fourth of his refrain from the previous duet characteristically returns:

The principle of the character moulded from one block is revealed again in the next duettino sung by Don Giovanni and Zerlina (number 7). Although the experienced seducer keeps to the simple folk-song tone of the girl, even in the first half sentence

there appears the already familiar caressingly soft fourth interval of seduction (see examples on page 145). Don Giovanni comes straight to the point without even an orchestral prelude! In the first half of the first part of the duettino he is repeated word by word by Zerlina who even adds two bars to it (it will be an easy, quick victory), and in the second half of the part the girl takes over — indeed, she extends the second two bars of the half period. (The string third figuration of bar 22, recalling the end of the previous duet, alludes to poor Masetto who is apparently to be cuckolded.) In the return, this time with the previous upbeat extended first to a fifth and then to a seventh, the enchanted little bird finally falls into the tempting embrace of the snake. Dazzled by love, she now, almost in each bar, cuts into the words of her seducer. By the second part of the 6/8 duettino (the tone of the minuet again, but this time with a pastoral character suiting the occasion) the situation has matured for the long-awaited parallel third; and the tenderly erotic transitional bars of the second violins and the violas

anticipate almost visually the lovers' embrace. Victory is certain. Words are almost superfluous now; and with his traditional two caressing fourths

Don Giovanni only talks of essentials. Like Susanna's and the count's duet in a similar situation in *Figaro* (from the point

of view of social relationships as well), the duettino is in A major. No clarinet is to be heard: there is no need for it in such an insignificant little conquest.

Elvira's next aria (number 8) provides a new sound not only in its sharp contrast to the previous scene; moreover it is new not only in this opera, but in Mozart's whole oeuvre. This massive Handelian sound, recalling baroque oratorios and concertos grossos, was almost completely passé in Mozart's time, just as in the world of superficial sentiments and light flirtations Elvira's passionate love for the one man in her life was completely outdated. The intonation does not contradict what we already know about Donna Elvira, since her first aria — where she also thought she was alone — was of an antiquated baroque flavour, and her last one will be a period piece, too. Now, however, when she pretends to protect an innocent maiden from her seducer, while in fact she is keeping the seducer, her unfaithful lover, away from the innocent maiden (Elvira is not interested at all in Zerlina's fate), the old-fashioned sound also becomes the musical representation of jealousy for which even a hypocritical lie is a good enough weapon.

The quartet (number 9) actually starts with the end of the preceding recitative, that is, with Elvira's two bars modulating from E flat major into B flat major. Elvira's basic tonality in the opera is the solemn and majestic E flat major. Her first and third arias are in this key (perhaps this is the only case where Mozart gives two arias of the same key to one character); indeed, even the D major of the second aria is only half a note away from the basic tonality — and this slipping down by half a note is particularly appropriate since here Elvira uses lies to achieve her aim. So it is in her own key that Elvira interferes again when — soon after succeeding in leading Zerlina to safety — she again finds Don Giovanni in deep conversation with a beautiful woman. Poor Elvira does not want to cause any harm to Don Giovanni — but she does not wish him to enjoy the company of other women either. She simply wants to regain his love, to tie him down to domesticity — as if one could ever hold the ocean in a jam-jar!

The atmosphere of the quartet is created by the ill-omened murmur of the empty B flat which closed the previous recitative: as in the introduction here, too, the B-flat-major transition prepares the way for the dramatic eruption. Like the previous aria, Elvira's first sentence — which is now broad and dignified — is accompanied by the strings; it is only in the sixth bar of the second sentence (which is actually the fifth bar of the period, since the whole of the first bar is just an extended upbeat) that the sound of the clarinet — so closely associated with Elvira — appears in the orchestra. The closing motive of the period,

which stubbornly recurs throughout the quartet, is like a musical symbol of the suspicion that gradually increases in the course of the scene. Don Giovanni attempts to convince Ottavio and Anna of Elvira's mental instability, and this is made somewhat plausible by Elvira's hysterical behaviour, already shown in her first aria, and her appearing, first for the duration of a repeated bar, and then for two bars twice in the middle part of the quartet, and finally in the excessive coloratura cadenzas which completely break the flow of conversation. But Anna's feminine intuition recognises sincerity glowing through Elvira's unbalanced words, and Don Giovanni, driven into a corner, becomes more and more nervous and uncertain while insisting upon the truth of his words. The tense scene comes to an end with the suspicion motive repeated seven times in the dialogue between Anna and the orchestra, while Elvira and Don Giovanni stubbornly repeat what they have to say in excited semi-quavers. During the quartet Ottavio is only a musical shadow of Anna: he does not suspect anything and does not understand the situation at all. He is the only one in whose part the suspicion motive does not appear. From Don Giovanni, too, we hear it only once, at the beginning of the quartet, in an altered, slightly embellished form,

as if he were mockingly distorting the accusations of the 'poor mad woman'; later, when put on the defensive, he does not dare to return to it.

The short secco, following the quartet, brings a dramatic turn of events: in Don Giovanni's feigned polite tone Anna recognises the voice of her masked assailant. In the recitative Don Giovanni's words — unconsciously but characteristically — recall the melody of Elvira's entrance which preceded the quartet and gave rise to the whole unpleasant situation; even the process of modulation leading from E flat major to B flat major, and the double-phrased subito piano empty bass note — that closes the phrase and also commences the next number — are the same:

Using the principle of the 'hint' in Anna's recitativo accompagnato and aria (number 10), Mozart does not go to extremes in exploiting the possibilities offered by the situation; instead, he prefers to convey, to describe and to outline (with very concise instrumentation, excluding flutes and clarinets, but using horns and trumpets). The narration is tense, excitedly modulating (E flat, B, G, E, A minor).

I would like to point out a serious mistake of Schurig's relating to this part of the opera. He describes Anna's narration – following her recognition of Don Giovanni – as 'musically the weakest point in *Don Giovanni*', and from this he reaches the conclusion that 'Mozart was not a conscious dramatist'. 'Mozart should not have used a secco recitative form for the solution of the scene that was so effectively placed and constructed (in contrast to Bertati) by da Ponte.'* It is incredible that Schurig, that thorough critic, should commit such a great mistake! The scene in question, as we have seen, is not secco but accompagnato, and indeed a very dramatic accompagnato that makes use of the whole orchestra, even of the otherwise so economically used trumpets. So let us exempt Mozart from Schurig's accusation: there is no musically weak point in *Don Giovanni*!

By the way, it is very interesting that Einstein interprets Anna's situation like this: '[Anna] has undoubtedly fallen victim to our hero who, disguised as Don Ottavio in the darkness of the night, achieved the fulfilment of his desires; and the curtain goes up at the moment when Donna Anna becomes convinced of the horrible certainty of her mistake. Nobody was in doubt about this in the eighteenth century. It is self-evident that in her famous recitativo accompagnato, where she reveals to her fiancé that Don Giovanni is the murderer of her father, that she cannot tell the complete truth to Don Ottavio, in whose "respiro", by the way, every initiated member of the audience feels the spirit of tragicomedy.'† Through a score of examples we have seen so far that Mozart, whenever he wants to, can express more than the libretto tells us; indeed, if necessary, he can express other things in addition – and he can even contradict the words of the libretto. Had his conviction dictated him to do so, he

* Schurig, q.v.
† Einstein, *Mozart,* 1956.

could certainly have thrown more light with his music on Donna Anna's narration: '. . . Trembling and pale, I could finally force myself out of his embrace!' And with the help of a few simple purely musical means he could have unambiguously brought it to our knowledge that Anna was now telling a lie to her fiancé: her trembling and paleness were true, but she did not succeed in forcing herself out of the embracing arms. As in Ottavio's naïve reaction, too ('Oh, I can breath again!'), it would not have been a moment's problem for Mozart to illustrate with a little irony the tragi-comedy heard by Einstein. Instead of all these, however, the transparent string accompaniment of the four bars of the scene

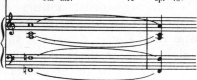

with its declining bass sequence and above it the syncopated violin motive repeated three times in an identical way, with its almost motionless recitative melody within a small third, and finally with its simple interrupted cadence, fail to express that which dreamers with psychoanalytical pretensions have been alluding to for more than a century and a half. A characteristic trait of the aria, incidentally, the tonality and basic approach of which — presenting a disciplined lady — are identical to those of the revenge duet, is the sudden halt in the coda and the following subito piano cadence which unexpectedly and significantly annuls the previous forte pathos.

The same halting conclusion, 'the native hue of resolution sicklied over with the pale cast of thought', is also characteristic of Ottavio's next cavatina (number 11) of outstanding beauty. Don Giovanni is a direct contrast to Hamlet — he does not indulge in monologues and self-scrutinies, but lives intensely, his actions obeying his instincts. On the other hand 'conscience makes coward' of Ottavio: he only meditates on life, psycho-analyses himself and the world about him (but mainly himself!); and meanwhile life passes him by and he is left there by the wayside. In his two arias Ottavio sings the most beautiful melodies in Mozart's oeuvre — they are so beautiful as to be almost unmanly.

It is in keeping with his character than in both his arias Ottavio sings the old-fashioned, schematic cadences of Italian opera seria (in the first aria only a few notes before the recapitulation — while at the same place in the second aria six full bars!). And Ottavio never forgets the good manners and polite behaviour compulsory to people of his rank: the conscientious closing of forms and parts of forms, for instance, at the end of the first aria:

and then in the orchestral introduction and postlude of the second aria:

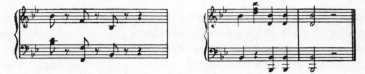

Verbosity is also part of Ottavio's character: modulating further after a regular cadence turn, the first aria repeats itself in a stereotyped way:

and so does the second, where, following the extended coda of the vocal part, and the twice repeated closing bar of the ensuing orchestral postlude, we hear again — now for the fifth time — the theme of the aria in subito piano chromatics:

This gentle sequence of femininely graceful chromatics, that returns to its starting point and leads from nowhere to nowhere, is also one of Ottavio's musical characteristics; its appearance in the first aria was identical to the fourth bar:

and then, as its reverse, before the recapitulation of the second aria:

Incidentally, Ottavio's first aria was not composed and put in place by Mozart until later on, on the occasion of the first performance in Vienna; and with this Mozart once again gave evidence of his ingenious feeling for drama and psychology. After his fiancée's call for revenge Ottavio, instead of challenging the murderer and seducer to fight a duel with him, or at least doing something appropriate (or if nothing else, at least singing about what he would do if for once he did something), he merely admits that when Anna is sad, he is sad, too; and life is only good if one is not alone. All this completely fits in with and adds to what we already know about Ottavio; and this time Abert really draws a blank when he refers to the *'Dalla sua pace'* as a 'grave mistake'![2] Moreover, what a wonderful contrast is provided by this lyrical intermezzo, placed as it is between Anna's dramatic narration and Don Giovanni's champagne aria (number 12).

Apart from some small 'confessions' in the recitatives, the champagne aria is the only part of the opera in which Don Giovanni talks about himself. Now we do not see our hero in action, or hear what others think about him, but see him as he sees himself. The basic mood of the champagne aria is that of unrestrained hurry, with a ceaselessly clattering quaver movement and with hard, transitionless dynamic contrasts. Its main element of composition is rhythm; its melodic line, on the other hand, is almost primitively simple, while its harmony is practically limited to changes of tonic and dominant only, and in tonality – apart from a short, close deviation – it remains in the basic key all the time.

In contrast, Zerlina's next aria (number 13) is full of tenderly coquettish, graceful melodies, with a loving and naïvely contrapuntal 'cello solo. Abert justly points out that Don Giovanni's love technique did not lack effect upon Zerlina, and that during their short flirtation the girl became aware of her womanly attraction: the form of the aria and the metre of the two parts are identical to those of the duet, and the andante/allegro relationship also represents a similar development of situation in both numbers.[3] To this observation we can add another characteristically conspicuous parallel which, it seems, has escaped Abert's attention, and which gives even more musical evidence of Zerlina's readiness to learn about love. The second half-period of the aria

is note by note the same as that particular recitative melody with which Don Giovanni courted Zerlina immediately before the duet, and even the caressing accented step of a fourth, characterising Don Giovanni's method of seduction all through the opera, returns a score of times:

Even if Don Giovanni did not achieve his aim as far as Zerlina is concerned, he found in her a talented and willing pupil.

But however pleased Zerlina is to continue to flirt with Don Giovanni (or with anybody else), really her heart only beats for her clumsy Masetto. At the beginning of the finale (number 14) while the girl's words reveal her anxiety for Masetto, we hear again the characteristic modulation of an augmented fourth, already heard twice from Masetto:

The key is identical with the key at the same place in Masetto's aria, while Zerlina's melody is almost completely identical with that of Masetto's refrain in the first duet.

However, when in the shadow of the trees Don Giovanni puts his arms round her slim waist, then — it's good-bye to common sense! Faithful to his habit, Don Giovanni takes over the girl's tone: word by word he repeats Zerlina's fragment of melody — and the well-tried method works again. By the second period Zerlina is already following the melody note by note with its tenderly caressing fourth, and even adds – as in the duet – two bars to it. At that moment, however, Masetto appears among the bushes and the music registers the unexpected and unpleasant surprise with a simple parallel minor modulation – another application of the 'hint'. Don Giovanni, caught red-handed, is confused for a moment, yet he manages to master the situation within the same period (this not being his first *in flagranti*!), and energetically, indeed aggressively, modulates back to his own ground, the previous key: the most effective means of defence is attack!

The eight-bar D-minor passage of the unpleasant surprise is only a slight foretaste of the inevitably approaching storm of the drama: some strange uncertainty, a hardly audible roll of thunder in the distance. The appearance of the revenge trio – Elvira, Anna and Ottavio – brings at last the genuine, serious D minor introduced by thorough modulation. The drama begins. The restless semi-quaver movement of the first violin is predominant throughout the whole scene (the conspirators are rather nervous). The augmented form of the violin motive is Elvira's opening motive:

which is also identical, both in its tonality and instrumentation, with the beginning of the first duet by Anna and Ottavio:

The two women — the instigators of the plan of revenge —
seem to have thoroughly discussed the strategy! As usual,
Ottavio is only a shadow of a personality stronger than
himself: his words repeat Elvira's melody, and even the
structure of the period extended to nine bars (with an
additional bar inserted between the sixth and seventh bars) is
the same. Anna's independent melody is softer and more
lyrical than that of Elvira, from whose dramatic D minor it
modulates towards the tragic G minor.

This scene is the demonstration of alliance between the
three of them; however, the actual carrying out of the play of
revenge is postponed for the time being. One of the windows
of the villa opens, and the faintly audible sounds of a minuet
take us back again to Don Giovanni's previous F major. The
minuet, which starts with the last two bars and only then
begins the melody, is Don Giovanni's music (in *Figaro,* too,
the graceful court dance of the minuet was the music of the
aristocracy); Don Giovanni's characteristic fourth dominates
the first motives of both its periods.

As in the finale of the third act of *Figaro,* the conversation is
carried on above the light dance music, while in the whirling
second violin figuration of the second period the tension
begins to accumulate, arising from the contrast of the two
different textures: the frivolous dance music, and the

suppressed, dramatic dialogue. After the acceptance of the invitation there is a modulation in key and mood to lead from the minuet into the 'mask trio' (Anna, Elvira and Ottavio wear masks as disguises at the ball), similar to the one that connected yet separated the previous D-minor trio and the preceding number:

(According to an anecdote, Richard Strauss once said that he would give up all of his operas if these two bars – second example above – could have been written by him, which 'lead from the most unrestrained joy to the deepest tragedy'.)

Following the sinister whirling under the surface of the 3/4 dance music, at the start of the adagio the strings of the orchestra modulate in unison motionlessly with this two-bar sequence that is broken and excited with punctuated rhythm. Its new 4/4 time, almost secretly sliding in after the previous minuet, only becomes obvious in the second bar.

A new tone is heard: F major followed by B flat major (as in the introduction and the quartet); and a new colour appears: an all woodwind accompaniment after the string background of the previous scenes. Dramaturgically, the B-flat-major trio is the continuation of the D-minor trio that was interrupted by the minuet. It opens a capella; the chords of the woodwinds entering in the second bar fulfil the function of a supporting accompaniment. Only the darkly-wavering clarinet triads (first only in semi-quavers, and for

166

the second time condensed into sextolets), the staccato bassoon notes, and the scale-melodies of the coda repeating Anna's last words, lead an independent life. Elvira's triad cadenzas, with their interruptions and stubborn repetitions, come naturally from her rather hysterical, monomaniac character; while Anna's delicate little embellishments and smooth scale roulades are created by Mozart from the texture of her disciplined, distinguished character. In the trio, Ottavio is again nothing but a mere shadow of Anna.

Once again there is new colour: a glittering tutti E flat major, a ballroom gaily awhirl. In parallel thirds the two hosts are talking to their guests of lower rank, for Zerlina's sake adopting a folk-dance tone to please them. Zerlina joins the two men's parallel thirds in the return, but in counter-motion, and repeating Masetto's last motive fragment: although she enjoys the distinguished company, and finds Don Giovanni's courting flattering, in the depths of her heart she still feels sorry for her clumsy fiancé who will be cuckolded in a matter of minutes (or at least she hopes so).

The gay whirling 6/8 E flat major is abruptly followed by stiff and reserved C major as the three masked people enter. There is a military flourish of trumpet, followed by the traditional civilities of Spanish etiquette; and the ordinary folk silently watch the starched and pompous aristocrats. From the solemn C major the words of Don Giovanni modulate into the repeatedly-heard minuet (this time in cheerful G major), above which the recently interrupted dialogue now continues. The contra-dance and waltz of the two peasant orchestras now join the 'aristocratic' dance: Zerlina and Don Giovanni (who wants to take her into a quiet corner) are accompanied by the 2/4 time of the contra-dance; Leporello, trying to get Masetto out of the way, manoeuvres in the 3/8 time of the Viennese waltz. When the voices of the three masked people are heard, the 3/4 time of the minuet takes over.

In the meantime Don Giovanni has succeeded in luring Zerlina into the next room; but it seems that the girl has changed her mind at the last moment. As she is heard screaming for help, the dance breaks off, and the G major is replaced by an excitedly turbulent E-flat-major unison tutti which, rising in sequences through B flat minor and C minor, reaches the dominant of D minor. Recovery from this scandal is achieved by similar musical means to those we came across at the unexpected appearance of Masetto at the beginning of the finale, because the situation is similar too – only even more unpleasant. Don Giovanni's quick reaction is also the same: he immediately takes the initiative, and preventing the fermata A-major chord to resolve into D minor, he immediately goes into the attack, accompanied by a new aggressive unison tutti, and in the hypocritical role of a champion of virtues, he peremptorily pulls the situation back to the F-major ground he believes to be safe. Leporello quickly sums up the situation and is ready to help (no doubt there have been other cases of this kind among the 2,065: the servant knows his role well!), and in sequences of descending thirds he gives Don Giovanni the often used, well-practised cues.

And then Ottavio – perhaps for the first time in his life,

but probably for the last, too – rises in defence of female honour; his first bar sets the basic tone for the ensuing united front against Don Giovanni, while his second motive is canonically taken up by Anna and Elvira who take off their masks as they enter the canon. Don Giovanni is now definitely pushed into a defensive position: being helpless, he is forced to put up with the irrevocable modulation from his own F major into the previous C major marking the appearance of the trio of revenge. It is worth noting that during the finale D minor has already been reached three times (first, only for the duration of six bars with the appearance of Masetto; second, for the extent of a whole scene when the three masked people appeared; and for the third time now, at the *in flagranti*); but still, the climax is not in this much-employed dramatic key, but in the relatively neutral C major of a lower temperature and looser texture. This relative decline in tension, however, has its well-considered dramaturgical reason: the end of the first act is no catastrophe, only a trivial scandal; the actual explosion into D minor for which the way has now been paved, and the real dramatic conflict, will only arrive in the second finale, with the entrance of the statue.

From the point of view of atmosphere, however, this is already anticipated in the heavy Cs at the start of the coda, this motive variant that first appeared in the overture, and which will gain a dramaturgical function later on with the knocking by the statue in the finale of the second act. This motive will there appear in F major (the reason will be explained later); here it is only in C major: two ladies, an effeminate gentleman brandishing a dress-rapier, and a few unarmed peasants are no opponents for Don Giovanni! On the other hand, even here, at the start of the coda, the motive of the later knocking by the statue unmistakably suggests that, although this time Don Giovanni can easily free himself from trouble, the clash with a worthy and equal opponent is yet to come.

Characteristically enough, Don Giovanni's first thought is not related to the heated situation and his possibilities of escaping from it (after all, he has managed to get out of trouble so many times before), but to the fiasco in which the gay party, that started so beautifully, finally ended. The suppressed subito piano words that follow the first offensive of the united front, while Leporello courageously holds out on the side of his master,

recall the melody fragment inviting the guests at the start of the finale:

Even the graceful trill of violins is the same: 'A gentleman is a gentleman even in hell!' (Later on Don Giovanni will be able to prove literally the truth of this proverb commonly used only in a figurative sense!) But the noose is tightening, and Don Giovanni, together with faithful Leporello, is already trying to find a way of escape. Their scale-exclamations, and the increasingly excited triplet passages of the orchestra clearly describe the two men's state of mind.

Incidentally, no chorus takes part in this affair. The country people do not take sides in the aristocratic quarrel – they would not even mind if the opponents were to kill one another!

Finally, Don Giovanni becomes exasperated with the unworthy situation and prepares to free himself with his sword from the threatening ring. Leporello has no weapon: the duel is an occupation for gentlemen only. A small but very fine and characteristic phenomenon is that this is the only moment in the coda when Leporello does not – and cannot – imitate his master. With a fanfare motive of heroic character Don Giovanni pulls out his sword: 'I am not wanting in courage.' This time, however, Leporello does not take up the melody of his master, but very modestly takes shelter behind it (as if we heard the voice: 'Pa-pa-pa-pa-pa-pageno', and Papageno's words: 'Fighting is not my business!'), repeating, 'He is not wanting in courage,' and hoping that one sword will do for the two of them!

The stretta starts with the variant of the sword-fanfare and with the statue's knocking motive in the orchestra. Another telling idea that also gives evidence of fine psychological observation is that for sixteen bars the three women (Anna, Elvira and Zerlina) imitate canonically Don Giovanni's heroic

171

fanfare-theme with its syncopated rhythm.[4] Their hearts are stronger than their reason: they should hate the unscrupulous seducer, yet as they throw all logical thought to the winds, Don Giovanni's courageous, grandiose, self-assured conduct makes a great impact on them – much greater than the cowardly timidity of the fiancés, Ottavio and Masetto.

Among other things, it is a combination of these fine details of situation, character-drawing, and psychological observation, condensed into the microcosm of a few bars, that raises the genre of the opera in its dramaturgical possibilities well above the more clumsy and limited means of expression that stage genres without music have.

The finale of the first act ends with the inverted variant of the motive of the statue's knocking. In the construction of the libretto this finale remains below the particularly high standard of the *Figaro* finales – at least as regards da Ponte's conception of what a finale should be like: the fact that the action is woven with several threads disrupts the unity of the finale, and the scenic change after the mask trio breaks the so-far evenly rising tension. However, as always, Mozart's music helps the libretto through the dramaturgical diffi- culties, and by joining the two broken threads to the mask trio's hauntingly lyrical intermezzo, which in its turn is connected with the ingenious trouvaille of the triple orches- tra of the brilliantly unfolded ball scene, Mozart closes the first act with a gradually rising dramatic climax that prepares the way for the real conflict of the second act, and even ensures its further rise in tension.

Having set out to extend Bertati's one-act work into a full two-act opera, da Ponte was compelled to spin out the action; thus the whole of the first finale, and more than a half of the second act (eleven of the eighteen scenes) is new material. Da Ponte was forced to grasp the eternal life-line of all stage authors, that of *allotria,* dramaturgical stuffing, and he draws out the time with a whole series of delaying scenes until the cemetery scene where he again returns to the Bertati libretto. So a good part of the second act, including Elvira's aria, is alien material, dramaturgical tautology, a loose chain of inserted episodes, only filled with life and dramatic content through Mozart's linking of them to the main line of events by purely musical means.

The first duet (number 15), in harmony with the principle of continuous action, takes up the thread where it was broken with the last sounds of the first act. It introduces a new aspect of our hero: he can not only find the tone that is most suitable for the partner and the occasion where women are concerned, but also with men – as now with Leporello who is fed up with all the excitement. Way back in the introduction, the servant told the world that he wanted to play the gentleman too. It is this – obviously often repeated – desire of Leporello's that Don Giovanni now quenches. The whole of the duet carries on in Leporello's buffo tone, and in the waltz rhythm that was his during the ball scene. And the next recitative concludes the tiny conflict between master and servant that lasted for the duration of only one number. Don Giovanni's character has been further enriched as a musical formulation has been given to his 'principles for the conquering of women' expressed in the self-confession monologue of Molière's hero.[5]

The trio (number 16), sung by Don Giovanni, Donna Elvira and Leporello, is yet another peerless example of how to render a transparently clear description of a complex situation, and how to achieve the creation of psychologically well-founded characters. Don Giovanni and Leporello have exchanged clothes, and Leporello, pretending to be his master, mimes to Don Giovanni's singing in order to lure Elvira from her room so that the coast can be left clear for Don Giovanni to chat up her maid. The key is A major, Mozart's 'seductive' key; and in the beginning the idea is somewhat reminiscent of the first trio (number 3) where, similarly, the dialogue of the two men joined the words of Elvira who was singing her aria and believing herself to be alone. However, while there the two parallel themes of the play were separated throughout the whole scene, here, following the small interlude after the first period, it is Don Giovanni who takes over Elvira's previous sentimental melody – but now in the more heated dominant. Then in the middle part, with caressing chromatics, modulating suddenly and boldly from E major to a remote key, the mediant C major, he is back at his own tone, and – behind Leporello's back – he continues the manoeuvre with his own well-known 'seducing fourth'. Elvira's weak resistance is broken; and in the recapitulation we get back to the basic tonality through the transition of the previous chromatic modulation, extended this time into two bars. Elvira has failed again: her voice is interwoven in loving thirds with that of Leporello, who plays the part of his master reluctantly, for he is disgusted by the unkind trick; while Don Giovanni, in the cloak and the staccato manner of his servant, but in his own cynical way, enjoys the awkward situation and his power to manipulate the two people. The metre and main theme of the trio recall the letter duet from *Figaro,* probably not by accident: the dramatic situation is similar. There one man was deceived by two women — here two men set a love-trap for a woman. But while Susanna and the countess were dramatically and morally justified in joining forces to bring shame on the fickle womaniser — here Don Giovanni pursues a cruel game (and without any dramatic reason which would — to a certain extent — objectively minimise his crime!) with Elvira's sentimental, but undoubtedly sincere emotions. Instead of the transparent, two-part canzonetta accompaniment of the letter duet, with its pure and delicate oboe and bassoon colours, in the trio there is a rich, almost sensual orchestration, with dominating horns and clarinets. Characteristically enough, for the first time in the opera, the oboes are omitted: indeed, how would their innocent, virginal sound fit in with this cunningly-concocted plan?

A further means, rather unusual in this genre, is employed to extend the length of the opera: two arias by the same singer follow consecutively. This awkward idea must have been the result of da Ponte's endeavour to pile one imbroglio on top of another. Yet we know that Mozart was too mature and constructive a dramatist to allow such a grave dramaturgical *faux pas* to be committed without a serious reason. And indeed, if we take a look at the dramatic situations in the two numbers, we shall see that, although Don Giovanni sings both his arias wearing Leporello's cloak, the intonation and psychological content of the two numbers are entirely different. In the canzonetta (number 17) Don Giovanni deliberately plays the role of his servant: he is intent on courting Elvira's maid, and 'a gentleman of my kind has little credit with these characters'. On the other hand, the voice is unmistakably his own conquering fourth, and the melody

175

Deh, vie - ni al-la fi - ne - stra, o mio ____ te - so - ro!

is also identical to that with which, just a short while ago, in the C-major middle part of the previous trio, he succeeded in luring Elvira for the second time:

Di - scen - di o gio - ja bel-la, o gio - - - ja bel - la!

Lady or maid: it makes no difference — for Don Giovanni all women are the same! In its melody and accompanying mandolin figuration, the serenade shows a number of similar features to the song entitled 'Komm, liebe Zither', composed by Mozart about 1780-81; but while the predominant feature throughout the serenade is Don Giovanni's stressed glissando step of a fourth — an X-ray picture of the melody would show something like this:

— in the song this fourth is only a conventional, weightless standard upbeat, without any special significance:

Another interesting difference between the songs is that 'Komm, liebe Zither' consists of four-plus-three and four-plus-five bar periods, while in Don Giovanni's serenade there are only regular eight-bar periods. For the seduction of a simple lady's-maid he does not need any sophisticated gimmicks of form structure!

As we have seen, Don Giovanni deliberately played the role of his servant in the serenade. However, in the following aria (number 18) the situation is entirely different: Masetto is approaching with a mob of armed peasants, and if Don Giovanni wants to avoid being manhandled in the dark street he has no alternative but to go on playing the part. That is why he starts the aria in Leporello's buffo tone and in his key (the F major of the introduction), repeating with fine irony Leporello's melody from the first finale: 'He is not wanting in courage':

Se un'uome u - na ra - ga - za pas-seggian per la piaz-za.

Intoxicated by the role, however, he grows too bold, and if the ears of Masetto and his friends were just a little bit more sensitive, the supercilious and ironic voice of the actor would certainly be recognised. But the peasants are confused by Don Giovanni's glib tongue, and he makes short work of the clumsy conspirators.

Zerlina's second aria (number 19) seems to be another digression. This — like her earlier aria — is sung to Masetto, and Zerlina, in her attractively coquettish way, tries to console her fiancé. But though before there were undertones to her words, here she is completely sincere. The momentary dazzle is over, and her relationship with Masetto is finally sealed. Dramaturgically it is very important to point out that, having drawn her own conclusions from the incident with Don Giovanni, Zerlina voluntarily tears out from her heart the memory of his sweet words, and now she willingly and irrevocably binds her fate to that of Masetto. Without this scene — that is, if Don Giovanni finally disappeared from Zerlina's life only as a result of the Commendatore's intervention — what would then guarantee that tomorrow would not bring another Don Giovanni to awake in the girl's

177

heart the fragrant memory of attraction which, due to circumstance, remained unfulfilled? The matter can only be settled once and for all by Zerlina's spontaneous decision, when she raises the spirits of the defeated, humiliated Masetto, and before God and man swears to be his faithful wife. But it is primarily due to Mozart's music that da Ponte's somewhat vulgar words are filled with such content, and raised to the sphere of poetry.

In its structure the sextet (number 20) is a kind of miniature finale, with independent action and conflict, a gradually increasing number of characters, and inner changes in tempo and key.[6] Its basic tone is provided by Elvira in her characteristic E-flat-major tonality; the sforzato piano and subito piano dynamics of its broadly-arched, dignified melody, its violin roulades and chromatic passages, reflect her barely-concealed anguish, the almost visible fear of rediscovered, uncertain happiness. Anna and Ottavio enter with a boldly enharmonic modulation, accompanied by the timpani and trumpets already familiar from the first act; their brilliant D major disperses the dimness of the stage. Anna answers her fiancé's flowing cantilena in her familiar voice, yet in an unexpected D minor; her sad melody recalls their first duet and the first trio of the finale, and already in the first phrase it modulates again from Ottavio's glittering D major, first to B flat major, and then, through a dense and painful series of discords, to C minor. The following chromatic violin motive of punctuated rhythm rules the scene until the allegro molto, containing, as it were, in a concentrated form the complicated emotional and spiritual duality of the whole tragi-comic situation — with the miserably crying Leporello, unable to go on playing Don Giovanni's part, and Elvira praying for her 'husband's' life. (Again the Shakespearean dramatic unity of tragedy and comedy, condensed into a single situation, even a single musical idea!) In unmasking Don Giovanni's imposture the 'hint' is again employed, while the delayed reaction of surprise, and the gradual comprehension of the unexpected turn of events are demonstrated by a rising sequence.

In the allegro molto coda of the sextet the individual

character-drawing within the 'united front' deserves attention. So does the return of Leporello's self-assurance, for he
instinctively exploits the changed situation, i.e. that the
target is no longer he, but his master. (The previous declining
chromatic motive is now impertinently rising, and this
psychological reversal paves the way for his next buffo aria.)
Another motive to be noted is that, among the members of
the 'united front', Zerlina alone (in the bar and a half
following the two D-flat-major digressions) with her tender
heart musically sympathises a little with the man in trouble:
she has herself recently experienced such a narrow escape,
that she can understand, if anyone can, Leporello's dependence upon and subordination to the master he genuinely
likes and faithfully follows.

Thus by the end of the sextet, Leporello has regained his
self-composure, and, just as he took the initiative in the
allegro molto, so in his aria (number 21) he leads the whole
distinguished company up the garden path. In addition to the
above-mentioned psychological connection, musically, too,
the aria is closely linked with the sextet. Its opening theme
recalls Anna's and Zerlina's melody that followed the bars of
Zerlina's sympathy for Leporello, but while there the scale
sequences of the two women reflected a falling tendency:

here, the sequence is rising (like the previous chromatic
sequence), thus confuting Leporello's plea for mercy with its
downward trend of sham humiliation:

179

tà, pie - tà di   me.

Characteristically, however, this melody pleading for pity, borrowed from Anna, decisively stops in the seventh bar, never to return. As Leporello masters the situation, so he starts a new musical idea. It is a syncopated version of what we heard earlier, in the catalogue aria. The adventurous life at Don Giovanni's side has taught a number of things to Leporello who, like his master in his previous F-major aria, with his glib talking blunts the vigilance of the enemy; by the time they see through his plot, he has succeeded in escaping. He is out of reach.

In Ottavio's next B-flat-major aria (number 22) he asks his friends to look after his fiancée until he can hand over the murderer to the authorities (a naïve idea, typical of Ottavio). The aria was composed and put into the play later, on the occasion of the first performance in Vienna – like Elvira's third (once again E-flat-major) recitative and aria (number 23). Here not only does Elvira imagine she is by herself, but she is actually alone on the stage, just as she is alone in life, with passionate and ungratified feelings, longing in her heart for love. The baroque-flavoured recitative, with its dynamically sharply divided opening motive, broadly-arched Bachian melody, tone-painting violin roulades, and its rich emotional scale that falls from hard determination to tearful, wordless pain – and then the aria with the clarinet passages which continue and supplement the singing part, with its restless quaver-motion, its old-fashioned coloratura passages, its unrestrained modulations, its extensive, although entirely monothematic, melody line – all this adds to what we already know about Elvira, and at the same time prepares the way for her scene in the finale: the last attempt by a human being to save Don Giovanni before the intervention and judgement of the superior power.[7]

With the churchyard scene da Ponte's libretto returns to the action of Bertati's. At the beginning of the secco (strongly dramatic in its atmosphere in spite of a buffo tone) introducing the duet, we again come across that characteristic emphatic fourth with which Don Giovanni turned Zerlina's head in the first act; here he has just returned from a similar interrupted adventure.

This melody is repeated almost note by note twenty bars later when Don Giovanni describes his seduction of Leporello's sweetheart — to Leporello himself. The frivolous story is interrupted by the sepulchral voice of the statue. Compared with Poseidon's monologue in *Idomeneo,* the Commendatore — who is not a god, but a supernatural representation of human values — sings in a warmer and more touching tone.[8] This is backed by the tonality, leading from dramatic D minor into tragic G minor, and by the orchestration with the colour of the woodwinds joining the three trombones, as well as the painful chromatics of the bassoon, declining from F to A in the second four bars. It is with this impact — which is even deeper and more shattering than the third version of Poseidon's speech in *Idomeneo* — that Mozart creates the mood for the return of the Commendatore and makes it credible: once we have heard the voice of the motionless statue in the churchyard scene, we can believe in the appearance of the 'stone guest' conversing, arguing, and trying to save Don Giovanni in the finale.

The duet (number 24) is another succinct example of the 'hint'. Its key is E major (the first and the only one in the opera), its intonation is basically of a uniform buffo character until the middle of the scene. Leporello's fear is only revealed by his repeated sevenths:

Earlier, in the sextet (although in a diminished form), Leporello was frightened and begging in sevenths:

although there he faced people of his own kind; simple, everyday people whom he could cunningly lead by the nose. He could hardly treat the statue in the same way, though, and the number of seventh leaps increases: first only two, then three, and finally four — and the rising and falling of the violins with a gradually widening range also denotes that simple craftiness would not suffice here! Before Don Giovanni's invitation to the statue, the character of the music changes with an interrupted cadence at the lower mediant (although his voice does not lose any of its supercilious frivolity: the violin motive of the second and fourth C-major bars reacts to the situation with the ease of a *grand seigneur*), and only with the consenting answer of the Commendatore do we get back to the basic key, which is, however, again darkened by the entry of Leporello and the basses, accompanied by a string tremolo. The octave-by-octave declining, excited violin motive, augmented by the dark sonority of the violas, dies out pianissimo at the end of the scene. According to Schurig, 'one of the strange aspects, and dramatic weaknesses of the work is that Don Giovanni's main crime, which will ultimately cause his destruction, . . . comes to the surface only in the last quarter of the play'* (i.e. making fun of the dead). Here Schurig tries to plant extraneous moral norms and the romantic concept of 'crime and punishment' into the work — while Mozart, as we have mentioned, does not philosophise, does not analyse, but accepts life as it is, in its infinite completeness and contradictory character, acknowledging the order and laws of the world. With Mozart it is not a fight between Good and Evil, but two different ways

* Schurig, q.v.

of life face to face with one another, of which the one that falls is inevitably the weaker — not because virtue conquers sin, but because society (represented by the Commendatore) is stronger than the lonely revolt of the individual (represented by Don Giovanni). Mozart does not identify himself with either party, but does not pass judgement on them either. He does not criticise life, but describes it, with wise humour, well-intentioned irony, and with an affection that pardons all, and surmounts all: dramma giocoso.

Donna Anna's recitative and aria (number 25) are the last in the series of delaying tactics da Ponte employed before returning to Bertati's libretto; according to Abert, 'undoubtedly one of the dramaturgical weaknesses of the opera'. It is quite natural to assume that this so-called *Szene auf kurzer Bühne,* a scene acted in a small area of the stage, in front of the curtain, was only necessary because of the large-scale change of scenery between the churchyard scene and the finale. (Of course, the fact that today's ingenious methods of quickly changing scenery no longer make the intermezzo a necessity does not entitle us to re-group these numbers, or indeed leave them out altogether![9]) The recitativo accompagnato that characteristically (with the major deviations thematically anticipated from the aria) leads from G minor into D minor, and then the two-part F-major aria itself, with its smooth and elegant coloratura passages and important, rich orchestration, are in perfect harmony with Anna's cool, reserved, aristocratic personality. At the same time, by showing the utmost affinity in style with the intonation of Ottavio's arias, they musically prepare the happy ending for these two characters, that will also be alluded to by the finale's larghetto (even if with some reservation). It is worth emphasising in this context that, after the heroically vigorous coda of the aria, the last scene before the finale does not end with the expected three F-major chords attached like an appendix, but with Ottavio's melancholy, G minor bound secco which inverts this heroic character, thus exposing, as it were, its artificiality, and paving the way for the limited maxims of the closing fugue of the finale: the narrow-minded philosophy of life of this aristocratic petit-bourgeois!

The second finale (number 26) opens in a bright D major, with an unequivocal buffo sound similar to that of the churchyard duet. (More evidence of Mozart's instinctive dramatic sense is that throughout the whole opera he can retain the basic mood of buffo — the only opera seria tone belongs to Elvira: a caricature! — and this is the only medium in which Leporello's rustic jokes, Elvira's painful humiliations, and Zerlina's obvious sensuality can successfully co-exist, and in which we can witness Don Giovanni's doubtful deeds of heroism without their arousing either our disgust, or our moral condemnation. The Shakespearean unity of tragic and comic elements grows from buffo.) The improvised, commedia dell'arte character of the finale is corroborated by the evidence of the original Prague libretto, which proves that the idea of the three items of 'table music' only occurred to Mozart and were cast into final shape in the course of the rehearsals, and in these he could utilise the outstanding abilities of the world-famous Czech wind-instrumentalists to serve his elastic ideas.[10] The three inserts ingeniously correspond to the triple dance orchestra of the first finale, and also represent a brilliant trouvaille in that the melodies of three contemporary 'hits' are built into the action that takes place on the stage. Knowing the originals, the audience of the time must have appreciated the ironic humour of the musical allusions much more than the public of today. During the first two items of 'table music' the hungry and envious Leporello comments on the good appetite of his master who eats copiously at the festive table, while he has to be satisfied with the excellent smells only; and in the excerpt quoted by Mozart from the finale of *Una Cosa Rara*[11] by Martin y Soler, the hopeless lovers are forced to witness how the object of their love is conquered by their luckier rivals. The aria quoted from Sarti's opera (written on Goldoni's text, *Fra i due litiganti il terzo gode*[12]) cynically hints in its first line at Leporello's state of mind: '*Come un agnello che va al macello.*'[13] And finally, the third piece of 'table music' is the aria, '*Non piu andrai*', from *The Marriage of Figaro,* at that time whistled at every street corner in Prague (that is why Leporello says, 'I already know this too well!'), and in which Leporello — who has at last got something to eat — praises the delights of Don Giovanni's *cuisine* to the same melody to which Figaro praised the fictitious delights of military life.

Elvira's entry brings a new tone, although the key remains the same. As we have already heard several times in the opera, now we shall soon witness again the transition leading from B flat major through F major into the dramatic explosion of D minor. Elvira, however, has not caused a truly dramatic situation yet; the B flat major of the *Figaro* quotation does not change, only the tempo speeds up and the metre changes suddenly into 3/4 waltz time. It is a bright idea that Elvira's appearance should put an end to the music on the stage. Beneath Don Giovanni's continuously easy, light sound, we are warned of imminent catastrophe by the condensed and ill-omened quaver-movement of the orchestra. The airy wind-octet 'table music' is unsuitable now. In addition, the servants and the musicians have to leave the room. A lady visitor has arrived, and on such occasions only Leporello has the right to stay — for a time at least. The rhythm of the waltz throws a somewhat grotesque light on Elvira's slightly hysterical words. At the same time the waltz rhythm itself takes on the sinister and harrowing character of a *danse macabre,* due to the stormy violin roulades, the permanent clattering of quavers, and the frequent fortepiano accents. Don Giovanni raises his glass to beautiful women and good wines with another quotation from a popular song, an old Viennese Gassenhauer,[14] while — with all the sincere passion of her love — Elvira tries to rescue from damnation the soul of the man who continues to despise her politely. Elvira's words follow Molière's comedy[15] up to the point where, having realised the failure of her mission, she is compelled to leave, and on her way through the hall, she notices the sepulchral guest. Her shriek is answered by a subito piano string tremolo and threatening chromatics. And when, curiously peeping round the door, Leporello also perceives the approaching statue, even Don Giovanni himself is for a moment alarmed by his obvious horror. The music

185

stiffens for a fearful moment on the dominant of the inevitably approaching D minor.

The explosion, however, has not yet come: with wonderful dramatic sense, Mozart continues to stretch the cord. The dominant of D minor (as in the first finale) dissolves into F major, and in this last transitional episode before the final culmination of the conflict between the two extreme ways of life, the scene of this apocalyptic cataclysm is seen through the eyes of the everyday man — Leporello. Beneath Leporello's words broken chromatics reflect his panic. The tension is increased by the sound of foot-steps, and then by the motive of the statue knocking, already familiar from the first finale. While, after the scandal of the ball scene, this motive only appeared in the relatively neutral C major (*that* danger was not yet serious) — here, it is in F major, on Don Giovanni's home ground, directly beside the D minor of the clash. The Commendatore enters, intending to give Don Giovanni an opportunity of mending his ways. There is a modulation by an A-minor sext chord of dim and uncertain function, and the full orchestra plays a diminished seventh version of the opening motive of the overture.[16]

The andante, the più stretto passage, and the allegro that closes the scene, are the climax of the play, and at the same time they represent a peak that had never before and has never since been achieved in music-drama. The basic material of the music — the syncopated chords with the sinisterly sustained basses, the rock-hard, merciless punctuated rhythm, and then the syncopated melody with its augmented second, diminished to half value on the violins, and the scales rising in chromatic sequences to ever higher levels — are in symphonic form already known from the overture. Now, however, in this ingeniously prepared situation, in the dark sonority of the three deep male voices[17] — each preserving his own individuality — the musical material is given a tense dramatic content, and, like Atlas carrying the world on his shoulders, carries the full weight of the conflict.[18] The bass roulades in the più stretto passage refer to the duel scene in the introduction. Here we have the second round of what was then an earthly clash — this time, however, on a cosmic

level and in demoniacal proportions. In the moments of
dramatic crisis Don Giovanni's character rises to the heights
of tragedy: above all true to himself to the last, broken but
unbending, he drags with him into destruction the remnants
of the way of life he represented.

So the two characters who were rather more than human,
the petrified champion of law and order, and his adversary,
the ever-restless challenger of the status quo, have been taken
by heaven and hell — and the cataclysm is followed by the
dénouement: once again in the epilogue the everyday people
appear on stage to exchange their mundane and self-righteous
views about the events and pass pompous judgement, going
out of their way to point out that they had prophesied that
such behaviour could only lead to trouble! Only for one
more moment — at the end of the allegro assai part of the
epilogue, in the labyrinth of the eight-bar intricately twisting
chromatics — does the demoniacal shadow of Don Giovanni
appear again. Then everything returns to normal; life goes on;
yet it will never be *quite* the same.

Ottavio again begins to court Anna; and, although she
reservedly draws away and postpones the wedding-day until
the year of mourning the Commendatore's death is over, the
long third parallel after the counter-motion of the two bars
confirms their matrimony more definitely than any church
blessing. After all, that had already been anticipated in very
clear musical terms by Anna's previous aria. Their tenderly
sentimental G major is veiled by Elvira's C-minor music of
calm sorrow. With the melody of the trio from the first finale
Elvira recalls for the last time, with Don Giovanni's twice-
repeated fourth, the memory of her only love,

and announces that she wishes to spend the rest of her life in
a convent.[19] Her resigned minor, however, is at once
transposed into a transparent major key by Zerlina's and

Masetto's *joie de vivre,* as well as by the cheerful optimism Leporello has managed to keep despite all his troubles.

It is to da Ponte's, and especially to Mozart's, credit that Anna is given such an important role in the opera. Incidentally, in shaping Anna's personality da Ponte at one stroke eliminated two unnecessary elements from Bertati's libretto: first, the hastily outlined and exclusively functional (therefore dramatically superfluous — and what is superfluous is also harmful!) character of Ximena; and second, the dramaturgically unjustified, abrupt removal of Anna early in the play. This gave a jolting effect not only because the character, presented with considerable tension, was left in the air, but also because Anna's wish to retire to a convent, with no really adequate reason for doing so, weakened Elvira's later similar decision which in her case was a logical result of the development of her character. In Bertati's play Anna leaves the matter of revenge entirely to Ottavio, while da Ponte makes her an active participant in the events, and Mozart's music clearly reflects that, as far as the larghetto part of the closing scene, the initiative is always taken by Anna, who is intellectually and emotionally the superior of the two. Ottavio lags behind his fiancée in every respect.

Indeed, indirectly the leading role is taken by Anna even in the larghetto. Although both melodies of the G-major duet

are begun by Ottavio, we have already heard both of them earlier (and so has Ottavio) from Anna: the first at the start of the recitative (number 2) when Ottavio made his first appearance:

and the second in the closing melody of the mask trio, and in the orchestral postlude that grew from it:

In other words, Ottavio is only the shadow of Anna, even when he is apparently independent and taking the initiative! (Except for a single place in the first finale, noted earlier.) Anna would only leave her fiancé the task of actually carrying out her decisions — provided he was capable of even that! The effeminate stuffed shirt with his marvellous melodies thus not only becomes Don Giovanni's antithesis, but he also follows in the wake of Idamantes and Belmonte. On his own he is nothing — a mere reflection of the woman he loves — who in this case is utterly superior to him. Only love can make him a man worth his salt. Clearly it was Mozart who introduced this motive into the play — we do not find anything similar in the earlier versions of the legend. This idea, which must have deeply absorbed Mozart's attention, appears in a less extreme light and develops further in the three remaining operas, *Così, Titus,* and *The Magic Flute.*

Bertati took Elvira's character from Molière, and da Ponte borrowed it from him without alteration. With her love-hate complex, Elvira is the only character in the opera who, in spiritual intensity, is almost on a level with Don Giovanni. At the same time she is the only character in the opera who develops significantly in the course of the action. Her important role is stressed partly by Don Giovanni's and Leporello's cruel irony, of which she is the main target, and partly by her own social position which – in contrast to Anna, the noble aristocratic lady, and Zerlina, the peasant girl – gives her much greater responsibility, but at the same time much greater independence. The middle-class woman alone in the world, less restricted by the demands of society, has more freedom of emotion and action. In fact, Elvira, denied her own love, actively interferes with the lives of the other two women.

On the other hand, the village coquette, Zerlina – although she is in a more exposed situation than Elvira – is, as a peasant girl, less tied than both Elvira and Anna by the moral conventions of the age (as Blonde is freer in her behaviour than Constanze, and Susanna than the countess). It is logical, then, that of the three she is the only one who, of her own free will, is able to break away from Don Giovanni's influence, and is able, without having a nervous breakdown (this is a privilege for noble ladies!), to find the way back to the place she had held before the upheaval. Zerlina's character is raised by da Ponte, and particularly by Mozart, to a poetically higher level than that reached by any of her predecessors. Masetto, too, is taken out of his run-of-the-mill peasant-lad pigeon-hole and is presented in an individual light. Their reconciliation – with Zerlina's delightfully sensual second aria – shows them in a tender vein, and lends a touchingly human aspect to the babes-in-the-wood situation.

Just as Don Giovanni is not simply a profligate and philanderer,[20] the Commendatore is not purely a representative of a crumbling morality either. Mozart's music, as we have seen, does not pass judgement, and does not oversimplify. It does not state: this is good, and that is bad. The rebel falls and thereby the disarranged harmony of everyday life is restored – but without him the world has become duller and shabbier. And the triumph is not undisturbed. Among the members of the epilogue 'jury' only Anna and Elvira – those who, to a certain extent, were able to see Don Giovanni's demoniacal greatness side by side with his 'Satanic wickedness' – feel this more or less consciously; the ordinary person is now happy to realise much later, at some unexpected turn in his life, or when his personality undergoes some inexplicable change, that once he encountered the exceptional, the super-human, the incomprehensible. These people do not yet feel the strange magnificence of their experiences. In the epilogue all of them appear exactly as we came to know them in the course of the opera. Ottavio sings sweet melodies on his one and only subject, his love; Anna is as cool as a piece of sculpture and politely evasive; Elvira is resigned and somewhat bombastic; Zerlina, Masetto and Leporello are cheerful and rather superficial, and forget easily. However, from underneath the commonplaces and the slightly conventional counterpoint of the closing stretta, Mozart's dramatic irony – already recognised from *Figaro* – flashes: 'Those who act wickedly all come to this end, and for the evil life and death are alike.' The norms of society pass judgement here on the accidental, the extraordinary, the exceptional.

It is interesting to note that at the first performance in Vienna Mozart left out the epilogue: the opera ended with Don Giovanni's D-major journey to hell. This practice was adopted in a number of later performances, among them Mahler's revival in Vienna one hundred years later. This abridgement, however, is not correct, if only because of the structural gradation of the finale – not to mention the distortion of the basic dramaturgical principle of dramma giocoso. Among the romantic misrepresentations, a distinguished place is occupied by Wagner's performance. He even composed an additional scene for it, in which Donna Anna, having been seduced by Don Giovanni, confesses her ardent love for him! The other extreme is represented by Nietzsche who speaks about 'cheerful, innocent and harmless Mozartian happiness and tenderness'. Even Dent does not shrink from the suggestion of omitting the epilogue altogether, notwithstanding the consequent implication of Mozart being an ineffectual dramatist.

At the end of our analysis we may try to answer one more question: what is the explanation for the relative overbalance of arias as compared with ensembles in this most dramatic of Mozart's operas? In the analysis of *The Marriage of Figaro,* we talked about the significance of ensembles in carrying the action forward. Measured by this yardstick, the fourteen arias and twelve ensembles in *Don Giovanni* would mean a standstill, or even – if we include the arias in *Figaro* with an ensemble function – a regression.

But this is only an apparent regression, and the reason becomes clear as soon as we define the basic dramaturgical principle of *Don Giovanni*. We have already seen how flexibly Mozart's dramaturgy follows the demands of dramatic expression. The basic dramaturgical principle of *Figaro* was ceaseless action; this was served by the ensembles and those dynamic arias which carried the action and had the function of an ensemble. On the other hand, the basic dramaturgical principle of *Don Giovanni* is not action, but *character-drawing*: the succinct outlining of clashing personalities, the reflection of the events of the opera in the minds of the characters, and the reactions of the characters to the changing situations. This principle is realised in the somewhat static ensembles – which contain character-drawings rather than action – as well as by the huge portraits painted in the arias.

In addition, each aria is a double portrait, simultaneously reflecting the singer and his relationship with and understanding of the hero of the drama. No character in the opera could be free from the domineering influence of Don Giovanni, and thus when in their different self-confessions they paint their own portraits, they at the same time sketch a picture of Don Giovanni; more particularly, of Don Giovanni as they see and know him; or, to be even more precise, as they imagine they know him. For each of them sees just one feature, one detail of the whole portrait: there is not enough room in the narrow perspectives of these commonplace people for the gigantic figure of the hero, who kicks away all conventions and lives according to his own laws. Don Giovanni – as we have already mentioned – does not speak about himself, but acts, exclusively and intensely obeying his own instincts, while also exercising a permanent and direct

192

sensual, magnetic impact upon his environment. And this impact provides Don Giovanni's indirect characterisation through the eyes of those surrounding him. Apart from the champagne aria 'self-portrait' and some remarks in his recitatives, Don Giovanni provides no description of himself at all: the serenade and the F-major aria (Leporello's introductory tonality) are an actor's performance, and not revealing; it is only from his actions, and from the opinions of the others that his character, like a jig-saw puzzle, gradually takes shape.

This is then the explanation of the relatively high number of arias in *Don Giovanni,* and that is how even the arias carry forward the external, but mainly the internal psychological, action of the drama. It is not by accident that of the fourteen arias only two are 'still life' pictures, and these are Ottavio's two lyrical monologues. Ottavio can only speak about himself, his only thought is his own unparalleled love. While supernatural forces fight and people perish around him, he sings one beautiful melody after another about himself.

The legend of Don Juan has inspired a whole series of writers, poets and composers to create works of art during the past centuries. Mozart's opera has similarly evoked dozens of opinions and theories that are often diametrically opposed, and sometimes startling. Critics have tried to put it into all kinds of pigeon-holes, ranging from Greek fate tragedies, through Faust paraphrases, to Freudian psycho-analytical dramas, in an effort to force the non-recurring, the extra-ordinary, the exceptional into Procrustes's bed of the categories of the average.

And it was violently and desperately attacked, not only by dull and narrow-minded people, but also by such a genius as Beethoven, in whose opinion Mozart was frivolous, since he could write equally enchanting music for sin and for virtue, and was immoral for having veiled the character of an aristocratic rascal with the glory of poetry.[21] I have a strong suspicion that for Beethoven *Don Giovanni* contained too much that is tongue in cheek, subtle and sophisticated; nothing was more remote from Mozart's attitude than the so-called 'liberating opera' — like *Fidelio* — with its dramatically primitive, black and white pathos!

Nearer to our age G.B. Shaw, who considered Mozart's *dramma giocoso* the finest opera ever written, revealed a deep and intensive interest in *Don Giovanni*. In one of his music criticisms* he wrote: 'As to *Don Giovanni,* otherwise "The Dissolute One Punished", the only immoral feature of it is its supernatural retributive morality. Gentlemen who break through the ordinary categories of good and evil, and come out at the other side singing *"Fin ch'han dal vino"* and *"La ci darem",* do not, as a matter of fact, get called on by statues, and taken straight down through the floor to eternal torments; and to pretend that they do is to shirk the social problem they present. Nor is it yet by any means an established fact that the world owes more to its Don Ottavios than to its Don Juans . . . . The hard fact is that *Don Giovanni* is eminent in virtue of its uncommon share of wisdom, beauty, and humour; and if any theory of morals leads to the conclusion that it is foolish and monstrous, so much the worse for the theory.'[22]

* Published in *The World,* 2 May 1894.

Notes

(1) Schurig, q.v.; and Hermann Cohen, *Die Dramatische Idée in Mozarts Operntexten,* Berlin, 1915.

(2) See Abert, q.v. As the only possible solution Abert here proposes to leave out the aria and put it on the concert platform instead.

(3) See Abert, q.v.

(4) With the easy superciliousness of a man of the world, in this dangerous situation Don Giovanni recalls the following lines from an ode by Horace:

'Si fractus, illabatur orbis:
Impavidum ferient ruinae!'

No wonder the ladies are enchanted by his bravado!

(5) Molière, *Don Juan,* act I, scene 2.

(6) In Abert's opinion 'the sextet closes the buffo episode of the second act'. This statement is not quite correct, since with Leporello's next aria — which is musically, dramaturgically and psychologically linked to the sextet — the unequivocal buffo tone returns, which in the deeply human and sometimes almost tragic atmosphere of the sextet can only be recognised in traces, hidden in the delicate, fine patterns of the texture which melt almost unnoticed into the musical material.

(7) Abert would banish Elvira's third aria, together with Ottavio's, to the concert platform. Yet, it is this monumental monologue that lends the dramaturgical strength to Elvira so that she can justifiably be the last person to attempt to save Don Giovanni's soul. It is right that Elvira should finally try to save him from himself, that she should be his last human contact before his descent into hell.

(8) Abert states that originally the two phrases of the Commendatore were supposed to be accompanied by the trombones only. However, during the rehearsals Mozart was not satisfied with their sound, and therefore he strengthened these bars with woodwind as well.

(9) In the romantic age the performers arbitrarily handled the scenes of the opera. Schurig's proposal to place the last Anna/Ottavio scene, as well as Anna's recitative and aria, three numbers forward, that is, between Ottavio's *'Il mio tesoro'* and Elvira's recitative and aria, is relatively reasonable, although by this switch four arias would come one after another. But there is a precedent for this in the first act, immediately before the finale. Rearranged in this way, the logically and dramaturgically related churchyard scene and finale are no longer separated. However, what is gained at one point is lost at another, namely the contrasting effect that was so fortunate from the point of view of dramaturgy, atmosphere, and music, that was created at this point, before the action reaches its peak, by the temporary relaxation of the lyrical aria, inserted between the two dramatic scenes. (See Schurig, q.v.) In the Budapest revival of the opera in

1917, Sándor Hevesi placed Anna's recitative and aria even further forward: between Leporello's and Ottavio's arias. In an article published at about that time Hevesi wrote of Mozart's opera: 'Mozart's excellence ... exists truly in the fact that in one second, with the help of a single bar, he is able to switch from the tragic to the comic mood, and vice versa; and, indeed, within the structure of a single aria or trio he renders genuine horror, but at the same time the parody of horror. Therefore the greatest problem in any *Don Giovanni* performance is the question of how to present this duality on the stage.'

(10) See Abert, q.v.; and Leopold Conrad, *Mozarts Dramaturgie de Oper,* Würzburg, 1943.

(11) Trans: 'A Rare Case'.

(12) Trans: 'When two people quarrel, the third one is happy'.

(13) Trans: 'Like a lamb when led to the slaughter-house'.

(14) From *Dantzbuchlein* by D.F. Dreysser, 1720.

(15) Molière, *Don Juan,* act IV, scene 9.

(16) '... And now followed that long and horrifying dialogue which carries even the most sober soul to the ultimate border of human imagination, or even beyond, until we seem to hear and see what is inconceivable for our senses, and we feel as if something in the depth of our soul irresistibly threw us here and there, from one extreme to another.' (Mörike, q.v.)

(17) The registers of the three characters are identical; they are, however, sharply separated from each other by the dramatic characterization.

(18) The eight bars in which the Commendatore sings of 'celestial nourishment' include all twelve notes of the chromatic scale, thus symbolizing the statue's unlimited power.

(19) According to earlier versions of the legend, Elvira had once been abducted from a convent by Don Giovanni. Da Ponte makes no mention of this.

(20) 'Don Juan is actually neither Idea nor Individual; he hovers between both .... Therefore Mozart stands with his Don Giovanni first among the immortals.' (Sören Kierkegaard)

(21) Goethe, on the other hand, who did not like Beethoven ('This does not move me, only inspires my admiration,' he said of the fifth symphony, and also: 'One expects the house to fall on one's head from this music'), in his long life knew only one composer who could have set Faust to music of an equal standard; and that was Mozart.

(22) In the preface to his comedy *Man and Superman,* that brilliantly pungent modern version of the Don Juan legend (in which Mozart's music plays a dramaturgically active main role; score examples are marked in the text of the play), Shaw gives a wise and appropriate description of Mozart's opera.

WE HAVE seen how misguided people, making their own adaptations of *Don Giovanni*, distorted the structure of the opera, and we have also seen how this great work of Mozart's was misunderstood and misinterpreted by posterity. An even worse fate befell the next and last of da Ponte's operas: *Così fan tutte, or the School for Lovers*. 'Impertinent and unfunny; primitive and lacking in fantasy, awkward and improbable, cynical and frivolous, mocking at passion, and trampling over love' — the chorus of stuffed shirts chants indignantly and endlessly.[1] They did all in their power to rewrite the 'immoral' text, arbitrarily and mercilessly changing the sequence of musical numbers and rudely destroying the harmonious unity of Mozart's music-drama. They did not even refrain from 'applying' Mozart's music to entirely different plays — comedies by Shakespeare and Calderón.[2]

In fact, Shakespeare himself endorses all the features objected to in the libretto — whether we recall the numerous disguises, masquerades and mix-ups between characters, or the Boccaccio-like, cynical wager and love trial (from *Cymbeline*), or all those recurring features in Shakespeare which are constructionally justified in the service of dramatic expression, although often seeming improbable to the Philistine. And after Molière's two comedies, *The School for Husbands* and *The School for Women,* the idea of a 'school for lovers' also appeared on the stage in a number of versions.[3]

We have already talked about the problem of how to make the impossible believable in the analysis of *Idomeneo,* while in connection with *Don Giovanni* we touched on the dialectics of chance and inevitability. Exaggeration was an element in classical tragedy and comedy, and such an obvious means of dramatic condensation can only be denounced as a fault of the plot by the most narrow-minded critics. Although the libretto of *Così fan tutte* is no masterpiece (perhaps it does not reach the standard of its two predecessors), it is far from being as bad, and is even less as immoral, as posterity has tried to prove. This time da Ponte had a more difficult task than in *Figaro* or *Don Giovanni* where he had ready-made patterns to follow: here, all he had was the basic idea, allegedly obtained from Emperor Joseph II, based on a scandal which happened in Viennese high society. It is probable, of course, that all this is no more than an anecdote: the 'trial of faithfulness' was a favourite subject for comedies and comic operas, and had been sung hundreds of times since Boccaccio's and Shakespeare's times. In fact, almost every feature of the libretto is a well-known and often-used buffo motive spun by da Ponte on the single thread of the action with a skilful sense of the stage.

Actually, Mozart's three da Ponte operas represent a connected trilogy with a common basic idea: the spectacular disappearance of an out-dated society from the stage of history. Da Ponte continued the direction begun in *Figaro* with *Don Giovanni* and *Così fan tutte* undoubtedly according to a plan; and it is certainly no accident that the scene chosen for the third part of the trilogy was the fresh pastel-coloured bay of Naples with the tourquoise mirror of the Mediterranean, and the smoking crater of Vesuvius beyond – an oppressive background to the idyllic setting.

This symbol was an appropriate one. The last outbreak of Vesuvius, which took place in the first part of the eighteenth century, buried Naples with a layer of stone and ash a foot and a half thick, and threw hot lumps of stone weighing twenty-five tons to a distance of twenty miles. The six characters of *Così fan tutte* – on the eve of the French revolution – play their frivolous games at the very foot of the volcano.

So many critics have already 'discovered' the symmetrical structure, the almost geometrical accuracy of *Così fan tutte*, as well as the puppet-like behaviour of its characters,[4] that it would be utterly futile to repeat it here. And just as until now I have tried to avoid the 'rediscovery' of familiar facts as much as possible, I would like to pursue a similar course in the following chapters, too, and − if it is at all possible − say something new: to reveal things that have not previously been unearthed from Mozart's mine of treasures. Therefore, I will only try and supply a few signposts, which have not perhaps received much consideration from earlier authors, to the rediscovery of Mozart's much abused human comedy.

The first is again the proportion of arias to ensembles. In *Idomeneo* there were only three ensembles standing modestly in the oppressive shadow of fifteen arias; the proportion was 1:5. In *The Abduction* this relationship changed: seven ensembles, thirteen arias − the proportion was almost 1:2. In *The Marriage of Figaro* and in *Don Giovanni* − with twelve ensembles and fourteen arias − a certain position of balance emerged: and in *Così fan tutte* the scales have been tipped: there are seventeen ensembles as against fourteen arias! (With its fourteen arias and eleven ensembles, *Titus*, as we shall see, is a step backward in this respect too; in *The Magic Flute*, however, the proportion will once again show a predominance of ensembles.)

The composer of *Così fan tutte* avoids *l'art pour l'art* arias like the plague, and we can safely state that almost all the arias in the opera have, if not an ensemble character (as in *Figaro* or *Don Giovanni*), at least a dramaturgical function and dramatic role. Let us take just one characteristic example. At the beginning of the second act Dorabella yields to Despina's encouragement and of the two 'Albanians' she chooses the brown-haired one. Fiordiligi presents a more difficult case: she hesitates for the time being. The situation slightly resembles the opening of the fourth act in *Figaro*: there, too, it was the momentary balance, the equilibrium of the action that provided the opportunity for the logical insertion of a whole series of arias. There, however, this transitional pause was caused by the sustained tension of the action having come to a temporary standstill; whereas here the necessity for delay is due to the characters of the two couples. The light-hearted, sentimental Dorabella is brought together with the experienced and determined Guglielmo: the short courtship — on the first occasion when Dorabella is left without the moral support of her sister — leads to a quick success. On the other hand, the day-dreaming Ferrando starts courting the cooler and less impulsive Fiordiligi: success — due to the greater difference between the two characters — is somewhat slower in coming. This extra amount of time which the less experienced and less self-confident Ferrando needs for the conquest of Fiordiligi, who is more sensible and less easily taken in than her sister, is used by Mozart for the logical insertion of five (more precisely, five and a half) arias. Ferrando's attempt starts with his aria (number 24), but all his efforts fail because of the strong resistance of Fiordiligi. 'Your cruelty is a death sentence for me,' the rejected suitor complains gloomily, but the cheerful music reveals that he is actually very pleased with this failure: Fiordiligi's 'mortal cruelty' puts one hundred zecchinos into his pocket.

In the following recitative and aria (number 25) Fiordiligi's faith is perceptibly shaken for a moment as she is left alone (the three exposed horn passages of the rondo represent an ambiguous allusion, as in Figaro's last aria[5]), but she can still master her budding emotions. In the meantime, Ferrando learns from Guglielmo about Dorabella's betrayal, and Guglielmo is inspired by his friend's despair to sing a new aria (number 26).

The miserable Ferrando, disappointed in both women, helplessly struggles in the net of his own sentiments. He wants to take revenge, but he is still in love with his faithless fiancée — an excellent opportunity for a cavatina (number 27). Dorabella's ensuing coquette aria (number 28) aptly reflects her fickle nature and sensuality; and Fiordiligi's solid determination (in order to suppress her awakening emotions) to don a soldier's uniform and go to the front after her fiancé forms a clear contrast. It is in this mood that Fiordiligi starts the sixth aria of the series (number 29). Ferrando, however, steps in to restrain her: the aria is extended into a duet, the girl's resistance gives way and the temporarily suspended action can move on.

This is the dramaturgical background to a series of arias which, according to Abert, 'is without peer in its monotony among Mozart's mature works.'*

The other interesting problem is the question of tonality. We have several times referred to Mozart's strong feeling for tonality, as well as to the fact that for him certain keys always have a similar dramatic character and express the same emotions and moods.

In the mature Mozart's two comic operas, *The Marriage of Figaro* and *Così fan tutte,* the series of keys with a permanent 'meaning' is enriched with new colour. F minor is one of Mozart's most rarely used keys, and it is therefore of particular interest to compare the conspicuously similar features of the few F-minor moments in the two comic operas: the moments of pretended sorrow, and the situations which are tragic for the characters but comic for the audience. Such are for example the twenty bars in the trio of the first act of *Figaro* (from Susanna's first entry), with the girl's genuine, but for tactical reasons over-acted fear that is even supplemented with fainting; then the twelve bars of the finale in the second act with the sincere anger of the count and the no less sincere anxiety of the countess, while only we know that the page is no longer in the neighbouring room; and finally such is the cavatina that starts the fourth act with the deep pain in poor little Barbarina's heart, coupled with her fear of the consequences — the comically touching, tearful sorrow of a child whining because of a lost pin.

There is a similar duality of mood in the only F-minor piece in *Così fan tutte,* Alfonso's aria (number 5) in the first act. Pity, excitement and sorrow are mingled in his voice — only it is all make-believe; he brings terrible news — only the news is not true. Here the character knows that what he is saying is a lie, therefore the music is unequivocally ironic: it over-emphazises the excited fluttering of the breathless Alfonso. But at the same time it also reveals that for the girls the news is really tragic.[6]

We have already mentioned that the basic key of *Così* is C.

* Abert, q.v.

We have also seen that the actual happenings, and, even more so, the psychological manifestations, of decisive significance in the drama, as well as the various motives of general moral, ideological and philosophical messages, are mostly in the basic tonality.

The C-major passages of *Così* provide both dramatic and psychological cross-sections of the whole opera. The first is the overture which, as always, prepares the mood of the opera and — like the *Don Giovanni* overture, although of course in different form and character — it anticipates the final moral lesson. The third trio (number 3), the closing part of the homogeneous series of ensembles of the prologue-like exposition, is the spring-board of the action: the fatal bet has been made — the story can begin. (By the way, the keys of the three trios provide the basic chord of the opera: G—E—C = a full C-major harmony.) The next C major is the recitativo accompagnato following the small trio (number 10) of the two women and Alfonso, one of Alfonso's philo-sophising maxims. The core of the second trio (number 2) was somewhat similar. This time, however, Alfonso, being alone on the stage, as if stepping out of the play, tells us in epigrammatic form his opinion on the unreliability of a woman's heart — very important when we consider later developments in the story. (A counterpart to this scene will be the last C-major piece before the second finale: the résumé, number 30.) Although the recitative after number 10 starts in D minor, with a four-bar stubborn ostinato accompaniment, this in fact is nothing but the sub-dominant of the C major; by the final conclusion ('Don't believe women!') we have already returned to the basic tonality.

The following C-major number, the sextet of the first act (number 13), marks the beginning of the actual comedy. The two 'Albanians' enter to the march rhythm with which they previously pretended to join the army. The pseudo-exotic and slightly conceited character of the sham janissary march music, with its stupid tonic-dominants, support the comic aspects of the over-done masks and disguises. The first encounter between the ladies and the two Albanians does not bring the result prophesied by Alfonso: they indignantly protest against the shameful attempt on their honour. The elderly cynic and his young helpmate, Despina, however, receive with reservation the too-passionate outbreak; Alfonso's melody ('This anger, this rage makes me suspicious')

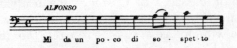

ironically quotes the first phrase of the second trio:

Woman's faith is like the Phoenix
In remote Arabia dwelling;
Travellers of such tales are telling —
Have they seen it? No, not they!:

Both dramatically and musically the next C-major music is the most significant in the opera. Although Fiordiligi has repeatedly rejected Ferrando's approaches — she now feels her resistance weaken, and wants to escape from temptation. The duet (number 29) starts out as a regular aria: Fiordiligi announces her firm decision to visit her beloved fiancé on the battle-field. She modulates from glittering A major into emotional E major and emphasises with an excited string accompaniment the joy of meeting him again, as if she wants to convince herself of the correctness of her decision.

This pathetic tone is deepened by the painful E-minor melody of Ferrando emerging from his hiding-place. The cheerful atmosphere of the light and frivolous play becomes serious in a second, and changes into sincere passion. From the violent emotional outbreak which might consume her, Fiordiligi escapes to neutral territory, into C major – as Susanna escaped from the count, also in an A-major duet,[7] in the third act of *Figaro* – and with the melody and violin figurations of the words 'fate' and 'hope' of the first quintet (number 6)

she tries to avert the feared and at the same time so much longed for consequence:

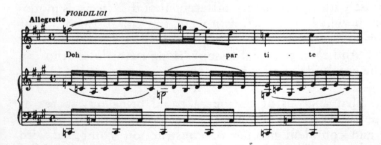

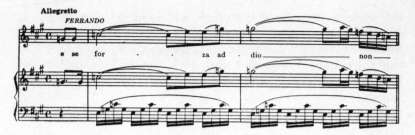

Ferrando takes over tone and tonality, and even the sword prepared by the girl for her long journey — and what was only play, a pretence and a comedy in the quintet, has now become a dangerous and genuine tragedy: the prospect of suicide, of death for the sake of love. Seeing this, Fiordiligi gives up her double fight — against Ferrando's advances and her own stifled emotions — and lo! she obediently imitates the man's melody. After a few bars, the fatal parallel sixths appear. Ferrando exploits the situation and, striking while the iron is hot, does his best to remodulate quickly into Fiordiligi's original A major. Although the girl tries once again to escape from him into D minor, this is only the last spark of her hopeless resistance. One more desperate outbreak — and then to the miraculously tender piano melody of the oboe, Fiordiligi finally yields. After a few unselfconscious third and sixth parallels, it is her turn to start the loving imitations.

After this love duet, supremely beautiful even by Mozart's standards, new C-major music follows as an immediate contrast with a completely different mood: Alfonso's monologue, in which he draws, as it were, the moral conclusion of the events (number 30): 'Così fan tutte': 'every woman's the same'. And then the final lesson: 'Happy are those who can see the good side of all things.'

A detailed analysis of the opera could bring out scores of wonderful examples of Mozart's ingenious ability of expression and confident manner of construction, combined with an endless supply of ideas and melodies, which make Così fan *tutte,* to use Dent's words, 'the most beautiful work of art among all of Mozart's operas'. Let us take — at random — a few of these pearls from the inexhaustible treasure-trove of *Così*. There is, for example, the first of the girls' duets (number 4) — a tenderly caressing wavering of strings under velvet clarinet thirds, two female voices softly blending into one: an enchantingly sweet sound. Sweet? No: *sugary.* A rococo *dolce vita* on the shores of the azure-blue bay of Naples. 'I am so happy,' they sing in flexible third scales, with their set smiles — and by the time we reach the allegro we are quite sure that the cynical Alfonso will have no difficulty with these empty-headed, superficial ladies of doubtful virtue who 'pursue love like a sport'; they really 'all behave like that'. If the rather naughty bet between the two men left us with a slightly unpleasant aftertaste, it would be resolved by this double portrait. These two women are not one jot better than the men who irresponsibly and heartlessly broadcast the virtues of their sweethearts and their own most intimate private affairs.

The characters, sharply outlined in the andante part of the duet, are further developed by Mozart with open irony in the allegro. After the two flirting clarinets above the empty bass sound, and the hard, cracking 'cello and bassoon roulades under the voices of the women, an irresistibly comic contrast is presented by the coquettish cadence in thirds of the two young women on the word *amore,* as well as by the hopping triads of a frivolous dance rhythm under a sentimentally long sustained note. The duet — the first appearance of the girls in the opera — provides a perfect picture of the *type* which will be later, in the arias, ensembles and recitatives, portrayed in more detail with the various already-mentioned individual features.

Mozart's usual dramatic irony almost becomes caricature in Fiordiligi's and Dorabella's duet (number 20) of the second act. They playfully divide the 'loot', and each chooses for a suitor the other's fiancé. In a gay, joking manner they repeat the expected, usual words of wooing — the sudden small excitement of the violins, however, denotes that this sophisticated nonchalance is not quite sincere: they would love to hear those stereotyped amorous phrases! After a new cadence in thirds the first idea of the duet returns, but the girls get so excited that they do not even listen to each other, and (as in the letter duet of *The Marriage of Figaro*), not even waiting until the end of the phrases, they cut into each other's words with canonic imitations and excited sequences.[8] At the prospect of 'a good time' – and anyway they are alone – all their social veneer disappears, and in the first thrill of their new emotions they fall into sensual day-dreaming: they frantically sing, in thirds, the coda that is crowded with its endless series of semi- and interrupted cadences.

The musical rendering of Despina's personality is characterised by the same volatile, staccato quaver-movement that characterised Susanna in *The Marriage of Figaro*. It has the same playful outlook as well as the acting ability also required by Susanna's role, and consequently provides an opportunity for various 'musical disguises'. In the 3/4 allegro time of the sextet (number 13) in the first act, for instance, Despina borrows the emotionally lyrical, chromatic tone of the 'Albanians', while in the quintet (number 22) and some ironic recitative outbreaks during the second act she ridicules the distinguished *grande dame* manners and artificial pathos of her mistresses.

Despina's two appearances in disguise are also in perfectly differentiated harmony with the situation. In the first finale, in the disguise of a doctor

she appears with the orchestral introduction of her first aria (number 12):

changed into 3/4 time and the men can't help but recognise her immediately. In addition, the voice is also her own glib staccato sound: Despina's first experiment at comedy-acting is far from perfect.

In the second finale where she appears in the excellent disguise of a notary (another allusion to Shakespeare: *The Merchant of Venice*), nobody recognises her. In a monotonous chant, she reads out the dull phrases of the official marriage contract. As the endless, dry, legal formulae become more and more complicated, the tiny violin variations evolving from the initial staccato theme paraphrase them, crowding upon one another above the solidly regular bass ostinato.

Tonality also has a distinguished role in the expression of various states of mind. Let us examine, for example, the development of tonality in the first finale. It starts in calm, serious D major: although the girls are a little sad, they have not actually realised the danger threatening their hearts. With the appearance of the two 'suicides', the tonality changes into G minor, Mozart's tragic key. After heart-beat rhythms recalling *Don Giovanni,* with diminished harmonies, chromatic melody- and chord-passages, a temporary relaxation of tension is brought about by Alfonso's pretended words of condolence in E flat major. But as soon as the ladies are left alone with their 'dying' suitors, and their resistance begins to weaken, the tonality again turns into minor, and sets off on an excited, indefinite journey – C minor, G minor, F minor, A flat major, B flat minor, and again C minor – reflecting the hesitating perplexity of the two girls. The pseudo-tragic situation comes to an end with cheerful G major, marking the appearance of the 'doctor'. With the miraculous 'recovery' the music turns suddenly, without transition, into a new key: B flat major.

Seeing the sympathy of the women, the two men become too self-assured – in spite of Fiordiligi's over-dramatised 'onore' cadences warning them still to be careful – and they commit a grave tactical error: with a sudden change into D major they ask the girls for kisses! This attack is, however, premature and thoughtless. D major is the tonality of Fiordiligi's and Dorabella's duet that began the finale – and is also the key reminding them of the march that called their two fiancés to the army! – and the girls are on home ground here. 'Go to hell, both of you, you miserable wretches! You will be sorry if you let my anger increase!' they both cry with more and more passionate chromatics, expressing the deep moral injury their womanly honour has suffered. But Dorabella already hesitates: while her sister gives expression to her anger with stormy scales and violent roulades, she slowly begins to adjust her rhythm to that of the men; and although she does – since she has to – mechanically repeat the indignant words of Fiordiligi, Mozart's music gives a clear indication that Dorabella has now more or less yielded to her inevitable fate.

This is how Mozart, making a virtue out of necessity, used the various abilities of the singers in order to achieve a differentiated rendering of character. While the qualities of Villeneuve, who sang Dorabella's part at the première of the opera, required a technically smooth texture, Ferraresi's coloratura capabilities and unusually wide register provided an opportunity for a bolder and more virtuoso vocal handling of Fiordiligi's part.

A similar solution is shown by the A-flat-major larghetto of the second finale. The two couples empty their glasses to celebrate the double wedding, and Fiordiligi toasts her fiancé with a sentimental commonplace which aptly suits the situation. The beautiful canon melody is imitated first by Ferrando and then by Dorabella with an increasingly colourful accompaniment and a richer contrapuntal background; but when Guglielmo's turn comes for his stanza, he – sur-

prisingly enough – does not enter with the canon melody
(Fiordiligi sings it for him), but separates himself from the
mood of the others with an angry staccato aside: 'I wish
these dishonest creatures had drunk poison instead!' Although Abert denies it,* I think the conclusion he quotes
from Julius Rietz is correct. It says that Guglielmo simply
had to be left out of the general wave of happiness, because
the melody is too high for a baritone singer. This is also
supported by the first conception, according to which all
four of them – Guglielmo included – were supposed to sing
their 'toasts', the present, final form of the canon having only
emerged later on (and even this has kept the four-part
character of the original plan, the difference being that
Fiordiligi is given two opportunities to sing). And Benucci
who sang Guglielmo's part at the Viennese première was not
even a baritone, but a buffo bass who was unable to sing the
high A flat of the canon melody.

The only argument raised against this by Abert is that 'if
he had wanted to, Mozart could certainly have mastered this
technical obstacle'.† But he did master it! What is the
dramatic situation when the canon is sung? Fiordiligi and
Dorabella are pleased about the marriage – that is all right.
Ferrando has got over Dorabella's faithlessness, and now his
soul is filled with the new, great love expressed in the
A-major duet; he is also pleased about the marriage – that is
all right, too. However, Guglielmo, who only a short while
ago so conceitedly felt himself secure in the affections of
both women – for Fiordiligi remained faithful to him, while
he also succeeded in winning Dorabella's love – has recently
witnessed his fiancée's ugly betrayal in the enraptured duet of
Fiordiligi and Ferrando. It seems that contrary to his
expectations he cannot have his cake and eat it! Guglielmo is
angry with his friend (he would never have thought that
Ferrando would be able to entice the girl from him – from
him, Guglielmo!), he is disappointed in women, he lost the
bet, he is at odds with the whole world; he has every reason

* Abert, q.v.
† Ibid.

to be in a bad mood. Therefore it is completely logical and dramaturgically justified if he withdraws from the general rapture.

Which is, by the way, a congenial idea from a dramaturgical point of view as well, because by bringing the ethereal atmosphere of the larghetto down to earth and by setting the slowed-down action into motion again it introduces and prepares the way for the new mood starting at Alfonso's entry with an unexpectedly sobering A flat/E modulation.

So Mozart, once again making a virtue out of necessity, overcame a seemingly insurmountable technical difficulty.

There are two additional pieces of evidence which prove indirectly the supposition that Mozart changed the musical conception in the course of the actual composition. In the dénouement of the second finale, the two men — as a sort of musical résumé — recall the strange events that have taken place. First Guglielmo reminds Dorabella of duet number 23, and then Ferrando and Guglielmo cite together Despina's 'cure'. Guglielmo's ironic hint is preceded by Ferrando's four bars which (according to what we know of the situation and the symmetrical structure of the opera) must relate to an earlier episode connected with Fiordiligi. However, the musical material of the quotation is new: one searches in vain for its origin in the earlier music. Ferrando probably cites here a number which was either omitted or changed in the course of composition (according to the rules of symmetry, he should have recalled duet number 29). Mozart, however, must have forgotten, or perhaps simply not bothered, to rewrite it in the finale in keeping with the subsequent alterations.

And our second piece of evidence is that originally, in the place of Guglielmo's first aria (number 15), there should have been a considerably longer one but, because it would have interrupted the swing of the ending of the act, Mozart replaced it with another, shorter aria: the present G-major rondo, *'Non siate ritrosi'*.[9]

We could spend dozens of pages analysing that 'extremely amusing irony'[10] in *Così* which in no other of Mozart's works has such a satirical edge of social criticism. Musical characterisation gives a truthful meaning to the mixing-up of couples: the decision dictated by their senses on the spur of the moment is more real than the 'objective' choice based on careful consideration, social convention and sober judgement! Although the bitter, resigned philosphy of the finale ('Happy are those who see the good side of all things') reinstates the status quo of the two couples at the beginning of the opera, Mozart's music does not leave us in any doubt that, due to their natures, the couples which would survive a long-lasting partnership would be Fiordiligi and Ferrando, Dorabella and Guglielmo.

One could also go on analysing the bitingly satirical development of the seducer type, the Almaviva/Cherubino /Don Giovanni line: the sharp caricature of the cheap woman-chasers, provincial Don Juans courting in disguise. Then there are the various formal solutions serving dramatic expression, and the orchestration, aimed at a more realistic character-drawing (with Alfonso's mocking bassoon, the voluptuous clarinets of the two girls, and the showy trumpets of the two soldiers). There is the fragmentary mosaic-dramaturgy based exclusively on situation and not on the development of characters and types, and the already-mentioned symmetrical architecture (with the similar, almost mirrored groupings of the arias and ensembles of the opera, as well as of the construction of the two finales). The multi-part seccos already discovered in *Figaro,* and the accompagnatos are here incorporated into the actual numbers; the opera marks the third appearance of exotic colour on Mozart's stage.

To conclude, however, I would like to speak very briefly about an important phenomenon which was a characteristic feature of the previous operas, too, but has become a basic principle of *Così fan tutte*: the means of expression by 'dropped hints'. I have quoted before that excerpt from one of Mozart's letters which is so characteristic of his music and his whole personality: 'You know that during a conversation one can often just drop a hint, and this produces a much greater effect than if one had announced the same thing

213

dictatorially.'* While in *Don Giovanni*, and particularly in *The Marriage of Figaro*, this principle was put into practice in dense series of abrupt, transitionless contrasts, subito dynamic changes, unexpected outbreaks and sudden stops — in *Così* we find it in the rounding off of sharp edges and corners, in the avoidance of clashes and sharp contrasts. The tone is soft, elegant, balanced: there is plenty of sotto voce, a sort of creative shyness which refrains from every harshness; and we also very frequently come across rare and very precise 'composer's instructions' as to the manner of performance, which perfectly suit the given situation; the men laugh *'moderamente'*, Ferrando renders his aria *'lietissimo'*, and the bogus notary sings *'per naso'*.[11]

And even if for a few moments Mozart sets free the passion of Alfonso, who gets very worked up about certain bees in his bonnet, as for instance in the recitative in the seventh scene of the first act — Mozart immediately curbs the excited philosopher at the peak of his outburst, as he is ready to be carried away on his favourite hobby-horse, and the old bachelor is left high and dry with only the support of two conventional closing chords. Even the characteristic means of expression used by Mozart in his previous operas, the repeated sudden alternation of forte and piano is now used with a delicate irony to mock unreal pathos and high-falutin', empty words. Thus for instance in Dorabella's E-flat-major aria (number 11) he parodies the flat, bombastic words like 'horror', 'disaster', 'death'. This is how the dramaturgical principle of the 'hint', self-control, moderation, grows in *Così fan tutte* into an attitude: 'For in the very torrent, tempest, and as I may say, the whirlwind of passion, you must acquire and beget temperance that may give it smoothness.' †

Wise humour, mild irony, quiet nostalgia, a profound love of life: *nil humani a me alienum puto*, says Mozart once again here, in his only opera to be published during his life-time. Although Einstein is right when he says that 'at the end of the opera we feel exactly the same aesthetic joy as one would

* Letter dated 17 August 1782.
† Shakespeare, *Hamlet*, act III, scene 2.

feel after a well-solved chess game or a successful conjuring trick',* Mozart's 'chess pieces' nevertheless live and feel, fear and hope, love and rage; and the composer sympathises with them. Although he smiles at the ridiculous bragging of his vain and narrow-minded characters, he still feels pity and affection for them. The twice repeated, sadly declining interrupted cadence of the 'All women behave like that' theme of the overture shows the helpless, shipwrecked victims of the turbulent seas of human passions in the tender, transparent light of compassion:

Both in its theme and message, *Così fan tutte* is a natural continuation of *The Marriage of Figaro* and *Don Giovanni.* In its theme which – after merciless, unstable and law-defying men (Almaviva, Don Giovanni) – now tells us about faithless and fickle women disregarding moral rules, Mozart paves the way for the final, great synthesis of flawless humanism, and happiness achieved through a real life and death struggle: *The Magic Flute.* And in the message of *Così* Mozart, for the third and last time, assesses the distorted manner of life of a decadent, obsolete society that will be swept away by the French revolution: it is weighed in the scales and found wanting.

For the sake of completeness we should mention here a composition commissioned and written for a particular occasion, *La Clemenza di Tito.* Mozart, who was already gravely ill, and struggling with constant financial problems and various family tragedies, only undertook this assignment in the hope of receiving a considerable fee, though this was only vaguely promised, and with a view to gaining the

* Einstein, q.v.

good-will of the new emperor so that he might have a chance of leading an easier life. Of all the stage works written by him ever since he was a child this was the only one in which he not only had no say in the text, but even part of the music was composed by someone else. The seccos, which almost solely carry the action, originate from his pupil, Süssmayr; indeed, some of his biographers claim that even a good many complete numbers were composed by Süssmayr.[12]

There would be no sense in making any analysis similar to the previous ones, since the dramaturgy of *Titus* is not Mozart's. Even if the glorification of the Christian teachings of goodness and forgiveness, projected into the setting of ancient Rome, might have to a certain extent attracted Mozart's interest, the rush job (twenty-six numbers within less than three weeks!) made any deep creative insight and homogeneous construction in music and drama out of the question.

In addition, the heroes of the opera are so stupidly good and noble that their sublime pathos often turns to ridiculousness: the emperor voluntarily renounces his loved one because she loves somebody else; a resolute assassin instinctively shrinks from carrying out the deed, and would not give away the name of his instigator even if he were torn to pieces by lions; the leader of the conspiracy voluntarily confesses her crime, etc. After the *Figaro/Don Giovanni/Così* trilogy, and living in the all-embracing synthesis of *The Magic Flute,* Mozart had by now left far behind this bombastic baroque world in which he had sincerely believed at the time of *Idomeneo.* He had progressed far beyond the opera seria that placed personified concepts on the stage and abstracted life into maxims and allegories. Since — as we have seen — Mozart was at home in every style, form and genre, he solved even this compulsory task with sure taste and an accurate sense of style. Only he did not feel it to be his own; he could not identify himself with it. The cool and objective baroque text evokes in Mozart an impersonal sound which only fills but does not explode — as it had so often before — the given framework.

Titus is beautiful concert music, a series of arias and

ensembles loosely strung together – a vocal and instrumental concert suite in which the text is not an 'obedient daughter' but only a pretext for music, and the music is not the mode of expressing dramatic action, character-drawing and psychological description, but – in the best sense of the phrase – *l'art pour l'art*. It is not a means in the service of an all-embracing conception that is beyond music, but it is the aim itself. (To avoid any misunderstanding, I should explain that is is not necessarily of a higher or lower standard: the difference between the *l'art pour l'art* G-minor quintet and the 'functional' *Don Giovanni* music is not qualitative, but a difference of genres.) It is only in the first finale and in the accompanied recitatives of the three protagonists that the old glitter of Mozart's instinctive dramatic sense appears, shining through even the most formal text.[13] The most important pièce de résistance of *La Clemenza di Tito* is the bel canto, the purely sensual beauty of sound. This is also emphasised by the transparent instrumentation and by the obligatory solo accompaniments;[14] and it is supported by the dramaturgical role of Mozart's 'hint' principle, which, from the means of expression in *The Marriage of Figaro* and *Don Giovanni*, and from the basic attitude with a dramatic function in *Così fan tutte*, stiffens in a smooth, polite and reserved manner in Mozart's belated opera seria.

Notes

(1) Beethoven not only stamped *Don Giovanni* as immoral, but also *Così fan tutte*; while according to Wagner: 'It is a proof of Mozart's greatness that . . . to the dull and insignificant libretto of *Così fan tutte* . . . he was not able to compose such music as he did for *Figaro,* for by this he would have shamefully desecrated music itself!'

(2) For instance Léon Carvalho, director of the Théâtre Lyrique in Paris, and later of the Opéra Comique, had,

according to Saint-Säens, an obsession for rewriting without exception every play performed by his company, irrespective of whether it was a classical work or a play by a contemporary author. He commissioned the popular play-wrights, Carré and Barbier, to write from Shakespeare's *Love's Labour's Lost* a new libretto for *Così fan tutte* entitled *Les Peines d'Amour Perdues.*

(3) One of its adaptations, a comedy entitled *The Latest School for Women,* was seen in Salzburg on 11 December 1780 by Nannerl, Mozart's sister. She mentioned it to Mozart, who was then in Munich, in her letter of 18 December.

(4) A superficial observer is easily misled by the seeming symmetry of *Così fan tutte*: two women – two men, two couples – two schemers, etc. Actually there is a much more delicate balance than that: the sisters are far from being identical, the characters of the men are also different, and Despina's cheerful light-heartedness springs from an entirely different root than Alfonso's cynical disillusionment.

(5) As Mozart in *The Marriage of Figaro* and *Così fan tutte* played on the double meaning of the word *corni* (horn: instrument, cuckold) to form a musical pun, Verdi used the same idea in an aria in *Falstaff.* And Beethoven, though rejecting *Così* itself due to its 'frivolous' text, was not at all averse to borrowing some of its ideas, for instance features of Fiordiligi's aria for Leonora's dramatic recitative and aria in *Fidelio*; even using the tonality and the solo horns, only – out-doing his model – he adopted three horns instead of Mozart's two!

(6) 'I wish to offer a depth-psychological interpretation which is hardly more than a rationalisation of purely musical reactions. For Haydn, F minor had a similar significance to that which G minor had for Mozart (and C minor for Beethoven). Mozart's admiration for Haydn was boundless, reinforced by personal friendship and Haydn's own admira-tion for him, and untinged – as far as reliable information goes – by hostility. Psycho-analysis has taught us, however, that where there is a father [figure], there is hostility towards him, overt, suppressed, or repressed by great love. Is

218

it too fanciful to assume that rendering the F minor ironic was a subtle means whereby Mozart's subconscious allowed itself to discharge its ambivalence, which would have been absolutely intolerable on the conscious level?' Hans Keller, *Tempo,* number 40, London, 1956.

(7) Mozart's seduction duets are generally in A major; in addition to those we have mentioned, this is the tonality of *'La ci darem'* in *Don Giovanni,* and of the trio of the second act: the 'duet of two men — one woman'.

(8) As in the first operas, the da capo form does not mean a mechanical repetition in *Così* either: the development within the number always coincides with musically-altered repetitions of text and composed recapitulation (thus for example Dorabella's E-flat-major aria is a parody of Elektra's madness aria, and the great dramatic monologues of opera seria.

(9) This omitted baritone aria was later registered as a concert aria with the number 6/45, and then under K.584 in the Köchel catalogue.

(10) E.T.A. Hoffmann. According to Richard Strauss, 'Mozart's art embraces every phase of the human world of emotions, ranging from the sombre and monumental magnificence of the Commendatore scene in *Don Giovanni* to the graciousness of Zerlina's aria, and from the heavenly frivolities of *Figaro* to the humorously pathetic and parodistically sentimental, delicate . . . irony of *Così fan tutte.'*

(11) *'Moderamente':* moderately; *'lietissimo':* very joyfully; *'per naso':* with a nasal voice.

(12) See Schurig, q.v.

(13) The first finale is of especial interest in that this is the only occasion when Mozart combines chorus and vocal soloists in an action-ensemble, making them sing simultaneously. The idea is certainly his: at first the off-stage chorus, which has a special dramatic function, sings without words.

(14) The basset horn that had only been tried out for colour effect in *The Abduction* (in Constanze's G-minor aria) now in *Titus* receives an individual role as an obligatory solo instrument (in the orchestral accompaniment to Vitellia's scene, at the end of the second act). The basset horn and its

older relative, the clarinet, receive added weight in Mozart's last creative period as a result of the friendship and inspiration of Anton Stadler, a Viennese clarinettist and musical-instrument maker (the clarinet concerto, two orchestral rondos, a complete and an unfinished clarinet quintet, basset horn solos in the *Requiem* and in *The Magic Flute,* an allegro fragment written for basset horn and orchestra, etc.). In connection with Stadler, see the letter of 7-8 October 1791, in which Mozart reports to his wife, staying in Baden, about a letter he has received from 'Stodla' in Prague with an account of the performance of *Titus* on 30 September (the date of the Viennese première of *The Magic Flute*). At this last performance Stadler once again played the clarinet and basset horn solos with great success: 'From the audience and even from the orchestra bravos were shouted to Stodla. "Oh, what a miracle for Bohemia!" he writes, "but I did my very best".'

The Magic Flute (1)

AT THE very end of the 1770s the idea that had pursued
Mozart throughout almost the whole of his career, the desire
to create a 'Deutsche Oper', became a real possibility. In
1777, when he was twenty-one, he had written to his father
from Munich: '. . . I am very popular here. And how much
more popular I should be if I could help forward the German
national theatre! And with my help it would certainly
succeed. For when I heard the German Singspiel, I was
simply itching to compose . . . . They would like to produce
[here] a German opera seria soon, and they are very anxious
that I should compose it.'*

After his third visit to Paris and his first unhappy
experience of love in Munich, Mozart returned to Salzburg
where he rewrote and supplemented with some new numbers
the *Thamos* music, written six years previously, and started
composing a German Singspiel (*Das Serail,* sometimes called
Zaïde) which has only come down to us in fragments. In the
Hannibalplatz, opposite the Mozarts' Getreidegasse house,
the hand-painted posters of the Salzburg Town Theatre
announced the forthcoming guest performance of the touring
company of Johann Joseph Emanuel Schikaneder, the
famous actor, singer, director and playwright.

At that time Schikaneder's company had been in existence
for only two years, but during that short period it had
already achieved considerable fame and prestige in such large
and culturally-aware towns as, for instance, Augsburg (the
birthplace of the Mozart family), Stuttgart, Nürnberg and
Linz. It had a rich and varied repertoire. Schikaneder not

* Letter dated 2 October 1777.

only directed their plays, but he acted in many of them too. In addition to works by less famous German contemporaries and by Schikaneder himself — musical plays and panto- mimes — their repertoire included works by Lessing (*Emilia Galotti, Minna van Barnhelm*), Goethe (*Götz von Berlichin- gen, Clavigo*), Calderón (*The Judge of Zalamea*), Gozzi (*Dreamless Nights*), Beaumarchais (*The Barber of Seville*), but chiefly Shakespeare; the director himself played Iago in *Othello,* Edgar in *King Lear,* and the title roles of *Hamlet, Macbeth* and *Richard III.*

After his journeys abroad and the years in Paris and Mannheim had opened his eyes and widened his horizons, the young Mozart took a great interest in the theatre, and particularly in new German drama and play-acting. Through Emanuel Schikaneder he became acquainted with the works of Shakespeare, too, and this acquaintance — as we have already seen — had a decisive effect on the further develop- ment of Mozart's music-drama. His acquaintance with Schikaneder soon deepened into a close friendship, and before long there emerged the idea of a jointly-written German opera, based on Gebler's *King Thamos.* But the preparations for *Idomeneo* called Mozart to Munich, and in the meantime Schikaneder, after his guest performances in Salzburg, was compelled to dissolve his company on account of various difficulties. References to Schikaneder, and the impact he made upon him, can occasionally be found in Mozart's later letters. However, the careers of the two men (at least according to the correspondence) now diverged for a period of time. (Of course this does not mean a complete break in their friendship: they lived in the same town, not too far from each other, and they had the same circle of friends, indeed, even the same patron: the emperor himself.[1])

The business-like Schikaneder did not remain a small-part actor for long: within three years he was already playing again with his own company, first in Pressburg, and then — at the emperor's personal invitation — again in Vienna, at the Kärntherthortheater. The company, however, was soon again disbanded; and Schikaneder, entering one of the Viennese freemasons' lodges, translated Beaumarchais's comedy *The Marriage of Figaro, or a Crazy Day,* that was having its première in Paris at that time, and creating quite a storm there. The Viennese Nationaltheater accepted it (in a somewhat watered-down form) and billed the play. However, the première did not take place: at the personal instruction of Joseph II, it was censored on the day of the dress rehearsal. Public performance of the play was prohibited. Most probably Mozart became acquainted with Beaumarchais's bitingly witty comedy through Schikaneder's adaptation (a few months after the first performance should have taken place, da Ponte was already busily working on the libretto), but the play remained on the black-list for another full year, and even after that it could only be performed at the court theatre of the imperial city, and only then in its musical version. By that time Schikaneder was again touring South Germany with a new company of his own; his repertoire included the latest prose and musical works of the new genre of German drama: *Doctor and Apothecary* by Dittersdorf, *The Abduction* by Mozart, and Schiller's dramas: *The Robbers, Fiesco, Intrigue and Love* and *Don Carlos.*

In the meantime Mozart, who had joined the Viennese freemasons' lodge called 'To Charity' one year before Schikaneder, stayed in Vienna, trying to find ways and means of establishing German play-acting, the new German Singspiel, and the German national theatre. However important a step *The Abduction* was on this road (and nobody knew that better than Mozart), it was nevertheless no more than *one* step. It was a new Singspiel, and although it differed in a number of aspects from its predecessors it still only continued in the style of works composed up to that time, consolidating and crowning the achievements of that style. It did not yet provide indisputable evidence that the German language could be as suitable as Italian and French for opera-singing. It was not yet German grand opera: grand in aspiration, message and artistic form alike. And it seemed that the attainment of the new German opera would not be through the imperial court theatre of Vienna: 'It seems to me that the directors of the theatre here are too thrifty and not

223

sufficiently patriotically-minded . . . . Were there but one patriot in charge — the situation would immediately become different! But then perhaps the now-budding German national theatre would start to flourish, and of course it would be an eternal shame for Germany if once we Germans seriously started thinking as Germans, acting as Germans, speaking in German and, indeed, singing in German!!!'*

In Wieden, a suburb of Vienna, a huge building stood on the right bank of the tiny river Wien, just beside the stone bridge that led into the town: Prince Stahremberg's customs house, the so-called Freihaus. In 1787, the year of *Don Giovanni*'s première, a shrewd theatre manager had a simple wooden barrack erected in the yard of the house, next-door to the pub. A year later the management of the new suburban Viennese theatre, called Freihaustheater auf der Wieden, was taken over first by Eleonora, Schikaneder's divorced wife, and in the following year by Schikaneder himself, who held it until 1801, when — together with his whole company — he moved to more elegant quarters, the distinguished Theater an der Wien, situated in the heart of the city. Ten years later, after a series of bankruptcies, failures, and an unsuccessful experiment to found yet another theatre elsewhere, Schikaneder, poor and ill, returned to Vienna, the ungrateful town of his earlier success and greatness, to die there forgotten.

Until his Freihaustheater period the majority of Schikaneder's repertoire was made up primarily of works of the new German dramatic literature — in addition to the ubiquitous Shakespeare. Now, at the Freihaustheater with a more or less permanent company, his repertoire contained for the most part works of the new German and Italian operatic literature: operas by Paisiello, Martin, Gluck and Haydn, and in first place Mozart's operas (*The Abduction, The Marriage of Figaro, Don Giovanni* and *Così fan tutte*), the most successful box office attractions of the second most important public theatre in Vienna. (The first was Schika-

* Letter dated 21 March 1785.

neder's great rival, the Leopoldstädter Theater; and one year
after the foundation of the Freihaustheater, a third one,
called Josefstädter Theater, opened its doors too.) The
slowly growing regular suburban audiences made the existence of so many theatres possible, but the struggle for
survival, the desperate fight against the rivals, made it
imperative for Schikaneder to be dissatisfied with the
standard repertoire, and to employ authors of his own, who
would write new and original works in accordance with his
ideas and in harmony with the aims of the theatre. One
among these dozens of 'new and original' works was Mozart's
Die Zauberflöte (*The Magic Flute*).

'New and original,' said Schikaneder proudly about his
own libretto. But is that really true? Faithful to the method
we have followed so far, we shall omit any comparison with
the familiar array of Magic Islands, Magic Pipes and Magic
Zithers, and examine instead a much less exploited but much
more exciting parallel, worthier of Mozart, which — due to
aspects of conception and principle rather than comparison
of plot and superficial stage-effects — tells us more and opens
up greater vistas. We do not want to waste time discussing
bad contemporary arrangements of similar themes. The unit
for measuring the cosmos is the light-year, not the inch.

'This very moment I have received a piece of news which
greatly distresses me, the more so as I gathered from your last
letter that, thank God, you were enjoying good health. But
now I hear that you are really ill. I need hardly tell you how
greatly I long to receive some reassuring news from you. And
I still expect it; although I have now made a habit of being
prepared in all affairs of life for the worst. As death, when we
come to consider it closely, is the true aim of our existence, I
have formed during the last few years such a close relationship with this best and truest friend of mankind, that his
image is not only no longer terrifying to me, but is indeed
very soothing and consoling! And I am thankful to God that
he has judged me worthy of understanding . . . that death is
the key to our true happiness. I never go to bed without
considering that, young as I am, I may not live to see the

225

next day. Still, none of those knowing me can say that I am sullen or sad in company — and for this blessing I express my gratitude to my Creator every day.'*

In 1787, at the time of writing this letter, Mozart was thirty-one; his father Leopold, living in Salzburg, sixty-eight. That was their last exchange of letters. Less than two months later Mozart concluded a letter to a friend of his with this brief postscript: 'I inform you that on returning home today I received the sad news of my most beloved father's death. You can imagine the state I am in.'† The principle of understatement, that of the 'hint', in life as in art! 'You can imagine the state I am in.' Can words express more than the mere fact, the short and objective item of news of death? They cannot: 'the rest is silence', the infinite empire of imagination. The imagination of the artist sees beyond the facts, and behind the phenomenon finds the essence, the very core of reality, which is richer and truer than the grey factual data squeezed within the narrow limits of our senses. On a sunny Sunday afternoon the people of Vienna make their way to the Prater: Blanchard, the French balloonist — inventor of the parachute — having developed further the Montgolfier brothers' decade-old discovery, is going, after several unsuccessful experiments, to make an ascent. The whole town is there, gazing admiringly at the miracle of the century, the flying man — with the exception of Mozart: 'I did not go to see the balloon, because I can imagine it for myself.'**Why should he go and watch it? His eyes see deeper: he established a whole world on the island of his imagination: 'I have bedimmed the noontide sun, called forth the mutinous winds, and 'twixt the green sea and the azured vault set roaring war: to the dread rattling thunder have I given fire, and rifted Jove's stout oak with his own bolt: the strong based promontory have I made shake and by the spurs plucked up the pine and cedar: graves at my command have waked their sleepers, oped, and let 'em forth by my so potent art.'‡

* Letter dated 4 April 1787.
† Letter dated 29 May 1787.
** Letter dated 7 July 1791.
‡ Shakespeare, *The Tempest*, act V, scene 1.

And for the last time, in order to carry out his life's purpose, Mozart 'requires some heavenly music; then he breaks his staff and drowns his book deeper than did ever plummet sound'. He knows there is no time to lose; he feels death round the corner, and he senses that the *Requiem*, composed at the commission of a mysterious stranger, will celebrate the end of his own life. His thoughts turn frequently to death.[2] 'I cannot chase away from my eyes the sight of that unknown man. Permanently and ceaselessly he begs and urges me and impatiently bids me to work. I go on composing because it is less tiring than idleness. However, I have nothing to be afraid of. From all I experience I feel that the great clock is soon going to strike, death is approaching; I come to the end before I can enjoy my talent. Life was so beautiful, and my career began amidst such good omens; but man cannot change the fate that has been assigned to him. Nobody knows the number of his days; we must acquiesce: everything should be as it is ordered by fate. I will bring my funeral music to an end; it must not remain unfinished.'* [3]

Since Mozart's earliest stage experiments, we have been following the development of his dramaturgy towards the dramatic completeness of the Shakespearean ideal. These two giants — who, each in his own genre, created a perfectly complete world — necessarily and inevitably had to meet; it is deeply symbolic, and at the same time tragic, that this finally occurred in the last stage work of each of the two lonely genuises. Quite inconceivably, the history of music, and within this the literature dealing with Mozart (that could well fill a whole library), has so far ignored the kinship between *The Tempest* and *The Magic Flute;* the most comprehensive biography, that by Abert, does not even mention it; others do not go beyond a few curt, skin-deep allusions which, even in the best cases, hardly go further than to point out the superficial similarities between some characters. However, the parallel we can draw between Shakespeare's and Mozart's swan-songs is much more funda-

* Letter dated 7 September 1791.

mental: there exists a deep conceptional, spiritual, dramaturgical and genre blood-relationship between the two. *The
Magic Flute,* intrinsically linked to the whole of the
Mozartian oeuvre, emerges from the foundation of Mozart's
Shakespearean ideal, and summarises in a final synthesis all
that the composer wanted to say once again — and for the
last time — about mankind: about life itself in the dramatic
unity of comedy and tragedy. In the following pages I shall
undertake to try and prove the fundamental connection
between *The Magic Flute* and Shakespeare's *Tempest* —
measuring the dazzling infinity of the cosmos with the
gigantic unit of the light-year.

Just as every age looked at Mozart through its own,
sometimes distorting, spectacles, in the same way every age
looked for and found its own ideas, desires and aspirations in
The Magic Flute. One found it to be a naïvely popular,
colourful fairy-tale; for another it was a historical allegory;
for a third the eternal, mystical struggle between light and
darkness; a fourth saw in it mankind's striving towards the
knowledge of truth; a fifth thought it to be an ancient
Egyptian ritual; for a sixth it was a freemasons' symbolic
ceremony; while for the audience of the Viennese première it
was a political pamphlet, a musical social satire, in which the
spirit of the 'good emperor', Joseph II, liberates the Austrian
people from the hateful despotism of the wicked Queen of
the Night, Maria Theresia.[4]

Dozens of different and antagonistic views — which of
them is correct?

None of them — and all of them. *The Magic Flute* is like a
mirror: anyone who looks into it, sees himself; and he will
find in it whatever he is looking for. It is a complete picture
of life, a mirror of the universe; in the beautiful words of
Bruno Walter: 'Mozart's spiritual testament'.

Just as *The Tempest* is Shakespeare's testament. Poetry
and clowning, fantastic fairy-tale and earthly, everyday
simplicity, childishly naïve play and the essence of philosophy and wisdom — all have a part. The resemblance
between the characters of the two works is obvious. Prospero

and Sarastro, the power of knowledge and love that is supernatural and rules the world – and their antithesis Sycorax, foul witch, expelled for her wickedness, and the Queen of the Night who lost her magic power with the death of her husband; Caliban, son of the Algerian witch, and Monostatos the Moor, stool pigeon of the Queen of the Night (the black Moor's Satanic origin is as accurately documented as by a birth certificate by the 'devil's instrument', the piccolo); Ariel, airy spirit, and the three asexual, *dues ex machina* genii; and finally the young couples, in each case two young lovers destined for one another, yet 'this swift business' must be made difficult 'lest too light winning make the prize light'.*

And with this – already leaving behind the question of characters – we arrive at the basic meaning of a long series of motives. The oneness and belonging together of Pamina and Tamino is – conceptionally, musically and dramaturgically alike – the central idea of *The Magic Flute*: the concise sentence '*Mann und Weib, und Weib und Mann reichen an die Gottheit an*'[5] (number 7) is the basic principle, almost the motto of the whole work. It is perhaps needless to prove that this conception was completely Mozart's own: it is from this same Mozartian ethical basis that the relationships between Ilia and Idamantes, Constanze and Belmonte, Susanna and Figaro, Zerlina and Masetto, and within a special framework Anna and Ottavio, and even the countess and the count, emerge in strength.

From this fact, there follow two other, extremely important conclusions. One is that amidst all the heterogeneous changes in genre of a whole creative decade, this natural development of the basic principle that leads from *Idomeneo*, through *The Abduction* and *The Marriage of Figaro*, to *Don Giovanni*, with its final and perfect formulation in *The Magic Flute*, undoubtedly proves Mozart's – during the past century and a half much-debated – active role in the realisation and detailed formulation of the libretto. The weight and central place of the motto is ensured first of all by its

---

* Shakespeare, *The Tempest*, act I, scene 2.

tonality, the E-flat-major basic key of the opera; further, by its dramaturgically distinguished position before the first finale that brings the decisive turn (we shall come back to that later); as well as by the piano sotto voce exposition with transparent flute accompaniment of the quoted sentence, based on the 'hint' principle; and last but not least by the fact that this final, epigram-like proclamation of the beauty, divine sanctity and transcendent power of love is not only heard in the basic key, at an important place in the opera, and with a special emphasis caused by restraint, but at the same time it is performed, we could almost say, in a sterile way. It is here that Pamina and Papageno meet for the very first time; there is no, and there will be no, other kind of relationship between them – that is inconceivable not only socially, and according to the strict laws of fairy-tale, but musically and dramaturgically as well – than the most chaste and pure friendship possible between two human beings. The tone is that of a folk-song; not a brilliantly individual tone, but the rather objective, everyday language of folklore. So, this abstract statement, lacking in personal interest or sensual feeling, with its complete absence of pathos and its sober objectivity, codifies, as it were, the enlightened formula of man + woman = god.

Which leads us again to Mozart's characteristic conception that held an important place in previous operas, first of all in *Idomeneo* and *The Abduction*: that only in love and through love, helped by the strength of the woman he loves, can our hero become a true man, and achieve full value both in the everyday and dramaturgical senses of the phrase. When we first meet him, Tamino, confused and helpless, is just escaping from a snake; and we bid him farewell when, having withstood the trials of fire and water, with Pamina at his side, he enters the Sanctuary of the Initiated. His development from a prince into a man is the skeleton of the story of *The Magic Flute*. And this relates not only to the action and its message, but primarily to the dramaturgical conception of the opera too (later on we shall return to that).

The other piece of evidence provided by the emphasis on the '*Mann und Weib*' motto concerns the blood-relationship between *The Tempest* and *The Magic Flute*. Right from their first meeting the suggestion that Miranda and Ferdinand are destined for each other continues through the whole play: 'They are both in either's powers: but this swift business I must uneasy make, lest too light winning make the prize light . . . . It goes on, I see . . . . At the first sight they have changed eyes . . . . It works [the plan],' says Prospero (*The Tempest*, act I, scene 2); and then later: 'Poor worm, thou art infected! . . . Fair encounter of two most rare affections: heaven's grace on that which breeds between 'em!' (*The Tempest*, act III, scene 1). And Ferdinand, who is 'in my condition, a prince', confesses to Miranda: 'the very instant that I saw you, did my heart fly to your service' (*The Tempest*, act III, scene 1), and he undertakes 'wooden slavery', and thus becomes, like Tamino, 'more than a prince: a man!' (*The Magic Flute*, act II, scene 1) to whom Prospero is justified in saying: 'All thy vexations were but my trials of thy love, and thou has strangely stood the test' (*The Tempest*, act IV, scene 1). The parallel is perfect: the two characters blend completely.

A whole series of other common features confirm the relationship between the two works beyond any reasonable doubt – first of all, their fairy-tale logic. Happiness in the world of fairy-tale hangs on a thread: Cinderella is allowed to put on the evening-gown woven from moonshine – provided she returns from the ball by midnight; Bluebeard's lady may open every door – except one. Little Red Riding-Hood would never have been in danger if she had not entered into conversation with the wolf; Sleeping Beauty would not have fallen asleep for one hundred years, had the king not forgotten to invite a certain fairy to the christening celebrations. There is this basic idea behind every folk-tale: that every prospect of perfect happiness depends on a single condition.

This fairy-tale logic determines a significant part of the dramaturgical motivation of *The Tempest* and *The Magic Flute* alike. The happiness of Tamino, his rise to a higher moral, emotional and manly sphere depends on a virtually passive test. The first stage of this test is an absolutely negative command: that of silence, or more exactly, the prohibition of talking to women. This, on the other hand, has its counterpart in *The Tempest*'s twice repeated brief sentence: 'Speak not for him!' — Prospero warns Miranda, referring to Ferdinand (*The Tempest*, act I, scene 2). In spite of its brevity this peremptory order is emphasised dramaturgically by its position as last sentence of the first act; and also by its significance as the first step in Ferdinand's trial. In *The Magic Flute* the prohibition of addressing a woman is dramaturgically emphasised in a similar way, when the forbidding words of the dialogue are immediately twice underlined by the music: in the duet of the two priests (number 11), and subsequently in the quintet presenting the first temptation (number 12).

Moreover, the form the trials take is also similar. It is not the spectacular, heroic deed of the fairy-tale — conquest over a Cyclops, a wicked magician or a seven-headed dragon, or even the unnatural task of, say, ploughing, sowing and harvesting a wheat-field within a single day — but a simple, passive sacrifice, the speechless and patient suffering of an ordeal, inflicted by a voluntarily-acknowledged supreme power. Tamino is silent, he does not even answer his beloved's words, but only plays his flute as he walks through fire and water, musically so abstract as to be reduced almost to mere symbols. And Ferdinand happily stacks the wood, for 'these sweet thoughts do even refresh my labours most busy lest when I do it' (*The Tempest,* act III, scene 1); and having recognised in the shackles of mundane activities the necessity of sacrifice, he finds here, in his prison, the true liberty of his soul: 'all corners else o' th' earth let liberty make use of . . . space enough have I in such a prison' (*The Tempest,* act I, scene 2). Neither of them is a hero in the usual dramatic, epic or fairy-tale sense — indeed, the contrary. Tamino, for instance, is not a very courageous lad: he runs in panic, not from a seven-headed dragon or even from a Cyclops, but from a common snake (abstracted almost to a symbol with baroque tone-painting) — a trifling danger in the hierarchy of fairy-tale beasts — and does not even make any attempt at self-defence; indeed, he faints in fear, and when he recovers and catches sight of the approaching Papageno, he is even frightened of him, too, and hides behind a tree. Not exactly what one might call typically heroic behaviour – and Ferdinand also lacks heroic pathos; yet both of them will be worthy of a throne (respectively the throne of the united empire of Sun and Night, and that of Naples and Milan) with the women they love beside them: for both of them are more than heroes: they are human beings.

The figures (as a type, almost allegorical) of Caliban and Monostatos provide a whole list of common features, motives, thoughts and ideas. Beyond the fact that, with his Arabic origin, Caliban is a blood-relation of Monostatos, the identity of the two characters is also emphasised by their almost raving desire to rape Miranda/Pamina,[6] the aggressive compensation required by an inferiority complex, due partly to their appearances and partly to their animal instincts being so near the surface (traces of this could be found in Osmin, too); as well as the limited development of inferior beings and the consequent lack of educational possibilities, expressed by Prospero and Sarastro in almost identical words. 'A devil, a born devil, on whose nature nurture can never stick; on whom my pains, humanely taken, all, all lost, quite lost – and as with age his body uglier grows, so his mind cankers,' says Prospero (*The Tempest,* act V, scene 1); while Sarastro says: 'I know too well that your soul is just as black as your face' (*The Magic Flute,* act II, scene 11). Through transpositions, the legal claim of the Queen of the Night on Sarastro's empire[7] is inherited directly from Caliban: 'This island's mine, by Sycorax my mother, which thou tak'st from me' (*The Tempest,* act I, scene 2); 'As I told thee before, I am subject to a tyrant, a sorcerer, that by his cunning hath cheated me of the island' (*The Tempest,* act III, scene 2). Also inherited from Caliban is her revenge plan for Sarastro's murder.[8] And dramaturgically Caliban, the treacherous slave, ridiculous and terrifying at the same time, embodies the Shakespearean dramatic unity of comedy and tragedy – that hair-raising buffoonery which (in a more primitive form) appeared in *La Finta Giardiniera* for the first time, to increase in perfection throughout the later operas, and find a harmonious, clarified and complete balance of its own in *The Magic Flute*.

Shakespeare's and Mozart's last works of art are also closely related from the point of view of genre. They are both adventurous, romantic fairy-tales with naïve magic and childish stage tricks (there is a table laid 'by magic' in both plays[9]), carrying — in peerless poetry — wisdom and ethics in the ornate, symbolic manner of the fairy-tale medium and bearing exquisite understanding of humanity. In *The Tempest* such an ambivalent moment that unites 'the majestic with the ridiculous' is the ending of, and transition from, the pastoral baroque masque, with Prospero's resonant, organ-like words which abruptly turn the mood into a serious, indeed, a gloomy tone ('And like the baseless fabric of this vision', etc., act IV, scene 1); in *The Magic Flute* such is the scene of the two men in armour in the second finale (number 21) where the majestic intricacy of the C-minor adagio (combining the Protestant choral melody with the counterpoint of Roman Catholic sacred music) smoothly blends into the childishly innocent, playful dance rhythm of the D-flat-major allegretto, and then, with a breath-takingly self-evident A flat/F modulation, into the majestic simplicity of the succeeding andante. When touching such extremes of characterisation, atmosphere and mood within the passage of a few minutes — and not only without any break but even without the slightest lurch in flying from earth to heaven and back again — in the wonderful magic of such moments Mozart, the 'Shakespeare of music',* encounters his dramatic ideal, the Bard of Avon. 'Every phenomenon of existence is lyrical in its ideal essence, tragic in its fate, and comic in its form of appearance,' says Santayana. On Shakespeare's and Mozart's stages all three categories exist simultaneously and melt into perfect unity.

Dramaturgically, another common feature is that the characters in both plays are *types* — even though they are

* E.T.A. Hoffmann.

deeply individualized types with subjective, lyrical souls. Of course this is nothing new for Mozart (e.g. *The Abduction, Don Giovanni, Così*); however, for Shakespeare it only appeared in the last plays on such an unambiguously general level. In addition, the beginning of the two works is similar: Man helplessly struggles in the lethal embrace of Nature. The brilliantly concise exposition, that divulges only the few most important facts with the most sparing means, does not reveal any further details about this man – who he is, where he comes from, or where he is going. Detailed information will not be given until later: the scene grasps the essence of the atmosphere of danger – there is no time now for anything else. A similar conception is reflected by the anticipated breaking up of the mood: with just a little ill-fortune the dramatic situation could well turn into a catastrophe – but the easy, frivolous tone of Gonzalo's and the boatswain's words, and similarly that of the three ladies-in-waiting, shows that there won't be any serious trouble, the danger will soon pass; this is a play, and a Singspiel, and not a tragedy.

At the same time the beginning calls attention to a significant divergence of dramatic construction, which reveals one of the very few basic dramaturgical discrepancies in the two works. *The Tempest* presents the final stage, one could even say the catharsis, of a long series of events; in fact, the whole play is an enormous last act, the antecedents of which are only known to us from the narration of the characters, primarily from Prospero; constructionally this is supported – as nowhere else among Shakespeare's works – by the classical unity of place, time and action. *The Magic Flute,* on the other hand, presents Tamino and Pamina actually in the process of development. Mozart is creating and using, more than one century before the birth of the film, something that is almost equal to the modern means of expression employed by the cinema!

The film approach which – identifying the camera with the eyes of the hero – presents the action, or part of the action, from the viewpoint of the audience, is now quite commonplace. But in Mozart's and Schikaneder's times it was a revolutionarily new form – so much so that even today the uninitiated are at a loss when faced with it and the egg-headed experts are still arguing about it. According to the infamous 'refraction theory' of the last century, in the first conception of *The Magic Flute* the Queen of the Night was intended to represent Good, and Sarastro was to be the personification of of Evil. However, in the course of the composition, with the first act almost finished, the plan had to be changed due to competition from a play with a similar subject at the rival Leopoldstädter Theater. Therefore the authors – according to the 'refraction theory' – proceeded by making a sharp-angle turn at the middle, and simply reversing the characterisation. This completely unfounded theory – doing an injustice to Schikaneder, but even more so to Mozart – has long been refuted by the more documented music history of the twentieth century, particularly by Abert. But even Mozart himself refuted it when, in one of his letters, he wrote the following about the so-called 'rival' play: 'In order to cheer myself up, I hopped over to the Kasperle to see the new opera *The Bassoonist* which is making such a sensation, but it does not offer anything.'* We also know enough about Mozart's personality to realise that not even on much less significant issues was he ever willing to make any artistic compromise – let alone a radical change in the basic idea and ethical message of a complete work!

Incidentally, a single sentence of a later letter throws light on Mozart's new attitude towards his audience, and towards success in general. One week after the première of *The Magic Flute* – and two months before his death – reporting on the performance of the opera on 7 October, he had this to write to his wife: 'As usual the duet *"Mann und Weib"* and Papageno's glockenspiel in act I had to be repeated and also the trio of the genii in act II. But what always gives me most pleasure is the *silent approval*! You can see how this opera is growing more and more popular.'† How far he has come since he wrote, only ten years before, about *The Abduction:* '. . . a great deal of noise . . . is always appropriate at the end of an act. The more noise the better; the shorter the better:

* Letter dated 12 June 1791.
† Letter dated 7-8 October 1791.

so that the audience have no time to cool down before they applaud.'* Is it still necessary to prove that this Mozart, the composer of *The Magic Flute,* who appreciated 'silent approval', did not and could not sell the message and essence of his work for the cheap reward of loud success?

What then is the explanation of that undoubtedly strange and unusual character-drawing which changes the Queen of the Night — for whom we learn to feel sympathy in the first act — and her frolicsome ladies-in-waiting into intriguing, murderous furies in the second act — and which presents Sarastro, formerly spoken of as usurper and kidnapper, as the incarnation of superhuman beauty, goodness and wisdom at his very first appearance? What is the reason for this apparent contradiction, this strange character-drawing that, from one act to the other, turns through 180 degrees?

After all, Tamino is in fact rescued from the snake by the three ladies, and it is also from them that he receives Pamina's picture which is of decisive importance in the imbroglio (E-flat-major aria!) and indeed even the magic flute itself (while Papageno receives the magic bell). They teach Papageno the virtue of always speaking the truth; and they lead Tamino onto the road at the end of which await him in turn Pamina's love, the Sanctuary of the Initiated, and eventually the united empire of the Sun and Night. And the first aria of the Queen of the Night (number 4) — despite its cold, faraway star-light glitter and baroque opera seria character — is, in its middle section, in tragic G minor, expressing maternal sorrow that sounds sincere and is plausible, even if it is harder and stiffer than any other of Mozart's G-minor arias. But only we are aware that there can be any comparison: Tamino does not know *Idomeneo* or *The Abduction,* and therefore he can easily accept (and he does, too) the outlook of the Queen — particularly since its truth is strengthened by Pamina's picture and the good deeds of the three ladies-in-waiting. Had Mozart wanted to, he could easily have given us a glimpse of the Queen's real face as early in the opera as during her first appearance (this real face will be reflected later in the demoniacal D-minor aria) — for we have

* Letter dated 26 September 1781.

seen more than once how Mozart's music can reveal more than the text, or even contradict it. Here Mozart did not do that — or if he did, then in such a delicate and refined way that neither Tamino nor the audience could be suspicious: they accept the world-order, as presented by the Queen, at its face value.

To us, however, who not only have eyes to see, but ears to hear as well, with the magic means of his music Mozart soon suggests that the whole first scene is in fact a play — skilfully directed by the Queen — with the help of which she sets out to gain Tamino's soul for her own purposes. Five strong, emotional pressures follow one another with dazzling impetus — shock tactics! No wonder the young prince, inexperienced in such intrigues, falls prey to them:

1. Pursued by a snake, unarmed and completely exhausted, he is saved by the Queen's three charming ladies-in-waiting.
2. He makes the acquaintance of a strange but rather likeable character, Papageno the bird-catcher, also the Queen's servant, with whom he makes friends very soon, and who is supposed to accompany him on his way.
3. He receives Pamina's picture from the ladies and falls in love at first sight; he feels ready to do anything to save her.
4. Then appears — with an impressively theatrical display — the Queen herself, playing the suffering mother, to personally entreat him for his help.
5. And finally the ladies give him the magic flute — symbol of the power of music — as a means of protection and a weapon in the forthcoming struggle.

The young man cannot help but succumb to this series of faultlessly constructed and performed emotional attacks: he accepts the Queen's point of view without the slightest doubt.

Obviously, of the five, the last four occurrences originate directly from the Queen. But what about the first one, the exposition of the whole series: the fatal snake-attack? Had it been only an accident, the following chain of events — skilfully improvised as they are — could by no means be interpreted as a complete plan, conceived and carried out in cold blood by the Queen in order to mislead Tamino.

Mozart, however, proves — between the lines — that Tamino did not become a victim of the Queen by accident at all. The snake gives itself away as a creature of the Queen; its attack results in the first and strongest emotional impact, that of the deliverance from danger. The musical motive of danger at the beginning of the first scene and at Tamino's appearance has some similarity with the first appearance of the Queen (only there it is in the major key and one note lower). The triad is a sort of fanfare for the Queen: the quick part of her first aria starts with it:

and ends in the same way (although in a distorted form, owing to her blind rage), and her second aria, too:

The fact that Tamino, despite all the Queen's intrigues, gradually recognises her trick, is again shown to us by Mozart through the simple and ingenious means of the leitmotiv. (This is not an anachronistic supposition: as we have seen, Mozart, ten years earlier in *Idomeneo,* applied a well-constructed and consistently developed leitmotive technique, more than sixty years before Wagner.) It begins with the first appearance of the three genii, and the process of fermentation in Tamino's mind takes place in the first finale. Tamino's change in outlook starts with the dialogue with the

Speaker where he is confronted with Sarastro's world for the first time. And at the very moment when Tamino begins to doubt the Queen's good faith, the first sign of independent thinking on his part, Mozart shows it to us musically.

This decisive moment is the first sentence of the recitative, when Tamino (after the dialogue with the Speaker), remaining alone on the stage, begins to meditate: 'Oh, eternal night! When will you pass away from me? When will my eyes find the light?'[10]

This thought is a symbolic expression of Tamino's desire to free himself from the bonds of the empire of Night, and in its music it unmistakably refers to the Queen's very first words, emphasising his conscious reminiscence even to its identical harmonisation (with the dissonant tonic bass for the dominant chord under the word *'Nacht'* as for the Queen's *'nicht'*).[11] The broken triad motive is undoubtedly the Queen's, as we have seen; and it is hardly by accident either that in the opera the flute triad is heard for the first time after the Speaker's scene, symbolising – as a reverse of the Queen's motive – Tamino's first active step towards liberating himself from the world of darkness.

This is also Tamino's starting point: an unequivocal 'yes' to the empire of Night that had been offered to him in a sympathetic form, both in action and in words, and not least in the music.

But it is not only Tamino who initially believes in the genuineness of the Night — and this is the great trouvaille, the ingenious dramaturgical solution of *The Magic Flute*: we, the audience, also believe in it. We, together with Tamino, blindly accept a false concept, solely on an emotional basis and without the control of logic; and we also start our quest for truth loaded down with prejudices. The more imposing the catharsis will be, the greater the victory against our greatest enemy: ourselves. Only after having learnt to conquer all our emotional whims, can we free ourselves from our last superstitions. When at the end Evil sinks in its hopelessness with a despairing, steeply-declining form of the Queen's motive, it takes with it all the different prejudices with which we set out on our peregrinations at the beginning of the opera. Tamino's development from his blind faith in the sincerity of the Queen of the Night, through a gradual change in outlook, to his voluntary and deliberate attachment to Sarastro's world, is the development of the audience too, accompanying their hero through his suffering and trials, in order to reach, beyond the night's cold darkness, the exhilarating warmth of the sun.

Notes

(1) See letters dated 8, 22, 29 November 1780.
(2) At that time death was a regular visitor in the Mozart family. In the spring of 1783, Raimund Leopold, first son of Wolfgang and Constanze, died at the age of two months; three years later Johann Thomas Leopold was taken less than a month after his birth. Half a year later Mozart's father, Leopold, died; a year after him, Theresia, the first daughter,

at the age of seven months; and the next winter the second daughter, Anna, died the day she was born. The youngest child, Wolfgang Franz, was not quite five months old when his father died.

(3) The identity of the addressee of this letter from Vienna, written in Italian, is not known; but it was probably da' Ponte.

(4) Only as a grotesque curiosity is it worth mentioning that fantastic somersault of logic which wanted to discover in *The Magic Flute* a sort of reincarnation of the Parsifal legend, and thus a predecessor of Wagner's opera (Tamino: Parsifal; Sarastro: Amfortas; the Queen of the Night: Kundry; the priests: the knights of the Grail, etc.).

(5) Trans: 'Man and woman, woman and man together reach up to God.'

(6) *The Tempest,* act I, scene 2; act III, scene 2. *The Magic Flute,* act I, scene 9, number 6; act II, scene 7, number 13; act II, scene 10, number 21.

(7) *The Magic Flute,* act II, scene 8.

(8) *The Tempest,* act III, scene 2; act IV, scene 1. *The Magic Flute,* act II, scene 8, numbers 14 and 21.

(9) *The Tempest,* act III, scene 3. *The Magic Flute,* number 21.

(10) The text of the recitative is quoted almost word for word by Schikaneder from one of André Chénier's elegies.

(11) Probably quite unintentionally, Beethoven quotes the Queen of the Night's opening motive with identical harmonisation in Florestan's aria in the second act of *Fidelio,* in order to characterise the empty darkness of the prison!

THE MAGIC FLUTE is the rambling journey of a soul in search of truth, his voyage from darkness to light.

The first appearance of the three genii prepares – at the beginning of the first finale – the process of fermentation in Tamino's soul, as well as the decisive spiritual and dramaturgical turning-point of the play. Their place and function in the world of *The Magic Flute* is one of the most debated questions of the opera and one of the strongest arguments in favour of the 'refraction theory'. In the first quintet (number 5) as we have seen, the three ladies – that is, indirectly the Queen of the Night – designate the three genii to show Tamino and Papageno the way; while in the finale, and even more decisively in the second act, the three genii unequivocally represent the principles and support the plans of Sarastro's side. This ostensible contradiction cannot even be resolved with the dramaturgical method of 'camera's eye view', since from their first appearance the three genii exercise a positive influence – with them therefore there is no question of a gradual change in the visual angle.

The answer is again provided by the parallel with *The Tempest*. The analogous figure, the 'spiritual ancestor' (in both senses of the word 'spiritual') of the three genii is Shakespeare's Ariel who is unaffected by human morals, or by the categories of 'good' and 'evil'; a creature without body and without sex. Shakespeare gives a fairly thorough motivation to Ariel's relationship with Prospero, for whom the spirit – free and independent by nature – nourishes a feeling of gratitude, and for this suffers heavy, but voluntarily undertaken, servitude for a definite period of time. Because of the restrictions of the opera genre Mozart and Schikaneder do not and cannot provide a similarly detailed explanation for the roles of the three genii: but if we consider their four appearances in the course of the action, we will see that on each occasion they appear independently as sort of *deus ex machina* aids to the good cause — yet not once by directly accomplishing Sarastro's instructions, or being in any kind of subordinated relationship to him, as the three ladies are to their mistress, or Monostatos is to his master. The three genii, who are neither male nor female, remain detached from the struggle between Night — personified by the women — and Day — personified by the men. The Queen of the Night could have assumed (due to some reason unknown to us, and not important) that as neutral forces, they would take sides with her in this struggle; they, however, (again for reasons that are not explained) invariably interfere on Sarastro's side — but from outside. This is shown clearly by their musical characterisation, first and foremost by their only 'solo', the A-major trio (number 16): the only A-major music in the opera!

It is also the parallel with *The Tempest* that provides a clear answer to Monostatos's somewhat problematic position (the other grave argument for the 'refraction theory'). With a careful motivation for his relationship to his master, Shakespeare gives a many-sided characterization of Caliban's deeply individualised type. Although here again Mozart and Schikaneder do not explain the circumstances, the analogy is obvious: education is of no help to this sub-human being, for he uses anything he learns for base purposes, he has to be curbed, or, if this is not enough, annihilated. Shakespeare chooses the former solution — Mozart the latter. Prospero pardons Caliban, but Sarastro, in the interests of mankind, mercilessly destroys the creature of Evil. In *The Magic Flute* (in accordance with the symmetrical construction of the play) the destruction of the enemy takes place by means of the dramaturgical division of the storm of *The Tempest* exposition: the allegro (the snake episode) that starts the introduction, is completed by the più moderato passage of the second finale, thus framing the struggle of the Queen of the Night for Tamino's soul and for the acquisition of the seven-fold circle of the sun – a struggle which begins with temporary success, but ends in complete failure. The close coherence between the two scenes and the dramaturgical consciousness of this are proved by their common 4/4 time and C-minor tonality, as well as by an identical tempo: the più moderato has exactly the same tempo as the allegro which started the introduction.

This additional dramaturgical discrepancy between the two plays does not only originate from the principle of symmetry, but primarily from Mozart's and Shakespeare's heterogeneous conceptions of humanism which, growing from the same root, develop into different or even, from a certain point of view, contrasting conclusions. The starting point is the same. 'Though with their high wrongs I am struck to th'quick, yet, with my nobler reason, 'gainst my fury do I take part: the rarer action is in virtue than in vengeance: they being penitent, the sole drift of my purpose doth extend not a frown further,' says Prospero*; and Sarastro's E-major aria (number 15) and his whole attitude reflect this same mental greatness, this mature humanism rising above petty controversies. The same point was made in the analysis of *The Abduction* with regard to the character of Selim, which I think proves that it was Mozart's idea to incorporate this important principle as part of the ethical message of *The Magic Flute*.

So the humanist starting point is common – and yet the two works end on entirely different notes. (Mozart was thirty-five when he composed *The Magic Flute*; at the time of writing *The Tempest* Shakespeare was forty-seven.) 'O wonder! How many godly creatures are there here. How beauteous mankind is! O brave new world, that has such people in't!' exclaims Miranda, sincerely enraptured. Prospero, however, cools with deep scepticism the girl's naïve enthusiasm: 'Tis new to theé.'†

This disappointed, resigned, and, in spite of all its basic humanism, to a certain extent misanthropic attitude is as

---

* Shakespeare, *The Tempest,* act V, scene 1.
† Shakespeare, *The Tempest,* act V, scene 1.

absent from the spirit of *The Magic Flute* as the hostility to civilisation, or indeed, almost to culture – following Morus and Montaigne, and foreshadowing Rousseau – of Gonzalo's completely retrograde utopia (*The Tempest,* act II, scene 1). Incidentally, this is hardly counterbalanced by Gonzalo's eventual regaining of his former self in the catharsis (act V, scene 1).

How tragically moving the contrast is between the brilliant optimism of *The Magic Flute,* and the utter resignation of Prospero retiring from the abounding empire of his small island to the loneliness of the throne of Milan – to a people that has now become indifferent to him. He abjures for once and for all the rough magic of his still so potent art, and looks forward to his grave. When we come to think of it, it is at the summit of Shakespeare's financial, social and artistic success, at the greatest period of his life and in the fullness of his creative energy, that he withdraws from the world he has created about him, into the voluntary exile of Stratford's loneliness, never to write another word – while Mozart, miserably poor and mortally ill, begging for paltry jobs [1] and suffering in the irreparable disharmony of his family life, writes the joyful, glorious finale of *The Magic Flute,* this wonderful hymn to the beauty of life, to the goodness of man, and to the worthiness of eternal struggle.

And he never did voluntarily 'break his staff': death struck it out of his hand, in the full vigour of his creative energy. Mozart lay dying at home; *The Magic Flute* was being performed in the Freihaustheater, and he looked at the clock. 'The first act ends now – soon the second will begin. I wish I could hear my *Magic Flute* just once more!' he whispered to his wife, and, breathing heavily, he softly hummed Papageno's song: *'Der Vogelfänger bin ich ja!'* By next morning he had died.[2]

The Magic Flute is the only opera of Mozart's last creative period in the tonality of E flat major, so rarely used by him. Most of Mozart's masonic music was also written in E flat major (with a similar use of wind instruments, including the basset horn). The timelessly-valid, constantly real, humanist

message of the sublime fairy-tale is reflected in the composition. The naturalness of the music hides a very deliberate
and firm construction.

As we have seen, the characteristic feature of Mozart's
tonality ethos is that every decisive action, every turning-
point, and every situation that communicates the message of
the opera, appears in the work's basic key. In *The Magic
Flute*, E flat major includes the following: the overture, the
entry of the Speaker (from A flat it modulates immediately
into E flat), the trio of the three genii (the announcement of
imminent victory), and Sarastro's recitative (the official
proclamation of victory, achieved again with a sudden
modulation from B flat into E flat in the following bar),
Tamino's picture aria and Pamina's and Papageno's duet
'Mann und Weib' reformulating once again and for the last
time the basic idea of all Mozart's operas. Dramaturgically,
these last two are especially worthy of attention because they
introduce the personalities of the two main characters. The
first appearances of Tamino and Pamina in the action take
place in dangerous situations (they are threatened respectively by the snake and by Monostatos), therefore they sing in
the key determined by their distress. However, afterwards
they express themselves at the first opportunity in E flat,
suggesting that both of them have, right from the beginning,
irrevocably been tuned into the wave-length of the Sun
empire – even if they still have a long journey to make from
Night to Day.

If E flat major is the 'good' key, then C minor is the 'bad':
it is the tonality of the exposition and of the last desperate
attack of the Queen of the Night against Sarastro's empire
(both the metre and the tempo of the two scenes are
identical). Pamina's suicide attempt is also in C minor: she
had been driven to it by her unscrupulous mother, for whom
she – like Tamino – served only as a tool. Mozart's characteristic G minor (remember Ilia and Constanze) is again the
key of despair in *The Magic Flute:* for instance Pamina's
aria and Papageno's attempt at suicide. The three ladies-in-
waiting are permanently acting a part: at first they appear in
the Queen's hypocritical B-flat-major key (her real face is

revealed eventually in the demoniacal D minor); later they try to bedazzle the two candidates in Papageno's key, employing the line of least resistance. They only remove their masks at their last appearance where — after having realised that the only way out is an open attack — they finally acknowledge their real C minor. The upper mediant of the basic key (G major) belongs to Papageno, while the lower (C major) is that of the flute; although both of them originate from the Queen of the Night, they serve, by their very nature, the good cause. The situation regarding the three genii is similar; they appear in the basic and in the flute key, and once even in the seemingly very remote A major. This, however, is on one hand closely related to Sarastro's E major that directly preceeds it, and on the other hand, the three sharps of this key correspond — as a reflection — to the three flats of the basic key. Likewise the E major of Sarastro's second aria (number 15) is on the one hand a strong contrast to the previous D minor of the Queen of the Night and an approach to the A major of the unearthly ambience of the three genii; on the other hand, in the circle of fifths lying furthermost from the basic tonality, it gains added emphasis and significance as the most succinct musical formulation in the whole opera of the principle of humanism, and being chromatically in the immediate neighbourhood of the basic tonality, it stresses the ethical message.

The three flats of the basic key belong at the same time to the opera's system of numerical symbols, too. In the rich lore of the fairy world two numbers play important roles: three and seven. The first of these, as well as its various multiples, being a mystic number for the freemasons, plays an especially decisive role in the structure of *The Magic Flute*: three chords, three temples, three ladies-in-waiting (with three appearances), three genii (with three different orders), three appearances of the Queen of the Night, three questions put by the priests to Sarastro in connection with Tamino, three trials, and a three-fold playing of the flute. Added to these there are — as a specifically musical solution — first of all the three flats of the basic key and the almost leitmotiv-like role of the triad (in the musical characterisation of the Queen and, in the C major, of the flute), the three-fold thematic connection between the opening bars of the priests' chorus (number 18), the scene of the men in armour, and the final chorus. It should be noted that all three of these places are divided, quite unusually, into six-bar entities (2+2+2, 3+3, 3+3). Then there is the priests' march (number 9), the conclusion of which is confirmed three times (the last seven bars), with the three chords linked to it. And finally the number three also appears in the architecture. In the first act there are three arias (numbers 2, 3 and 4) and three ensembles (numbers 5, 6 and 7) one after the other. In the middle of the second act there are three consecutive arias (numbers 13, 14 and 15); three more arias (numbers 10, 17 and 20), and three ensembles (numbers 12, 16 and 19) and the three priests' scenes (numbers 9, 11 and 18) in an alternating, embracing order; and the whole structure is held together by the three large ensembles (numbers 1, 8, 21).

The role of the number seven is less obvious in the construction of the opera; in the symbolism of *The Magic Flute* story it appears only once — but then with special significance: in the motive of the seven-fold circle of the sun. This symbol is reflected in the musical construction by certain tonal and thematic affinities, shown by the following table:

OVERTURE	E flat major = Light	SCENE 13
NUMBER 1	C minor = Darkness	SCENE 12
NUMBER 2 First appearance of Papageno	G major (upper mediant)	SCENE 11 Last appearance of Papageno
NUMBER 3 Tamino: 'Dies Bildnis . . .'	Motive parallel	SCENE 10 Pamina: 'Tamino mein! . . .'

Tamino

Dies Bildius ist bezaubend   schön, wie   noch kein Auge je   ge - sehn!

NUMBER 4   Motive parallel   SCENE 14
Queen: Queen:
'O zittre nicht . . .'   'Hört, hört, . . .'

SCENE 3   C major (lower mediant)   SCENE 11
First appearance of   Last appearance of
genii   genii

SCENE 3   E flat major + motive   SCENE 11
              parallel

Speaker: '. . . was suchst   Sarastro: '. . . vertreiben
du hier im Heiligtum?'   die Nacht . . .'

Tamino's first encounter   Proclamation of Tamino's
with the Sun Empire   definitive adherence to
                              Sarastro's world

The ostensibly spontaneous intuition and simple musical language of *The Magic Flute* covers a perfect order as well as an extremely precise and systematic construction.

And finally, may I call attention to one more point that has a particularly important dramaturgical role in both *The Tempest* and *The Magic Flute*. This is *the power of music*. Tamino (and Papageno, too) tames the wild beasts and wild people with music and, having drawn strength from music, passes through fire and water unharmed, to gain at the end the woman he loves. Ariel leads the lost, shipwrecked men

250

with his song, and so Ferdinand and Miranda are brought together. Prospero enchants the afflicted senses with celestial music because 'A solemn air, and the best comforter to an unsettled fancy cure thy brains, now useless boil within thy skull'*; and even the distorted soul of the monster Caliban is inspired to wonderfully poetic words by the all-ennobling power of music:

Be not afeard, the isle is full of noises,
Sound and sweet airs, that give delight and hurt not.
Sometimes a thousand twangling instruments
Will hum about mine ears; and sometimes voices,
That, if I then had waked after long sleep,
Will make me sleep again; and then, in dreaming,
The clouds methought would open, and show riches
Ready to drop upon me: that when I waked
I cried to dream again.*

Although in *The Magic Flute* Tamino gains the power of music from an evil source, it is not by accident that the flute remains silent as long as its sound would intone the 'music of Night': it is only after the turn in the plot that its pure sound is heard for the first time! The power of knowledge, thought and art is immense: in evil hands it can become harmful and inhuman – in the service of a good cause it can move mountains. Shakespeare's choice of title symbolises the raging storm of nature and of the passions of the human soul; Mozart's choice of title symbolises art's animating power and the wonderful creative strength of the human spirit. Both works are fairy-tales moulded into words and sounds (and in the fairy-tale, music and song are perfectly suitable means of expression); and each contains an infinitely rich variety of human, sub-human and superhuman types, spanning a wide range of characters, from the monster through different grades of human evolution to the pure spirit, free from all earthly ties.[3]

* Shakespeare, *The Tempest*, act V, scene 1.
* Shakespeare, *The Tempest*, act III, scene 2.

Notes

(1) See letters of the first half of May 1790 and from the beginning of May 1791.

(2) As to the cause of Mozart's death — for a long time it was held that he died of tuberculosis, while others thought the reason was a rheumatic heart complaint; later research, however, revealed that he suffered from uremia, an illness of the kidney resulting from scarlet fever in childhood.

(3) '[Shakespeare and Mozart] are the greatest artists in the world, for in one scene, or in one finale they can intone the whole world . . . . Among the various composers of the world, Mozart is the only one who introduced every musical subject into the charm of a fairy-tale — in whom the rejuvenating strength of fairy-tale lives so vividly, that every sorrow, every pain turns into pure beauty that enchants the audience.' Sándor Hevesi.

APPENDIX

MOZART'S DRAMATIC WORKS

Title	Librettist	Köchel Number	Composition or Première	
Die Schuldigkeit des ersten Gebotes	Wimmer	35	Salzburg	1766-7
Apollo et Hyacinthus	Widl	38	Salzburg	1767
Bastien und Bastienne	Weiskern	50	Vienna	1768
La Finta Semplice	Goldoni/ Coltellini	51	Vienna	1768
Mitridate, Rè di Ponto	Racine/ Cignasanti	87	Milan	1770
Ascanio in Alba	Parini	111	Milan	1771
La Betulia Liberata	Metastasio	118	Milan (?)	1771
Il Sogno di Scipione	Metastasio	126	Salzburg	1772
Lucio Silla	Gamerra	135	Milan	1772
La Finta Giardiniera	Calzabigi/ Coltellini	196	Munich	1775
Il Rè Pastore	Metastasio	208	Salzburg	1775
Les Petits Riens	Noverre	—	Paris	1778
Semiramis	Gemmingen	—	Mannheim	1778-9
Zaïde	Schachtner	344	Salzburg	1779
Thamos, König in Aegypten	Gebler	345	Salzburg	1779
Idomeneo, Rè di Creta	Varesco	366	Munich	1780-81
Die Entführung aus dem Serail	Bretzner/ Stephanie jun.	384	Vienna	1782
L'Oca del Cairo	Varesco	422	Salzburg	1783
Lo Sposo Deluso	da Ponte (?)	430	Salzburg	1783
Der Schauspieldirektor	Stephanie jun.	486	Vienna	1786
Le Nozze di Figaro	Beaumarchais/ da Ponte	492	Vienna	1786
Don Giovanni	da Ponte	527	Prague	1787
Così fan tutte	da Ponte	588	Vienna	1790
Die Zauberflöte	Schikaneder	620	Vienna	1791
La Clemenza di Tito	Metastasio/ Mazzolà	621	Prague	1791

BIBLIOGRAPHY

The Letters of Mozart and his Family (translated and edited by Emily Anderson), Macmillan, London, 1938.

H. Abert, *W.A. Mozart,* Leipzig, 1924.

E. Blom, *Mozart,* J.M. Dent, London, 1935.

H. Cohen, *Die dramatische Idee in Mozarts Operntexten,* Berlin, 1915.

L. Conrad, *Mozarts Dramaturgie der Oper,* Würzburg, 1943.

E.J. Dent, *Mozart's Operas,* O.U.P., London 1960.

O.E. Deutsch, *Mozart: A Documentary Biography,* Cassell, London, 1961.

A. Einstein, *A. Mozart: His Character, His Work,* Cassell, London, 1956, Panther, London, 1971.

A. Hyatt King, *Mozart in Retrospect,* O.U.P., London, 1955.

L. von Köchel, *Chronologisch-thematisches Verzeichnis sämtlicher Tonwerke Wolfgang Amade Mozarts,* Reprint House International, New York, 1968.

H.C. Robbins Landon and D. Mitchell, *The Mozart Companion,* Rockliffe, London, 1956.

E. Lert, *Mozart auf dem Theater,* Berlin, 1918.

B. Paumgartner, *Mozart,* Berlin & Zurich, 1940.

S. Sadie, *Mozart,* Calder & Boyars, London, 1965.

E. Schenk, *Mozart and His Times,* Secker & Warburg, London, 1960.

A. Schurig, *W.A. Mozart,* Leipzig, 1913.

T. de Wyzewa & G. de Saint-Foix, *W.A. Mozart,* Paris, 1936.